Surviving in the Newspaper Business

Newspaper Management in Turbulent Times

Jim Willis

PRAEGER

New York
Westport, Connecticut
London

Library of Congress Cataloging-in-Publication Data

Willis, William James, 1946–
    Surviving in the newspaper business : newspaper management in
turbulent times / Jim Willis.
        p. cm.
    Bibliography: p.
    Includes index.
    ISBN 0-275-92862-4 (alk. paper). ISBN 0-275-92863-2 (pbk. : alk.
paper)
    1. Newspaper publishing.   2. Newspapers—Management.   I. Title.
PN4734.W54   1988
070.5'7'068—dc19
87-37685

Library of Congress Catalog Card Number: 87-37685
ISBN: 0-275-92862-4
        0-275-92863-2 (pbk.)

First published in 1988

Praeger Publishers, One Madison Avenue, New York, NY 10010
A division of Greenwood Press, Inc.

Printed in the United States of America

The paper used in this book complies with the
Permanent Paper Standard issued by the National
Information Standards Organization (Z39.48-1984).

10 9 8 7 6 5 4 3 2 1

To Diane

CONTENTS

EXHIBITS

PREFACE

Newspapers are facing turbulent times as we approach the last decade of the twentieth century. The obituary notices of several metro dailies during the first half of the 1980s has prompted a spirit of crisis management by some publishers who see similarity between their newspaper's situation and those of the *Washington Star, Cleveland Press,* and *Philadelphia Bulletin.* In America, where optimism normally reigns, businesses don't like to think about the possibility of hard times up ahead, yet failure to plan realistically and to monitor conditions in the marketplace can lead to a quick failure. When that happens, even crisis management may not be sufficient to save the company.

This book is dedicated to the principle that the newspaper is one of the most valuable assets of the United States, and that those who manage these institutions should do so in a responsible and enlightened manner.

The past two decades have witnessed many changes in both the internal and external environment for newspapers. Internally, new technologies have made the job of producing the newspaper much easier and faster, but labor problems have caused many newspapers some headaches. Part of this trouble is brought on by union reaction to the technologies that are putting computers in place of skilled craftsmen. Part of it is brought about by arbitrary newspaper leadership styles which were out of date a decade or two before many newspaper managers bothered to notice.

Externally, both the marketplace and the competition have changed. It is now harder than ever to get people to read a newspaper, especially when they are faced with an abundance of local and national television news programs which can provide much of that information. Newspaper readers want some of the traditional things they have always received from newspapers—such as a comprehensive display of the day's news—but they also want more. They want information designed to help get them through their daily problems, and they expect even more in the way of entertainment and color.

The following pages look at this changing newspaper environment and assess what it takes to compete successfully in it. Although the book is entitled *Surviving in the Newspaper Business,* it is hoped that future publishers reading it will see that success is much more than mere survival and that they should work toward putting out newspapers that excel. Nevertheless, in order to succeed, newspapers must first survive, and survival is no longer a given in the newspaper industry.

At times, the newspaper industry will be taken to task for its reticence in adopting more enlightened styles of management. At times, there will be numerous examples of newspapers that have gone the extra mile in search of excellence. Overall, the newspaper industry is probably no better or no worse managed than any other industry, but, because of the individuality and skepticism of many journalists and because they realize they are in a business that has great social impact, it is sometimes forgotten that the newspaper is a business. The first goal of any business must be survival. Otherwise, whatever mission it has will never be realized.

Because of the differences existing among management styles of U.S. newspapers, some things discussed in this book will not be universally true. For instance, it is probable that the organizational chart presented in Chapter 2 will differ at some newspapers. Similarly, while most newspapers have different managers in charge of the editorial and circulation departments, a few large dailies give their executive editor jurisdiction over both because of their symbiotic nature in this day of newspaper marketing. Also, many newspapers farm out the job of delivering the newspaper to circulation agencies, while others will field a full circulation staff.

The principles stressed here are universal for the industry. Few newspaper managers could, for instance, argue against the need for successful newspaper marketing or for the need to balance the market ethic with the service ethic. Few could criticize a newspaper philosophy that takes into account the service goals of the newspaper—as well as the bottom line—before arbitrarily making budget cuts in a non-revenue-producing department like the newsroom. (Of course, it would be foolish to accept the idea that news is a non-revenue-producing item in the first place.) Few could also argue against the need for newspapers to protect their market shares from encroaching shoppers and direct mail competitors. Finally, few could doubt the necessity of adopting the Total Newspaper Concept, discussed in Chapter 1 and built upon the philosophy that the newspaper is a living, breathing body made up of various parts, each vital to the well-being of the other. Some of these parts are the different newspaper departments; some are the market segments which the newspaper serves and on which it depends.

Beyond the internal and external environmental studies presented in this book are discussions of the day-to-day workings, problems, and opportunities of each department in the newspaper. No chapter is meant to be an exhaustive study of departmental operation. That would be beyond the scope of any one book. It is hoped, however, that each chapter will whet the appetite of the reader to adopt a regular habit of reading more about the different phases of newspaper management in such excellent publications as *Presstime, Editor & Publisher, WJR, Advertising Age,* and *Publisher's Auxiliary.* Changes in newspaper management are occurring every month, and it is important to keep an up-to-date understanding of how various issues—such as how the ABC counts bulk sales of newspapers—are being resolved.

This book is meant to be read primarily by undergraduate and graduate students of media management. Even though it is primarily a text on newspaper management, we live in a day when any media manager must have an understanding of newspapers, because he or she either serves them or competes with them. It is encouraging to see so many schools of journalism offering newspaper management courses and—in some cases—entire newspaper management programs. Universities such as Northeastern, Virginia Commonwealth, the University of Miami, and the University of Minnesota are on the leading edge of those schools recognizing the importance of instilling an appreciation of media management in their journalism students.

This book is also meant to be read by working professionals who may have always wondered "what goes on in advertising or circulation," or why management makes some of the decisions it does. Such knowledge can only serve to make that journalist more of a likely prospect for a future newspaper management opening when it occurs. Some of the information in the following pages may seem too basic; some of it may seem too advanced. All of it is important.

ACKNOWLEDGMENTS

Any book is, to a large extent, built upon the ideas of authors and practitioners who have done previous work in the field. This book is no exception. I am indebted to the publishers of *Presstime, Editor & Publisher, Publisher's Auxiliary, Advertising Age, WJR* (and, especially the thinking of John Morton), the *Bulletin of the American Society of Newspaper Editors,* seminars and publications of the American Press Institute, Associated Press Managing Editors, Inland Daily Press Association, the International Newspaper Marketing Association, and the American Newspaper Publishers Association for jogging my thinking and keeping me up to date on the changes in the newspaper industry. I am grateful also to editors David Lipman, Jim Standard, and Bill Evans, who graciously granted me interviews when I was teaching at Southern Illinois University in Edwardsville.

An author is also dependent upon the moral support of friends and loved ones. I am unbelievably fortunate in having the support of Diane, Molly, Jim, Hazel and C. J. Willis, Mark and Barbro Bruhn, my colleague Pat Kelly, and H. S. Sandhu.

Surviving in the Newspaper Business

1

SURVIVING IN THE NEWSPAPER BUSINESS

The newspaper business is a lucrative and rewarding investment for those modern-day entrepreneurs who own one or more of the approximately 1,660 dailies and 7,600 weeklies in the United States. At the start of this decade, the median net profit margin for all U.S. newspaper groups was 9.6 percent, or about double the median profit margin for the Fortune 500 Industrials.[1] In addition, return on sales was ranging from 14 to 18 percent, which is way over the national average of 6 percent for other types of companies. Third, daily newspaper circulation was 62,489,360 in 1986, about even with the circulation at the start of the decade. However, newsprint consumption climbed to a record 8.9 million metric tons in that year, showing a real growth in the size of newspapers. Fourth, newspapers continue to garner the largest single share of available advertising revenue for all news media.[2] Fifth, most newspapers still represent monopolies in their respective, local markets. Only about 25 cities still have competing daily newspapers. Finally, to generalize somewhat, 1986 Audit Bureau of Circulations figures showed most of the nation's top 25 daily newspapers showing circulation gains in that year.[3]

The problem is that, while the above figures are all valid and can be supported by numerous other positive indicators about newspapers, the entire media mix is changing to the point that many newspapers are finding themselves an endangered species. Some have already become extinct. On this negative side, the years 1981–1983 saw the deaths of several notable metro daily newspapers such as the *Washington Star, Philadelphia Bulletin, Buffalo Courier and Express, Cleveland Press,* and *Memphis Press-Scimitar.* Later, in 1985 and 1986, some 38 smaller daily newspapers ceased publication. Some were merged with other newspapers, some were converted to weeklies, and a few were just shut down. Also in those years, however, several new dailies were begun. In sum, the number of U.S. daily newspapers dropped from 1,772 in 1950 to about 1,657 in 1986,[4] and although total circulation of dailies has jumped nine million or 20 percent since 1950, the population has increased even more.[5] Finally, although total daily newspaper advertising rose from $25.2 billion in 1985 to $27 billion in 1986,[6] it is barely keeping pace with the country's Gross National Product increase.

Clearly all is not well in the newspaper publishing business. An industry that for decades did not see much need for changing its management or marketing structure has today been confronted with the demand to change. Publishers realize that if they don't wake up to the changing nature of their cities, news consumers, and advertisers, they may find their products have become dinosaurs in an electronic world populated by consumers and clients with needs of immediacy, intimacy, specialized reporting, deep market penetration, and target circulations.

NEWSPAPERS AND THE MARKET ETHIC

For decades much of the newspaper business has been characterized by well-insulated publishers and editors who dictate the daily news agenda along with the emphasis given certain categories of stories. At least one recent study by the American Society of Newspaper Editors found much of that arrogance is still in place in the 1980s among journalists.[7] Among its findings are that many reporters and editors still distance themselves from their readers, underestimate their readers' intelligence, and develop a limited tunnel vision about conditions that really exist in the outside world. Many editors feel they know their town or city simply because they have lived there a while or because they feel people and local governments are really about the same anywhere they go, yet if there is one single reason why newspapers are having difficulty in the 1980s, it is this very isolation. The warning of newspapering in the 1980s and beyond is that no newspaper can afford to distance itself from the readers and advertisers. On the contrary, any newspaper must stay attuned to the changes, both obvious and subtle, taking place in its local market. The byword in the newspaper business—as in any business today—is competition. If a newspaper is not doing a good enough job in meeting the demands of the consumers, another entrepreneur with another type of product will step in and fill the gap.

Enter the *market ethic*, so welcomed by advertising and circulation executives, but so dreaded by editors and reporters. The reason for the different reactions is normal. Most newsrooms value the concept of the service ethic, which, to an editor, states that the public good takes precedence over making a profit—a profit that might come by pandering to the public's whims. The market ethic rests on the concept of identifying, addressing, and supplying the feasible desires of the consumer. Still, no polarity should exist between the two ethics. The reason is that the mission of the news, advertising, and circulation departments is basically the same. That overall mission is to provide a quality newspaper to the breadth and depth of the newspaper's geographic and demographic market.[8]

Few would disagree that newspapers must first cover their own local markets first. That is one difference between newspapers and television, especially television networks. Newspapers are locally oriented media, entrusted first to cover that local market and deriving most of their advertising revenue from that market. If the news department fails to cover events in a particular circulation area, the circulation manager will become upset. If the news department regularly fails to cover events in an area of the market containing several advertisers, the advertising director will become upset. In similar fashion, the editor should be upset if the circulation department doesn't do its job in extending delivery of the newspaper to the widest feasible area, and if the advertising department doesn't sell advertising in these areas. Why is this so? It is because the editor should be concerned about how many readers are exposed to the news. Is not the implied mandate of the First Amendment to inform the people? Also, the editor should realize that, like it or not, many people buy newspapers as much for their advertising content as for the news. Therefore, the more advertising sold in the market's far corners, the more papers will be bought, and the more people informed.

However, there is yet another reason for a cease-fire between the news and advertising departments. It is no secret that the lion's share of a newspaper's revenue (and therefore the resources to run the news department) comes from the sale of local advertising. For a metro daily, that can amount to 85 percent of its total revenue; for a smaller paper, it can equal up to 100 percent, if the paper is a shopper for instance. As Jon G. Udell notes in his book, *The Economics of the American Newspaper,* the newspaper that is financially independent generally is the one that will be the more editorially independent,[9] for the larger the advertising base a newspaper has, the less chance its publisher will ask the editor to back off a story which may alienate a few advertisers. Keeping that advertising base as broad as possible is the job of the advertising department, but it must have help from the news and circulation departments to succeed.

Also, this question should occur to everyone on the newspaper staff: is it feasible to think readers will continue to spend money every year for a newspaper that is not giving them what they want and need? After all, it's not as if the United States were in an information vacuum: quite the contrary. What is to prevent readers from getting all their news from television and buying a couple of special-interest magazines to quench their thirst for news about their particular fragmented interests?

For years, communication theorists have debated the rhetorical question of whether a tree falling in the woods makes any sound if no one is there to hear it. The same debate could be waged over the editorial content of the newspaper. Is the story really getting through if only a small percentage of potential readers see it? Whether one accepts the philosophical argument or not, the argument of reality is inescapable. If a newspaper does not keep track of its changing market, it may find itself failing entirely in its mission. It may sound facetious, but it is hard to get any news out to readers after the newspaper has folded for good. This being the case, what are some of the changes that can occur in a newspaper's market that could spell trouble for the paper if they go unaddressed? The following are some possibilities.

The Changing Nature of Readers

In 1979, and again in 1984, the American Society of Newspaper Editors hired researchers to conduct studies on the nature of readers' wants and needs concerning their newspapers. Ruth Clark, who headed the research project, said that, whereas in 1979 readers wanted less news about the world and more about themselves, the 1984 study showed almost the opposite. "Then it was me, my life, my problems, my environment; now it is news, facts, basic information the public wants out of newspapers," she says in the 1984 report.[10] The new study, "Relating to Readers in the 80's," concludes that the public wants hard news, and though some question whether papers are fair or biased, people by and large think newspapers are "indispensable" for their lives. The important thing is that those desires did not remain static over the years between the two studies. For instance, whereas the 1979 study showed readers to have more of an interest in lighter, consumer-oriented pieces, the 1984 study showed readers returning to the hard, local news as never before. Market-conscious newspaper editors should have picked up on these changes and adjusted their news emphasis accordingly. This is probably the hardest pill for any editor to swallow, but it deserves strong consideration.

Another recent study conducted among New England editors showed many editors disagreeing with readers over the ranking of particular news items.[11] The study further showed that many editors felt it was their job to "give the readers what they *need* rather than what they *want*." The image occurs of a determined mother trying to force-feed castor oil to her reluctant son. As admirable as this editorial determination sounds, the question arises: how does an editor know what his or her readers need if the editor doesn't stay in touch with those readers? Does every reader in every market need the same thing? Just because a daily newspaper in Los Angeles is leading with a story about Mexican refugees doesn't mean the daily in Des Moines, Iowa, does the same. For this reason, many newspaper publishers like to set up regular meetings with townspeople to keep their hand on the pulse of the readers. To be sure, television has long been interested in market research studies, but many newspaper managers have only recently begun paying attention.

Changes in the Age Demographics

The nature of readers can also change in a market when a city's population experiences greater emigration or immigration from one age group than another. Take for instance a Southern community to which retirees have recently begun to flock, or take an old, traditional city that has been losing its young college graduates to a more progressive locale. When the age profile of a community changes, story interest will definitely change. A newspaper that has been dishing out a steady diet of consumer pieces for expectant mothers or first-time home buyers will find it hard to sell those pieces to a preponderance of readers interested more in retirement plans, Social Security benefits, and special-interest hobbies.

Another practical reason for keeping track of the age demographic, especially among current subscribers, is that certain age groups are deemed better target audiences by advertisers. Especially attractive are the people between 18 and 49, who do most of the buying in the retail outlets. If a newspaper finds, such as the *Christian Science Monitor* did several years ago, that the median age of its subscribers was 60 years old, far beyond that optimum group,[12] then efforts must be expended to attract more of the younger age groupings.

The Competition

Even if the news consumers in the market don't change in terms of reading needs or age demographics, the market can still change if the competition itself changes. If competitors start doing something different, such as putting out a Sci-Tech Section and drawing in more computer advertising, then the market has changed. If a competitor folds and leaves town, the market has changed, and if a new type of competitor enters the marketplace, as happens when a shopper moves in, the market has changed. All these changes and many others have definite implications for the newspaper that wants to survive.

In the late 1970s and early 1980s the competition between the *Dallas Morning News* and the *Dallas Times Herald* reached a fever pitch. Prior to the 1970s, Dallas had been dominated by the home-owned *Morning News,* but when the *Times Herald* was purchased by the *Times Mirror* group, things began changing. The *Times Herald* found greater financial resources at its disposal and a more savvy management team running the operation. That translated into the paper improving its pool of reporting and editing talent. As a result, more and more prestigious news awards began going across town to the *Times Herald,* culminating in that paper receiving a Pulitzer Prize. Soon the once-dominant *Morning News* was being beaten in several important journalistic areas. The *Morning News,* a paper which many of its reporters had characterized as a hard place to get hired but an even harder place to get fired, soon realized what was happening and joined in the battle. In the past few years it has reclaimed its former glory and has outdone itself in producing a newspaper which is on most top-25 lists in the country for journalistic excellence.

The situation was similar on the advertising side. As one newspaper would begin a more comprehensive and aggressive advertising campaign, the other would follow with a similar campaign. Special sections were launched by both papers to draw in more readers and advertisers. These sections were well planned and executed, and top-notch designers were laying them out. No sooner would one of the two papers announce a special section than the other would begin a similar one. In the clothes-conscious world of Dallas, a high-quality fashion section seemed a sure hit, yet neither paper had one until the late 1970s when both papers launched their own within months of each other, making full use of color, good reporting, and state-of-the-art design techniques. The competition reached peak levels when the circulation department of each paper began aggressive marketing campaigns to increase circulation numbers. Some of these efforts even gave rise on both sides to charges and lawsuits of inflated subscription numbers. Many of these same charges were still flying in 1987.

The point is that if either of the newspapers in Dallas had chosen to ignore any of these changing market conditions, it is likely that paper would not be in existence today. Since both did join in the battle, however, Dallas remains one of the very few cities with aggressively competing daily newspapers, and both are considered better products because of the competing influence of the other. Now both newspapers have won Pulitzer Prizes and are considered among the better papers in the nation.

A second change in competitive market conditions can come about when one newspaper suddenly finds itself the only daily in town, or at least one of a smaller number of dailies. Such has been the situation in New York on several occasions over the past five decades when worthy competitors such as the *New York World* and *New York Herald-Tribune* closed their doors, leaving fewer New York Dailies to divide the spoils. In more recent years, the *Washington Post* found itself the recipient of several thousand potential subscribers and many advertisers as a result of the death of the *Washington Star*. No sooner had the *Post* a chance to implement strategy to claim some of those potential subscribers and advertisers, than it had to face a new competitive challenge in the form of the *Washington Times*. Therefore, in a period of just a couple of years the market conditions had changed twice in drastic fashion for the *Post*. Had analysts in the marketing and advertising departments—as well as the news department—not taken early notice of these pending changes, and had they not developed strategies to address these changes, the *Post* could have missed a growth opportunity.

So far we've discussed what can happen when a newspaper faces a new challenge from existing competition, and when a newspaper finds itself losing an old competitor, but what happens when a new competitor enters the franchise area, and what if that competitor is of a more nontraditional nature? Such was the case in St. Louis several years ago when both the prestigious *St. Louis Post-Dispatch* and *St. Louis Globe-Democrat* found their existence threatened not by a new metro daily, but by a well-organized group of free-distribution, suburban weeklies. None of these weeklies would have claimed to have the consistent reporting power of the two St. Louis dailies, but they did have a few advantages over the two powerhouses. For one, they had total market coverage—or at least something close to it—of the St. Louis suburban area. Second, they offered advertisers more specific target customers. Third, they offered it all at lower advertising rates than the metro dailies. Since most newspapers get the majority of their advertising revenue from local advertisers, and since local advertisers are looking for high penetration of the newspaper into the market area, the St. Louis group of weeklies began taking large chunks out of the advertising base of the two metro dailies. In the end, after the dust had settled, both dailies emerged somewhat scarred, and the *Globe-Democrat* is no longer publishing.

To meet such challenges as those posed by free-distribution newspapers and shoppers—which generally have no news content at all—more newspapers are converting to Total Market Coverage (TMC) products. Today it is not unusual for a paid circulation daily or weekly to publish its own weekly shopper which covers the entire market, or at least the portion of the market not already covered by the paid counterpart. Publishers around the country have found advertisers to be low on newspaper loyalty and high on the need for such total market coverage. This is one reason why not only shoppers—but also direct mail firms—are garnering large chunks of local advertising revenues.

For the newspaper publisher who has always considered himself an editorialist only, and stayed relatively removed from the business side of the operation, the times are changing. Now, more than ever, publishers must be expert planners, strategists, and market-oriented business people. This doesn't mean they cannot continue to publish high-quality news products, but it does mean the publisher must first focus attention on the financial underpinnings of the business and the threats and opportunities posed by the changing nature of the market's competitors.

General Societal Changes

A newspaper's management team must also keep track of the changes occurring in the market which affect everyone and influence other changes of day-to-day behavior. One change that has affected residents of large cities is the increasing difficulty of physically moving around in the city. Traffic patterns on city streets and highways are heavier today than ever before. Motorists are spending more time sitting in traffic jams, are leaving for work earlier in the morning, and arriving home later in the evening. These changes affect the way in which many people obtain their news and information on a daily basis, and it also affects—and in most cases hampers—the delivery methods of metropolitan daily newspapers. A publisher may chalk up these problems to progress, joke about them with the rest of the city, or curse them, but eventually he or she must deal with them or the newspaper may lose ground to suburban papers, radio, and television.

For instance, what happens to an adult's newspaper reading habits if she must begin her morning trip to work at 6:30 instead of 7:00 or 7:30? That half hour may mean there is no time for even scanning the morning paper—assuming it even got there by 6:30—especially if this commuter is driving to work, and especially if the newspaper is a broadsheet and not a tabloid. That means the commuter's attention will possibly turn to the afternoon daily, if there is one. However, this is not automatic, for if that same commuter doesn't get home until 6:00 or 7:00 P.M., then even the afternoon daily is old news because its deadline was probably 1:00 or 2:00 P.M. at the absolute latest. The evening edition of television news is carrying material that has occurred in the five-hour interval. Of course the commuter may pick up a paper any time during the day, but leisure reading time is scarce during the day, and advertisers like readers to take their time going through the newspaper.

A related problem which is occurring in many cities, especially on the East and West coasts, is that commuters are living further out from the cities because of the high price of housing closer in. That poses a problem in that the metro daily must somehow get the paper past the traffic jams and out to the outskirts early enough for a commuter who is going to be leaving very early indeed. It also means that that commuter is going to be interested in the news of that far-out region as much—or more—than the news of the city itself.

Still another related problem is that when a city's work force changes over time from primarily white-collar to blue-collar, or vice versa, the reading habits of the news consumers also change. Many blue-collar workers have overnight shifts and sleep in the mornings. Therefore they would generally prefer to subscribe to an afternoon paper that is on the doorstep about the time they wake up in mid-afternoon. If a publisher has not been keeping aware of the increase or decline in the number of blue-collar workers in the city, he or she may be unaware of such changes in reading habits going on in his or her own market.

Still another reason many afternoon dailies are experiencing trouble is that the trucks which carry these papers out to the drop-off points in the suburbs and far reaches of the city get caught in the same traffic jams as the rest of the city's motorists. Certainly the delivery vans can beat the rush-hour traffic by leaving earlier, but that means the deadlines for these afternoon dailies must be shoved back to even earlier times in the day. The earlier the deadline, the older the afternoon news is when it hits the doorsteps in time to beat the 6:00 television news, which in content it can't really do, anyway. One solution to this problem has been the installation of satellite printing plants so that newspapers can actually be published in the suburbs, thus making it easier and quicker to get the papers to the doorsteps without compromising the deadline situation.

IT TAKES A SENSE OF BALANCE . . .

These then are just some of the changes that can occur in a market and can have direct impact on the local newspaper's chances of survival and success. Before moving on, however, it seems appropriate to inject a note of caution: it is possible to go too far in trying to satisfy the market ethic. One New England television station, for instance, dreamed up an idea a few years ago to form a sort of community advisory committee of several hundred leading citizens to decide what stories needed coverage and what emphasis the station's newscast would assume. A few times a year, so the plan went, this group was to gather in some high school auditorium and become, in effect, a pool of amateur editors and producers for that television station. Fortunately that idea was never implemented, and the station's management changed shortly thereafter. If the idea had been put into effect, the station would have abdicated its responsibility to present a daily news agenda based not just on market considerations, but also on the experience of seasoned news producers and reporters.

There is nothing wrong in listening to representative groups in a community, but there is something wrong in turning over the editorial decisions to them. This then becomes an important qualifier for a news operation intent on addressing the market ethic: taking market considerations into account when planning a community news agenda does not mean turning over the decision-making responsibility to amateur journalists. The newspaper's editors still have responsibility for the news product, so they must also have the authority to develop it, and with good reason: newspapers generally employ competent, highly skilled journalists who understand the history, context, and significance of stories as well as their probable interest among readers. The market ethic should imply that in performing a responsible job of news gathering and presentation, editors will consider their reader's wants and needs as prime criteria of what the daily news agenda will resemble.

. . . AND AWARENESS

Surviving and growing by responding to challenges in the market take a newspaper management team that stays aware of the current and potential market conditions, tracks them over time, compares and contrasts them, sees the connections and impact on the newspaper, and responds quickly with sound planning and measured strategies for implementation. The newspapers that grow and prosper will be the ones led by enlightened managers who direct fully integrated newspaper operations. The classic pyramidal management structure may cause problems for such integration, however, because it has a tendency to separate departments into neat units that develop tunnel vision about their mission and how to achieve it. This is one reason why advertising, news, and circulation departments have for so long been at each others' throats instead of operating in a more coordinated way. Thus, several years ago, a more enlightened concept was introduced in the newspaper industry to complement— and even take the place of—this classic pyramidal structure.

THE TOTAL NEWSPAPER CONCEPT

Developed by the International Newspaper Marketing Association (INMA), this new structure has been called the Total Newspaper Concept. It rests upon several beliefs, but chiefly the following:

1. To be effective and efficient, a newspaper's various departments must communicate, cooperate, and coordinate efforts at becoming a superior newspaper ready to meet the challenges of the changing market.

2. To meet those challenges, a newspaper must be concerned about—and respond to— the needs of four external target groups: its readers and nonreaders, advertisers and nonadvertisers. In fact, many newspaper marketers are even more concerned with the infrequent reader and infrequent advertiser than the people not reading or advertising in the newspaper at all. They feel it may be more feasible to try and convert these infrequent customers to steady customers than to try to interest nonreaders and nonadvertisers in using the newspaper. The best newspaper marketing departments try to go after all these market areas, however. Failure to meet the needs of any one of these groups will mean the newspaper is failing to reach its potential and fulfill its mission.

Exhibit 1 is a diagram of the Total Newspaper Concept showing the importance of the various interfaces between newspaper departments and between the newspaper and the four broad target groups in the market. The departments represented in the core of the diagram are the offices of publisher, personnel, promotion, accounting, marketing, and the mechanical department. They must constantly interface with the three main newspaper departments: advertising, news-editorial, and circulation. These departments, in turn, must coordinate work with each other and conduct two-way communication with the newspaper's four broad target groups outside the newspaper. It is imperative that the entire newspaper staff realize it is on the same mission: to produce a quality newspaper that will reach the breadth and depth of its geographic and demographic market. With that mission understood, it is easy to see why communication and cooperation are the chief features of the Total Newspaper Concept.

An example of how a newspaper can develop an integrated approach to opportunities in its market was demonstrated by an Illinois daily when it seized its chance in 1981 to capitalize on a high-interest news event, which was long-awaited by the public. The event was the pending release of the U.S. hostages from Iran in January 1981. The newspaper's management knew the day would come when these men would be released, and they also knew that this would be a wonderful day to spread the news to the far corners of the newspaper's market, to readers and nonreaders alike. To take full advantage of this saturation coverage on that day, the advertising department began a campaign to solicit welcome-home ads from businesses that had not advertised with the paper in some time, as well as from the regular advertisers. The circulation department worked out a sampling procedure and had contingency plans for extra carriers in place. The news department worked up special advance sidebars chronicling the history of the hostage incident. The production department was alerted to expect a larger press run that day and had its people in place. Finally the hostages were released, and the entire team, which had met several times in earlier weeks, went into action to implement the plans for saturation

Exhibit 1
The Total Newspaper Concept

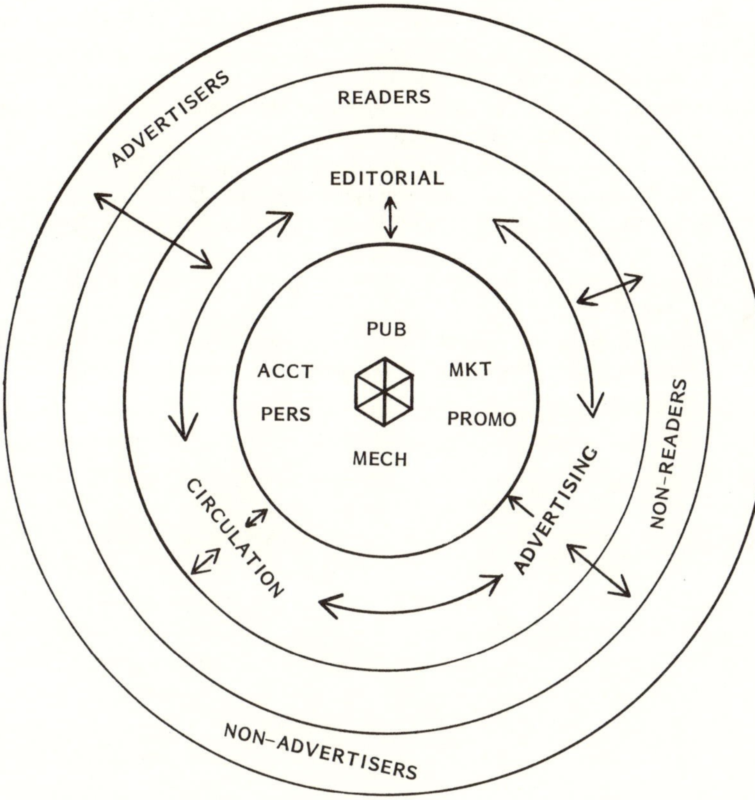

The Total Newspaper Concept portrays the fully integrated newspaper interacting with its market of readers, nonreaders, advertisers and nonadvertisers. In addition to nonreaders and nonadvertisers, newspaper marketers are becoming more interested in the infrequent reader and the infrequent advertiser.

Source: Reprinted with permission of the International Newspaper Marketing Association (© International Newspaper Marketing Association).

coverage. As a result, at least on that one day, this newspaper came very close to reaching its mission and getting out the word to all four target groups.

NOTES

1. Benjamin Compaine, *Who Owns The Media?* (New York: Harmony Books, 1979), p. 13.

2. "A Year of Ups and Downs," *Presstime* (May 1987), p. 124.

3. "Most Top 25 Newspapers Show Circulation Gains," *Editor & Publisher* 15 November 1986: 14.

4. "A Year of Ups and Downs," p. 124.

5. Jon G. Udell, *Economics of the American Newspaper* (New York: Hastings House, 1978), p. 31.

6. "A Year of Ups and Downs," p. 124.

7. Celeste Huenergard, "Study Says Reporters are Cynical, Arrogant, Isolated," *Editor & Publisher* 22 May 1982: 14.

8. Udell, "Economics of the American Newspaper," pp. 55, 57.

9. Udell, "Economics of the American Newspaper," p. 25.

10. Marcia Ruth, "Readers Now Want Hard News, New Clark Study Says," *Presstime* (May 1984), p. 52.

11. Jim Willis, "Editors, Readers and News Judgment," *Editor & Publisher* 7 February 1987: 14.

12. William M. Bulkeley, "Staid *Christian Science Monitor* Changing Its Look to Restore Readership and Profits," *Wall Street Journal* 1 October 1983: B1.

2

NEWSPAPER MANAGERS: WHO DOES WHAT?

Walter Goldsmith and David Clutterbuck write in their book, *The Winning Streak,* that good leaders possess at least three overall attributes. First, they are visible, traveling throughout their departments to discuss with their people where and how the business is going. Second, leaders provide a clear vision in which they believe passionately and which they encourage others to embrace. Third, leaders have clear objectives and are provided the resources needed to strike out after them.[1] The need for good leaders in the newspaper industry is as strong as in any other industry. In fact, with the abundant evidence that the media arena is growing more and more competitive, strong newspaper leaders who encompass these attributes are more valuable now than ever before.

THE MAJOR DIVISIONS OF A NEWSPAPER

Newspapers are generally divided into news-editorial and business divisions. Within each large division are more distinct departments. For instance, within the business division would come the revenue-producing departments like advertising and circulation, along with mechanical and the front-office departments such as marketing research, promotion, accounting, and personnel. News-editorial would contain both the news and editorial departments.

Newspapers vary, according to size, as to how elaborate and distinct each of these divisions is. On metro dailies, the distinctions between divisions and departments is very clear. On smaller dailies and weeklies, the distinctions are somewhat blurred and overlap occurs. The publisher, for instance, may serve both as editor and general manager. The following descriptions generally characterize the scope and nature of each division at a large daily newspaper.

News-Editorial

This division is charged with producing all reading material, except advertising, that is published in the newspaper. Also included is all visual material encompassing news photography and artwork done by the newsroom's art department. The news-editorial division will have several separate departments within it.

The News Department. This department encompasses the city, state, national, foreign, features, sports, business, science, entertainment, and travel desks, with editors overseeing each. The newsroom is presided over by the executive editor or managing editor. The copy desk operation is a part of the newsroom but has a distinct function from the newsgathering and reporting duties. This is where the stories are checked and double-checked for grammatical, factual, and contextual accuracy, where style is checked for consistency, where headlines are created, and where stories are assigned positioning in the newspaper. Usually the news editor presides over the copy desk operation, and he or she is assisted by a copy desk chief and several copy editors and layout editors. This is the newsroom unit that interfaces directly with the backshop, and it is thus sensitive to both the news and production schedules and requirements. It often becomes a separate island of activity in the newsroom, however.

The Editorial Desk. This department is responsible for producing the opinion and commentary section of the newspaper. It is presided over by the editorial page editor, who generally reports directly to the editor or publisher of the newspaper.

The Photography Department. This is presided over by the photo editor, who is responsible for all the original news, sports, and feature photography done by the newspaper.

The Art Department. It produces all graphs, charts, line art, and retouchings for news-editorial. It is presided over by an art director.

The Morgue or Library. This unit provides the historical research for all reporters requesting it for their stories. A chief librarian directs this staff, which is responsible for maintaining up-to-date files of stories produced by the newspaper, as well as storing data from other news and feature services. With the dawn of the computer age, most large daily libraries have gone on-line with their information retrieval services. This facilitates the accessing of information by the news staff, and it also makes it easier to store more information from a variety of sources outside the newspaper itself. In fact, there are several software packages that allow networking with a variety of informational services. This may be one of the most significant applications of computers to newspapers.

Business

The business division is responsible for the efficient operation of all the newspaper's revenue-producing divisions. It is presided over by a business manager or general manager, who oversees all sales, collections, budgets, and capital expenditures. It receives, spends, and invests money, and supervises everything pertaining to the business side of the newspaper, including advertising, circulation, and job printing. The following departments are usually under its direct control.

Advertising. This is the most important revenue-producing center in the entire newspaper. It is presided over by an advertising manager who is in charge of generating and directing sales in all advertising categories: retail, national, classified, and preprints. The advertising manager is assisted by managers who have hands-on supervision over each of these separate categories.

Circulation. This department is the lifeblood of the newspaper. Without it the newspaper would carry no advertising, and without advertising the paper would not survive. Presided over by a circulation manager, the circulation department is split into smaller units, consisting of district and state circulation.

Job Printing. Many smaller dailies and weeklies engage in job printing. Generally these printing jobs are handled on smaller presses in the newspaper, unless the printing jobs consist of producing other area weekly newspapers. In that case they are done on the large web presses that produce the daily itself. This department is presided over by a job printing manager.

In addition to having direct supervision over these departments, the business manager usually serves as the reporting officer for the manager of the mechanical division as well.

Mechanical. Most newspaper plants use newer cold type or photo-processing techniques instead of the old hot lead/linotype processes. In fact, among almost all newspapers, the linotype has gone the way of the dinosaur. Some newspapers, which cannot afford an immediate gutting of their old presses and installation of new ones, have found ways of combining phototypesetting and their existing letterpress units. The result is usually better reproduction than the hot lead system, but not as good as the offset presses. This new process of flexography is discussed in Chapter 7. For newspapers using offset processes, the following units comprise the mechanical department.

Composing. This department is responsible for all typesetting (and some is still required, even with the most advanced newsroom computer systems), and paste-up. It should be mentioned, however, that with the rapid advances in computerized typesetting and pagination (computerized page design), the clear distinction between the composing room and the newsroom is vanishing.

The Reproduction Camera Unit. This division is responsible for taking all art shot by photographers and reproducing it into halftone art for the page negatives. This unit also shoots the pages, forwarding page-size negatives stripped with halftone negatives to the platemaking unit.

Platemaking is the process by which page negatives are photographed onto light-sensitive aluminum plates that are then "developed" into positive images and placed on the offset presses.

The Pressroom. This is where the actual printing of the newspaper occurs. The pressroom is presided over by a foreman who synchronizes his unit's schedule with the other mechanical units before it, and with the mail room and circulation after it. If the plates haven't been made on time, the presses won't roll; if the presses don't roll on time, the delivery trucks won't roll either, and the paper winds up late on the doorsteps around the city.

The Mailroom. This is where the preprinted inserts are stuffed into the newspaper and the newspapers that are to be mailed are prepared for their journey. It is presided over by a mailroom foreman.

Data Processing/Accounting. The addition of the computer to newspaper operations has necessitated the development of an entirely new section of highly trained personnel and sophisticated equipment. The data processing department fulfills several functions, all related to the purchase or leasing of computer hardware and software, analysis, and dissemination of useful information so newspaper executives can make better, more informed decisions. As the years proceed, the need for efficient management information systems will increase, and this department will grow in importance. Taking advantage of the data processing system is the accounting department, charged with keeping accurate records of expenditures, purchases, and investments by the newspaper.

Other Administrative Departments. These would include such departments as marketing/research, personnel or employee relations, purchasing, and promotion, all of which are vital to the successful newspaper's operation.

KEY NEWSPAPER MANAGERS

Exhibit 2 shows a typical organizational chart for a large daily newspaper. Although this chart shows the reporting relationships and the responsibilities of each manager, it should be interpreted in conjunction with the Total Newspaper Concept, presented in Chapter 1. The reason is that the Total Newspaper Concept stresses the interrelatedness of all these departments and their managers.

Among the key newspaper managers are the publisher, business manager or general manager, advertising director, editor-in-chief, executive editor, managing editor, circulation manager, production manager, marketing research manager, and promotion manager.

Publisher

For some reason, to many people inside and outside the profession, this title is synonymous with "owner." It shouldn't be, especially in this era of group-owned newspapers where the owners and chief stockholders sit in New York or on the West Coast, and the papers and their individual publishers are scat-

Exhibit 2
Organizational Chart for a Metro Daily Newspaper

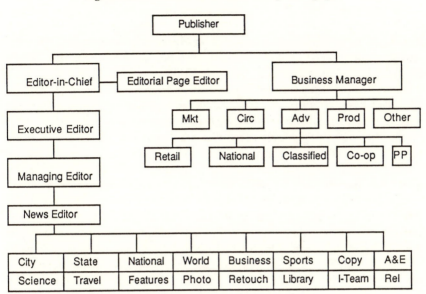

Key: PP = Preprint   A&E = Arts and Entertainment   I-Team = Investigative Team
Rel = Religion   Copy = Copy Desk.

tered across the country. The publisher is simply the chief executive officer at the individual newspaper. He or she may indeed be the owner if the paper is home-owned or is part of a closely held corporation, but few large dailies fall into this category. Nevertheless, whether the publisher is a majority owner, minority owner, stockholder, or simply an employee of the corporation, the person who holds this title is responsible for everything that goes on at the paper. As such, the publisher is charged with directing and coordinating the efforts of all the various departments within the newspaper.

The publisher is also the chief policy-making officer at the paper, although if the paper is group-owned, he or she must answer to headquarters in areas of budget approval and profit planning. Although the tradition has been for the publisher to rise from the ranks of the advertising department, there have been numerous cases in recent years where publishers have instead come out of the news-editorial department. A reporter who does have aspirations of going through the editing ranks and emerging as a publisher, however, must understand that he or she will be expected to have a thorough knowledge of the function and importance of sales to the newspaper, as well as budget preparation, planning, and implementation.

The ranks of publisher are opening up more to women as well as men. One recent study done at the University of Missouri, however, shows that the climb to the top is still difficult for women journalists. (That study, done by Jean Gaddy Wilson, will be discussed in Chapter 8.) Nevertheless, some newspaper groups, like the Gannett Co., pride themselves on moving women into the managing editor and publishing ranks. As a result, several Gannett newspapers are today operating with women chief executives.

One of the problems facing the publisher in the 1980s, according to a study by University of North Carolina journalism professor Philip Meyer, is the fact that many in the newsroom distrust publishers, because they don't believe they can be "good guys."[2] Meyer found that the happiest newsrooms were those where the publisher became involved and was perceived as "only doing good things." Meyer suggested that publishers should become more active in the newsroom, thereby breaking down some of the barriers existing between the news and business sides of the newspaper. He added that this also opens the door for editors to feel they can have more of an impact on the business side, learning some of the problems faced by that half of the newspaper. Meyer's study grouped publishers into one of four categories or types: the statesmen, who score high on "benign" involvement in the newsroom; the politicians, who score high in both malign and benign involvement; the partisan, who is high in malign involvement and low in benign involvement; and the absentee, who is low in both areas. His survey of editors showed that 36 percent said they had absentee publishers, 26 percent said they had politicians, 19 percent said partisans, and 19 percent said statesmen. Publishers, meanwhile, perceived themselves differently, with 36 percent seeing themselves as statesmen. Newsroom morale was found to be lowest at newspapers with absentee publishers and highest with statesmen.[3]

Business Manager

The business manager is the chief financial officer of the newspaper and, as such, is responsible for financial matters relating to all departments. If there is one individual at the newspaper who must have a thorough understanding of the financial threats, trends, and opportunities facing newspapers like his, it is the business manager. This individual must be adept at planning, budget building and implementation, revenue collection, and cost control. This is a good spot for an MBA or a graduate of one of the newer graduate programs in news media management like the one at the Northeastern University School of Journalism in Boston. The business manager should have an understanding of the uniqueness of the newspaper's mission in contrast to other types of businesses, but the main goal of this manager is to insure a profitable bottom line for the newspaper company through careful planning and cost-control strategies.

Editor-in-Chief

This is the manager who has full responsibility for the news and editorial content of the newspaper. Two things should be noted about this position, since some confusion has attended it over the years. First, the editor-in-chief is a manager: this individual's job is to successfully manage the people who produce the news and opinion pieces of the newspaper, to chart an appropriate news and editorial philosophy for the newspaper, and to insure that the philosophy is implemented. Second, different newspapers refer to their top editor by different titles. At one daily, the chief editor is known simply as the editor. At another, he or she is editor-in-chief. Yet another daily might attach top editorial responsibility to an executive editor or managing editor, although these titles usually connote day-to-day management responsibilities instead of overall planning and policy-making responsibilities. Some dailies, generally smaller ones, will find themselves edited by the publisher himself. In large metro dailies, the editor-in-chief usually assumes little if any direct, hands-on control over the newsroom's operation. Instead, he or she is the chief policy-making officer and planner in the newsroom and must battle at times with other newspaper departments to get a fair share of the company resources for the newsrooms.

Executive Editor and Managing Editor

These two management positions are lumped together in one section because sometimes a newspaper will sometimes have only one or the other, and will sometimes have both, especially at the metro daily level. The executive editor is like the executive officer on a naval ship. He or she is charged more with the day-to-day implementation of the overall news philosophy (often the editorial page editor reports directly to the editor-in-chief or publisher). For all intents and purposes, at many metro dailies the executive editor is the most visible chief news manager to the news staff as he or she translates news policy into implementation to be carried out by the managing editor and the newsroom staff.

The managing editor has a direct interface with the various desk editors in the newsroom, including—but not necessarily limited to—the news editor, city editor, state editor, national editor, foreign editor, lifestyles editor, arts and entertainment editor, sports editor, business editor, travel editor, and so on. The managing editor generally runs the daily editorial conferences which feature input from the various desk editors and discussion of the daily news agenda. The managing editor, assisted by several assistant managing editors, also handles the deployment of the editorial staff and the acquisition of new equipment for the newsroom. In short, he or she manages the newsroom.

The executive editor and managing editor are both former newsroom staff members, and it is not uncommon for them to have risen through the ranks on the copy and news desks, to assistant news editor, news editor, assistant managing editor, and then managing editor. The reason for this is that staffers graduating from the copy desk operation have a more thorough understanding not just of newsroom procedure, policy, and requirements, but also of production department procedure, policy, and requirements. A good knowledge of both departments is essential for the executive and managing editors.

Advertising Manager

The advertising manager is responsible for the largest single revenue-producing center of the newspaper: the advertising department. A veteran of advertising sales and a former manager of one of the advertising units (retail, national, classified, or preprints), the advertising director must have a thorough understanding of the relative importance of each division; the latest in time-tested sales techniques; the best methods available to motivate and pay ad reps; the most efficient measures of collection; the advertising potential available in the market, and the best ways of going about tapping it. Like the editor, the advertising director is not just a senior advertising salesperson; he or she is a manager in charge of producing the ad revenue through the efficient management of employees in the advertising department. Among the specific duties of the advertising director are the following:[4]

1. Know the market and the potential advertising revenue.
2. Set quarterly goals.
3. Transmit the above two goals to the staff.
4. Take standard call sheets and sales reports regularly from the staff.
5. Plan sales strategy with the sales reps.
6. Hold regular sales staff meetings and make the ad reps feel a part of the overall sales process.
7. Make sure the sales reps know the newspaper as well as the territory.
8. Know the competition and the nature of it, and look out for antitrust abuses.
9. Keep tabs on competitive strengths of the newspaper.
10. Interface with the marketing research department for optimal results.
11. Hire new sales staff members, coach current ones, and dismiss those who continually fall below the newspaper's standards.
12. Work to continually tailor the sales compensation strategy for sales reps to obtain the maximum motivational benefit.

Circulation Manager

Long a forgotten department in some newspapers, possibly because of its relatively lackluster nature, the circulation department has grown a larger profile in recent years because of the importance advertisers attach to the quantity, as well as quality, of subscribers. Because of its importance and volatile atmosphere in which it operates, the circulation department needs top-notch professionals staffing it. The three major goals of circulation management are to increase penetration into the market's households, provide a good distribution system and plenty of newsracks for single-copy sales, and collect payments in full. Circulation managers are often former district circulation managers who have risen through the ranks because of their commitment to the circulation effort and their understanding of its many, varied aspects.

Production Manager

This individual is in charge of all the components relating to producing the physical newspaper product and delivering it to circulation for distribution. The production manager is a veteran of the backshop and hopefully has had experience both in composing and in the pressroom. This can be a volatile management position at times because the production manager must mediate not only between upper management and the backshop, but also between management and organized labor. The Pressmen's Union is a strong one at most large newspapers and has a tradition of making tough demands on newspaper management and of striking if those demands go unmet. Sometimes the trouble has gone beyond striking to sabotage and personal injury, as the *Washington Post* discovered with its labor trouble in the pressroom during the early 1970s. Therefore, the person occupying the role of production manager must have a good deal of tact and people skills. Furthermore, he must feel equally at ease in the pressroom and in the office of the business manager.

Marketing/Research Manager

Many metro dailies have set up a distinct marketing/research department in recent years, and this is a testament to the importance these newspaper executives attach to the marketing approach to newspapering. The marketing/researching manager should be an individual who is thoroughly schooled in the types of research methods and designs available to newspapers to produce appropriate, specific, and reliable data that can be used to predict reader patterns. Once this data is in hand, the newspaper management team can then go about assessing whether they can feasibly construct or modify a newspaper to appeal to these readers. Once these changes are made, it is the job of the promotion department and the advertising department to make these changes known to the readers and advertising clientele.

For too long the duties of the marketing/research manager have been buried in the advertising and circulation department. Certainly a great deal of interfacing is needed between all three departments, as well as the newsroom, but the tools of research methodology have become so sophisticated and time-consuming that a separate department presided over by a trained researcher is necessary. In many cases, this marketing/research manager will be working with outside researchers hired by the newspaper. Two of the largest such research consultants are Simmons and Scarborough. Even if much of the larger research is actually carried out by outside consultants, however, the marketing/research manager must advise as to the focus and scope of that research, and help to interpret the findings to the rest of the newspaper.

Promotion Manager

The job of the promotion manager is simply to promote the newspaper and the modifications in it to the readers and advertisers. This individual should be thoroughly familiar with the newspaper industry, the latest research showing needs and wants of readers, and—of course—he should be familiar with his own newspaper. Promotion managers come both out of the news and business sides of newspapers, and sometimes come directly from the world of professional public relations. They are entrusted with taking the data collected and interpreted by the marketing/research department and translating it into winning appeals for their newspaper. One promotion manager at a mid-size daily describes his job this way:

Our staff consists of eight people including myself. Over the last three to four years we have centralized all marketing service functions. Before that it was a dispersed system with circulation doing its own promotion, advertising doing its own, etc. Now it's all done in one department. We handle all promotion for the paper. I think we have a strong creative team in-house and a strong advertising agency. In-house we do all collateral material: direct mail, rack cards, market research and most in-paper print. We work cooperatively with the agency on our trade press ads, some in-paper and all broadcast. Almost all in-paper print tied directly with broadcast is done with the agency, but there are no strict rules. Our budget is 2 percent of our gross revenue.[5]

Indeed, the median total promotion budget for all newspapers participating in the 1987 Newspaper Promotion Operations Survey is $809,377, according to the International Newspaper Marketing Association.[6]

WHERE THE MONEY IS

A 1985 survey, conducted by the University of Missouri School of Journalism and funded by various news and university foundations, showed the breakdown at that time of average and median salaries for some of the key managerial jobs at daily newspapers. The results are as follows, with average first, and then median salaries reported:[7]

- Publisher: $65,729; $55,000
- General Manager: $53,751; $45,000
- Advertising Manager: $34,768; $30,000

- Circulation Manager: $27,542; $25,000
- Managing Editor: $30,714; $27,000
- Production Manager: $32,722; $29,000

In addition, the Newspaper Promotion Operations Survey showed the median salary of promotion managers to be $37,500.[8]

It must be noted that the Missouri study responses represent both large and small newspapers, with more medium- and small-size dailies represented than metros. Therefore, the salaries are not the average of what one would find at a metro daily. As would be expected, salaries at smaller dailies are lower than for the same managerial position at large dailies. That fact comes to light if one analyzes the average top minimum salary for reporters and photographers at 126 daily newspapers under contract with the Newspaper Guild. That average salary was just over $585 per week as of December 1, 1986,[9] meaning the average reporter at a large daily made about $30,420 annually at that time. Obviously the top editing positions would be substantially higher than that average reporter salary and, thus, substantially higher than the salaries quoted above for editor and managing editor. The same holds true for the salaries of other departmental managers as well. For instance, a 1987 study by the Southern Newspaper Publishers Association showed the average managing editor at a large daily makes $82,429.

NOTES

1. Walter Goldsmith and David Clutterbuck, *The Winning Streak* (New York: Random House, 1984), p. 13.

2. Andrew Radolf, "What Kind of Publisher Are You?" *Editor & Publisher* 12 November 1983: 26.

3. Radolf, "What Kind of Publisher," p. 26.

4. Christopher Eddings, "Management of the Weekly Newspaper," seminar, American Press Institute, Reston, Virginia, January 22, 1983.

5. Terilyn McGovern Mazza, "An Interview With a Winning Promotion Manager," *Editor & Publisher,* 19 July 1982: 19.

6. "INMA Study Shows Promotion Budgets, Salaries at Papers," *Editor & Publisher,* 29 August 1987: 30.

7. "Where the Money Is," *WJR* (March, 1986), p. 14.

8. "INMA Study," p. 30.

9. "Top Minimums for Reporters Average $585," *The Guild Reporter* 19 December 1986: 3.

3

NEWSPAPERS AND THE BOTTOM LINE

The newspaper that is financially independent has the best chance of being editorially independent. There is interplay at work between these two variables, and each rests heavily upon the other. If a newspaper must worry about where its next dollar is coming from, chances are its publisher will not allow the news staff to go out and alienate—or even disturb—readers and advertisers with hard, investigative stories. In addition, a newspaper is unlikely to have enough money to even field an expensive investigative team if its revenues are low. Therefore, everyone on the newspaper should be concerned about the financial health of the newspaper. On the economic side, any entrepreneur must see a profit ahead before taking a risk investing in a newspaper. On the altruistic side, the services that a newspaper provides the public cost money, and usually a lot of it. Without that money, those societal needs will go unmet.

The good news for newspapers is that, in 1986 profits were up for most public newspaper groups. For instance, Gannett Co.'s net income for 1986 rose 9 percent from 1985, while its revenues for the year increased 27 percent from the previous year; Knight Ridder Inc.'s net income for 1986 rose 5.5 percent, and its revenues were up $2 million from 1985; and net income for the Times Mirror Co. almost doubled in the two-year period, partially due to after-tax gains on the sale of assets.[1]

HOW NEWSPAPERS MAKE MONEY

Basic to any study of the newspaper's bottom line is an overall understanding of where that money comes from. What are the various revenue sources of the newspaper? How dependent is the newspaper on each of these sources? The Inland Daily Press Association (IDPA) publishes cost and revenue data for subscribers that detail both the sources and the destination of newspaper funds. The IDPA, headquartered in Park Ridge, Illinois, issues data for more than 350 participating dailies ranging in circulation from 3,000 to more than 500,000. In addition, the association collects and distributes data for weekly newspapers. Collectively, this data forms one of the standards many newspaper publishers and business managers use to assess the financial performance of their own newspaper. The following discussion is excerpted from the 1986 IDPA study for daily newspapers in two circulation categories: 115,800 to 230,400 and 10,000 to 11,100.[2]

Large Dailies

In 1987, the average large daily in the circulation category 115,800 to 230,400 grossed a total operating revenue of $81,891,500 and spent $62,251,800 for a total gross profit of 24 percent. Advertising revenue accounted for an average of $67,384,900 of that operating revenue (82.9 percent of newspaper revenue), and it came from local ($31,134,000), national ($4,699,200), classified ($24,236,700), legal ($353,000), and preprint ($7,677,800) advertising sources. Revenue per inch of local advertising averaged $23.72, while revenue per inch of national averaged $43.55 and classified averaged $32.47. The bulk of preprint advertising was from local advertisers ($6,386,100), and the rest from national ($1,212,800). Circulation revenue averaged $13,245,200 (16.3 percent of newspaper revenue), while other revenue averaged $620,900.

Small Dailies

Smaller dailies (circulation 10,000 to 11,100) averaged total operating revenues of $2,595,300. They had total operating expenses of $2,145,700, for a total gross profit average of 17.3 percent. Advertising revenue accounted for $1,628,000 (72.6 percent of newspaper revenue), and that was made up of local ($1,054,600), national ($69,100), classified ($327,800), legal ($48,400), and preprint ($169,200) advertising sources. Revenue per inch of local advertising averaged $4.29, while national averaged $5.27, and classified averaged $3.73. Legal advertising averaged $6.37 per inch. The bulk of preprint advertising was from local advertisers ($167,500), with the rest from national advertisers ($6,400). Circulation revenue averaged $533,500 (23.8 percent of newspaper revenue). Nonnewspaper revenue averaged $423,900, and was made up largely of commercial printing jobs which grossed $359,000. Revenue from newspaper-published shoppers averaged $191,800.

HOW NEWSPAPERS SPEND MONEY

Newspapers have little difficulty in finding ways of spending all this money, as the following discussion shows.

Large Dailies

The same Inland cost and revenue study showed the large daily category to spend an average of $7,405,600 (9.1 percent of newspaper revenue) on the news-editorial department; $4,322,500 (5.3 percent) on the advertising department; $9,977,600 (12.3 percent) on the circulation and distribution department; $6,674,500 (8.2 percent) on the mechanical department, and $19,915,800 on general and administrative departments. Another $13,411,200 (16.5 percent) was spent on newsprint, ink, and handling charges.

Salaries occupied a prominent part of these expenses, with news-editorial salaries averaging $4,676,300 (181 full-time and 17 part-time employees); advertising averaging $3,468,000 (138 full-time and 17 part-time); circulation and distribution averaging $5,086,300 (191 full-time and 159 part-time); and general and administrative averaging $3,366,000 (130 full-time and 16 part-time).

The other large expense was newsprint, ink, and handling costs of $13,411,200. Depreciation averaged $3,314,200. Other interesting findings of this study are that newspapers of this category averaged 32,519 tons of newsprint per year, and wasted 4.7 percent of that; grossed $75.73 per subscriber while spending an average of $57.05 for each; and published 16,882 pages annually of news-editorial content, 23,077 pages of advertising content, and 1,213 pages of unpaid (house) advertising. Bad debts averaged 1.1 percent of newspaper revenue.

Small Dailies

Small dailies spent their operating revenues of $2,595,300 as follows: news-editorial operation cost $249,300 (11.1 percent of newspaper revenue); advertising cost $196,100 (8.7 percent); circulation and distribution cost $207,000 (9.2 percent); mechanical cost $267,600 (11.9 percent); newsprint, ink and handling cost $235,500; and general and administrative cost $708,700 (31.6 percent). Nonnewspaper expenses were $337,700. The total gross profit was 17.3 percent, and 38 percent of the newspaper revenue went to payroll. Of the payroll expense, $174,800 went to news-editorial (10 full-time and 3 part-time); $158,800 went to advertising (9 full-time and 2 part-time); $94,200 went to circulation and distribution (4 full-time and 11 part-time), $193,800 went to mechanical (12 full-time and 6 part-time); and $230,400 went to general and administrative (8 full-time and 7 part-time). Other large expenses were $708,700 for newsprint, ink, and handling; $149,500 for putting out a shopper; and $290,200 for commercial printing expenses.

Other key findings were that an average of 473 tons of newsprint were used by the average small daily in this category, and 4.5 percent of that was wasted; 3,641 pages of news-editorial content were published, along with 2,822 of advertising and 157 of unpaid advertising; bad debt expense totaled .6 percent of newspaper revenues; and average circulation revenue per subscriber was $49.86, while the circulation and distribution cost per subscriber was $19.35.

COST AND REVENUE DATA FOR WEEKLIES

A National Newspaper Foundation (NNF) cost and revenue study showed the following data breakdown for weekly newspapers.[3]

Revenues

Revenues for weekly newspapers averaged as follows: retail advertising: 38 percent; classified: 8 percent; national: 1 percent; preprints: 3.5 percent; legals: 1.5 percent; commercial printing: 38 percent; circulation: 7.5 percent; and other: 2.5 percent. It should be noted that these percentages are in relation to gross revenue for weekly newspapers printing at home. The figures differ for weeklies printed by others, with the chief difference being that total advertising revenue amounts to about 77 percent of income and commercial printing brings in only about 9 percent.

Costs

Costs for weeklies averaged the following: news-editorial: 6.5 percent; advertising: 6 percent; production: 16 percent; administrative: 7.5 percent; printing: 22 percent; operating costs: 20 percent; depreciation and leases: 5 percent; other: 2 percent; and pretax profit: 9 percent. Again, these percentages are in relation to gross revenue for a weekly paper printing on its own presses. The chief difference for a weekly printing elsewhere is that editorial and advertising payrolls are higher, while in-house production expenses are down to about 13 percent. Pretax profit is also less, averaging 7.5 percent.

NOTES ABOUT COST STUDIES

The 1987 IDPA study was the first one done totally in-house and designed the way newspaper executives might really use it. The format for this 67th annual study starts with a chart that plots the performance of newspapers from various circulation, cost, and revenue categories. The normal ranges are graphically represented by what Inland research director Don Beelow calls the "cone of OK-ness." Beelow says, "If a publisher finds his paper is way outside that area in some department, it can raise a flag."[4] This same information is contained in a "predicted value" table showing what a newspaper should be getting in a particular category, and what percent of that attainment a newspaper has reached. Following that are charts laying out specific performances in detail. Altogether, the reader can go from the simple picture, to a table, to the real data. Using a workbook included in the study, a newspaper business manager can plot his newspaper's financial performance against those of other similar newspapers. As of 1987, the IDPA was also planning to put its studies online to be accessed via computer terminals at newspapers.

In 1987, 308 daily newspapers participated in the IDPA cost and revenue study. Included in the study's findings were the following:[5] the average participating newspaper had 45,000 subscribers; the average small- to medium-size daily (10,000 circulation and up) had a 52.2 percent penetration into the city zone market; the average operating revenue was just shy of $2.6 million, 72.6 percent of which comes from advertising, 23.8 percent from circulation, and 4.3 percent from other sources.

In addition to the NNF and IDPA studies, most state and regional press associations conduct periodic surveys of their member newspapers to obtain averages on expense and income figures. In fact, state press association directories offer some good, basic information regarding advertising rates, subscription prices, and so on for member papers. A national publication studying advertising rates of newspapers is the Standard Rate and Data Service (SRDS) publication. Still another way in which many publishers and business managers discover how they stack up to other newspapers is by participating in conferences and seminars of state, regional, and national press and publishers' associations, and by discussing cost and revenue data with fellow newspaper executives. Meetings and seminars helpful to such discussion are the American Newspaper Publishers Association Annual Convention, and American Press Institute seminars on newspaper finances.

Whatever the sources used, most publishers find it imperative that they understand what the cost and revenue averages look like for the industry so they can assess whether their newspaper is reaching its potential as a business.

NEWSPAPER FINANCIAL EXECUTIVES

The newspaper's chief financial executive, the business manager, has a great responsibility for insuring the health of the company's bottom line. In addition, the business manager's scope has broadened over recent years. For instance, although the news and business sides of the newspaper are philosophically separated, they have become more and more integrated over time. The person figuring prominently in that union is the business manager. Most top newspaper editors now consult both with the business manager and the marketing/research director on a regular basis. Although most editors report formally to the publisher, they have found it foolhardy to think they can ignore the newspaper's chief financial executive in times of planning, hiring, or acquisition. The basic role of the business manager is to provide the publisher with accurate, usable information to make profit planning possible. Generally, this individual, who is assisted by several assistants, will hold an MBA degree and may be a CPA as well. The person holding the office of business manager must have excellent people skills and be able to interface equally well with managers in the advertising, news, and other newspaper departments.

THE NEWSPAPER'S BALANCE SHEET

A newspaper, like any other business, records its financial data on two basic accounting forms: a balance sheet and an income (or profit and loss) statement.

Exhibit 3
Balance Sheet for a Small Newspaper

ASSETS

Cash on hand............................	$10,000
Checking account........................	25,000
Accounts Receivable.....................	55,000
Job paper inventory.....................	40,000
Office supplies..........................	30,000
Total Current Assets....................	160,000
Building.................................	200,000
Printing equipment......................	200,000
Total Fixed Assets......................	400,000
Total Assets............................	$560,000

LIABILITIES

Accounts Payable	
Job paper...............................	$40,000
Office supplies.........................	30,000
Total Current Liabilities.................	70,000
Building Mortgage.......................	50,000
Printing equipment loan..................	75,000
Total Long-Term Liabilities...............	125,000
Owner's Equity..........................	365,000
Total Liabilities........................	$560,000

A balance sheet, seen in Exhibit 3, provides a written photograph of the newspaper's financial health at any given time. It basically shows the overall assets and liabilities of the newspaper. Assets are all company resources (including cash, property, equipment, and supplies) that are available for use to the newspaper. An asset is usually owned by the newspaper, but need not necessarily be paid for. For instance, a small newspaper may have a $100,000 mortgage on its $200,000 building, yet the entire $200,000 is listed as an asset because it is available to the newspaper for use. The same holds true for supplies, which the newspaper may order on a 30-, 60-, or 90-day charge account. However, even though there is an outstanding balance on the supplies, the entire worth of the supplies is carried on the balance sheet as an asset.

If this seems a little unfair, the liabilities side of the ledger balances out the equation. Liabilities are basically monies owed. They can either be owed to other people (in which case they are true liabilities), or they can be money owed to the newspaper's owners—or investments in the newspaper—in which case they are equities. A bill owed to Ajax Office Supply Co. is a liability, as is the $100,000 owed to the mortgage holder of the newspaper building mentioned earlier, yet the other $100,000 already paid for the building is an equity claimed by the owners. Liabilities may be current or long-term, depending on the amount of time allowed to pay them off. Assets many times are divided into current assets, like cash on hand or in the bank or prepaid expenses; inventories like newsprint and ink; plant (or fixed) assets, like the land and building or equipment; and intangible assets like company goodwill, patents, and copyrights.

Liabilities represent the source of all assets, so total liabilities should equal total assets. If there is an asset listed on the balance sheet, the amount of that asset must be balanced out by a liability on the other side. The balance sheet does not show the sources of income on a month-by-month or week-by-week basis, nor does it show how that revenue is spent on a regular basis. The document showing all this is the income statement.

THE NEWSPAPER'S INCOME STATEMENT

This accounting document is probably the best tool for troubleshooting financial problems within the newspaper. It shows, generally on a monthly basis, the level and type of income generated by the different revenue-producing centers of the newspaper, and it shows the level and type of costs associated with running the newspaper for that month. Sometimes called the "cost and revenue statement" or the "profit and loss statement," the income statement pairs the income and expenses for a given month with the figures for the same month a year ago. Also, the income statement usually shows costs and revenues for the Year-to-Date (YTD) period for the current year and for the immediate past year. So, by studying the income statement for the month just completed and comparing it with the income statement for the same month a year ago, the business manager can assess whether the newspaper is growing, stagnating, or sliding backwards financially.

The income statement provides the bottom line—the profit or loss of the company for a particular period, usually a month. Income statements are given in report form, and the form may vary somewhat depending on whether the business is a manufacturing company or a service corporation. A newspaper really is both, but because a physical product is produced, its income statement generally resembles that of a retail or manufacturing company. The income statement shown in Exhibit 4 could be typical of such a statement for a small newspaper.

In spotting financial trouble or in looking for its causes, much attention should be paid to the income statement, which should be studied for trends. For instance, in Exhibit 4, the total income for March 1987 is ahead of the total income for March 1986. That is good, but these bottom lines can be somewhat deceiving and lull publishers into a false sense of well-being. Just because the bottom line is up does not necessarily mean all the revenue-producing centers at the newspaper are up as well. In this case, the most important revenue-producing center (local advertising) is indeed up, but national advertising is off by $2,000 in a time when most dailies are doing their best to attract more such advertising. Also, there is no growth in classified advertising. In addition, even though the March total income is up, the Year-to-Date total income is down by $3,000. Therefore, this is a newspaper which needs work if it is to show a gain at year's end.

Furthermore, the income side of the income statement tells only half the story. If one wants to assess the financial health of the newspaper, the expense side of the ledger must also be examined. Not doing so would be like considering yourself well off financially because you make $50,000 annually. If your expenses are $53,000 a year, however, you are in trouble. In the case of the income statement in Exhibit 4, the expenses are up for the YTD 1987, and—since income is down from the same period last year—that can only mean less profit at this year's end.

USING FINANCIAL RATIOS

Accountants and financial analysts have developed some easy-to-figure financial ratios which, if applied to the income statement and balance sheet, will help tell the publisher if his business operation is sound. Like all guidelines, these are rules of thumb, however, and special circumstances may call for violating one or two of them from time to time. Nevertheless, they have proven over time to be good indicators of the financial health of a company. Some of these ratios are strictly for the income statement, while others are for the balance sheet. Still other ratios require that you consult both the balance sheet and income statement.

Key Income Statement Ratios

Return on Sales. This ratio measures the operating effectiveness of the company. It can be found by dividing the total revenues into the net profit. In the case of the income statement in Exhibit 4, total revenues for YTD 1987 equal $192,000, while the net profit equals $15,500. Therefore, the return on

Exhibit 4
Income Statement for a Small Newspaper

	March '87	YTD '87	March '86	YTD '86
INCOME				
Advertising				
Local..............	$40,000	$118,000	$36,000	$120,000
National...........	4,000	14,000	7,000	15,000
Classified..........	8,700	24,000	9,000	24,500
Legals.............	2,500	7,000	3,500	6,500
Preprints..........	3,000	12,000	4,000	13,000
Total Advertising.....	58,200	175,000	59,500	179,000
Circulation...........	4,000	10,000	4,500	12,000
Job Printing..........	3,000	7,000	3,500	7,000
Total Income	65,200	192,000	67,500	198,000
EXPENSES				
Payroll				
Editorial...........	$8,000	$24,000	$7,200	$21,000
Advertising.........	6,500	20,000	6,000	18,000
Circulation	3,000	9,000	3,000	9,000
Production	6,000	19,000	6,000	18,000
Administrative......	4,500	13,500	4,000	12,000
Total Payroll.........	28,000	85,500	26,200	78,000
Other Compensation.....5,000		15,000	4,500	13,500
Printing..............	9,000	27,000	8,500	25,500
Postage...............	3,000	9,000	3,000	9,000
Other Operating.......15,000		50,000	13,000	39,000
Total Expenses 60,000		186,500	55,200	165,000
Pre Tax Profit	5,200	5,500	12,300	33,000

sales is 8 percent. That means that for every $1 in sales, 8 cents goes free and clear to the company.

Total Salaries to Gross Sales. This ratio determines the percentage of total revenue spent on labor (payroll plus other compensation). This is an important ratio, since payroll is the largest single expense a newspaper incurs, and the budgeted cap must be respected. In Exhibit 4, $100,500 was spent on labor for YTD 1987, while the company took in $192,000 in revenue. To discover the ratio of total salaries to gross sales, simply divide the total revenue into the labor expense. Here the ratio would equal 52 percent. In other words, 52 percent of the budget is going to payroll. Is this acceptable? To answer that, one should consult some of the industry averages provided by groups like the IDPA or the NNF. Generally the payroll expense for a small daily newspaper hovers around the 40-percent mark.

Total Presswork to Gross Sales. This ratio determines the percentage of total revenue spent on printing the newspaper. It can be found by dividing the presswork expense by the total revenue. If the presswork expense of the year is $200,000, while the total revenue is $1 million, then the presswork-to-gross sales ratio equals 20 percent, about average according to industry data.

Sales Margin. This ratio is found by dividing the net profit by the net sales (sales minus the cost of those sales). If the newspaper's end profit was $50,000 after taxes, and the net sales were $800,000, then the sales margin would be just over 6 percent.

Operating Ratio. You can use the operating ratio to compare current newspaper financial performance with its performance in previous years and also with operating ratios of other newspapers. In using the operating ratio, you can compare the sum of cost of goods sold and operating expenses with net sales. In so doing, the formula is the cost of goods sold plus operating expenses, divided by the net sales. For instance, if the net sales total $500,000, cost of goods sold is $250,000, and operating expenses are $200,000, then the operating ratio is 90 percent. You may also use the Operating Ratio to review the trend in operating expenses. In so doing, you can find the ratio by dividing operating expenses by net sales. For example: in 1987, operating expenses total $500,000, net sales $1.5 million. In 1986, operating expenses were $250,000 and net sales $1 million. The 1987 operating expense ratio is 30 percent, while the 1986 operating expense ratio was 25 percent.

Key Balance Sheet Ratios

Current Ratio. This is a so-called "liquidity ratio" that determines the newspaper's ability to meet current debt. It is found by dividing current assets by current liabilities. In the balance sheet in Exhibit 3, current assets total $160,000, while current liabilities total $70,000. Therefore, the current ratio is 2.28. That means the company has more than twice as many current assets as liabilities, and it is a nice position to be in. It also means the newspaper has leverage it can use for future loans if it needs money to expand or improve its facilities. Most analysts suggest a current ratio of two. A large current ratio is not always a good sign, because it may mean the company is not making the most efficient use of its assets.

Quick Ratio. This liquidity ratio determines the newspaper's ability to meet current debt quickly. It can be found by subtracting any inventory (such as newsprint, ink, and office supplies) from the current assets, and dividing that figure by the current liabilities. In the case of the Exhibit 3 balance sheet, current assets minus inventories equal $90,000, while current liabilities equal $70,000. Therefore, the quick ratio is 1.28. This newspaper would have no trouble meeting its current debt quickly. Financial analysts feel a quick ratio of one is good, although many companies that operate in stable environments can get by successfully with a lower ratio.

Working Capital Ratio. This ratio measures how much working capital the newspaper has to work with. It is found by subtracting the current liabilities from the current assets. In the case of Exhibit 3, the working capital is thus $90,000.

Total Debt to Equity. This is a so-called "leverage ratio" (leverage is the gap between debt and equity), and it records the debt pressure on the newspaper. It can be found by dividing the total liabilities by the owner's equity. In Exhibit 3, the total liabilities equal $195,000, while the owner's equity equals $365,000. Therefore, the total debt to equity is 53 percent. Because of the possible magnification of losses in bad economy years, debt-equity ratios over the 0.5 norm are usually considered safe only for the most stable of industries. The rule of thumb is that this ratio should not exceed one, although it often does when a newspaper is newly purchased and incurs a large mortgage. The lower the ratio, the easier the pressure and the greater the protection for creditors.

Return on Equity (ROE). This ratio measures the owner's percentage of return on his or her investment in the newspaper. Investments in any business enterprise are made in the anticipation of a return on that investment in the form of a profit. This ROE figure is used to compare alternative investment choices. Return on equity is found by dividing the annual net income by the owner's equity. You must refer to the balance sheet and income statement for this. In Exhibit 3, the owner's equity is $365,000, and in Exhibit 4 the projected net income for the year would be $16,500. Therefore, the return on equity would be 4.5 percent for that year. In this case, the return on equity is very low, and the publisher might wonder why, if he is concerned only about making money, he is not taking that equity and investing it elsewhere. Even a bank CD pays more than 4.5 percent. The return on equity issue brings up an interesting point and possibly a reason to not have so much equity capital lying around. If, for instance, the owners used some of their equity as leverage to assume a large loan for expansion purposes, that would decrease the net worth but increase the return on equity, assuming the profit level stayed the same.

For instance, if the owner's equity were only $265,000 (assuming the owners incurred a new $100,000 loan liability), then the return on equity would be 6.2 percent. Another way of increasing that return, of course, is to improve profits. If annual profits were $33,000 and net worth were $365,000, then the ROE would be 9 percent.

Return on Investment. If you are a stockholder in a large daily newspaper whose stock is traded on one of the exchanges, you can figure this ratio by dividing the annual dividend per share by the price paid per share. If the dividend per share were $4, and the price paid for a share were $5, then the return on your investment would be about 6.5 percent.

Return on investment can also be determined by dividing the company's net earnings by the total assets. If, for instance, the newspaper's net earnings for the year were $500,000, and the total assets equaled $20 million, then the return on investment would be 2.5 percent.

Other Ratios

Average Daily Sales. This is a ratio found by dividing the year's gross sales by the number of issues of the newspaper. For instance, if the newspaper took in $1 million last year and published 260 days (a 5-day daily), then the average daily sales would have been $3,846.

Accounts Receivable Turnover. This ratio shows how long, on average, it takes the newspaper to get its money from advertisers, subscribers, and printing customers. It can be determined by dividing the accounts receivable (from the balance sheet) into the annual sales revenue (from the income statement). For example, if accounts receivable total $97,182 and annual sales are $908,785, then the accounts receivable turnover is 9.35. On the basis of a 360-day year, the average collection period for this newspaper is 39 days (360 divided by 9.35). Just remember that your newspaper's ability to pay its bills monthly will depend on your customers' diligence in paying their bills monthly. If the average collection period for your newspaper is going beyond 45 days, you should work to shorten it, possibly by reviewing the payment history of your credit customers and tightening credit requirements.

Inventory on Hand. Do you have enough newsprint in supply or do you have too much? This ratio lets you know the answer. This is a two-part ratio you compute by, first, dividing the number of annual publishing days into the newsprint tons used. For instance, if you publish 260 days and use 100 tons of newsprint per year, you use about .38 tons of newsprint per each issue of the newspaper. Second, to get the inventory on hand, divide .38 ton into the tons of newsprint on hand. If you have 20 tons of newsprint in the shop, then you have 52 days' worth of newsprint on hand. The rule of thumb is that 1.5 months' inventory of newsprint on hand is enough. Too little can be a problem, especially if your newsprint mill experiences a labor strike, and too much can be a problem since warehouse space is expensive.

For up-to-date newspaper industry averages with which you can compare your newspaper's performance, the following sources are helpful: Moody's Manuals, Standard and Poor's Manuals and Surveys, annual reports to stockholders of newspaper companies, and investment essays from major brokerage houses.

TYPICAL NEWSPAPER EXPENSES

A number of varied types of expenses could appear on a newspaper's income statement. As with any business, these expenses are either fixed expenses or variable expenses. Examples of several different expenses in each category are as follows:

Fixed Expenses

These can include such things as property taxes; depreciation on the building, furniture, and machinery; feature and advertising services; professional services (accounting and legal); telephone, heating or air conditioning; rent or mortgage payments on the building; subscriptions to wire services or feature syndicates; office supplies and postage; and interest paid on loans or charge accounts. These and some other expenses are called fixed expenses because they don't vary much, if at all, over the course of a year. Most managers try to keep fixed expenses to a minimum to allow room for any needed cutbacks during times calling for retrenchment.

Variable Expenses

These can include such items as payroll, supplies for each department, promotion, travel, telephone, staff development fees, payroll taxes on wages, copy processing, press and plate costs, photo production costs, circulation, newsprint and ink, postage (second class), subscriptions to clip art, magazines and other newspapers, art services, dues, and memberships. These are called "variable" because their amount can and does vary with turnover on the newspaper or during personnel cutbacks initiated by management. Some of the expenses associated with physical goods, like newsprint and ink, can vary with the size of the newspaper, which is also determined by the management.

A WORD ABOUT DEPRECIATION

One of the fixed expenses just mentioned is depreciation. This particular expense differs from any other expense in its nature, in that it may not really involve an outlay of money at all, yet will still act as a tax deduction for the newspaper. It arises because the building, machinery, cars, trucks, and furniture are used by the paper over time to help produce revenue, so accountants adopt the practice of writing off the cost of such a fixed asset over a "useful life" selected for the asset.[6] This write-off is depreciation, and it constitutes an expense deduction from revenue produced by the newspaper. However, "useful life" of equipment or a building really bears no relation to actual use of the asset. This is particularly true because tax laws permit the use of accelerated depreciation rates and short, useful lives.

These shorter useful lives provide a newspaper—as any business—an opportunity to speed up the time of taking deductions. This, in turn, reduces income that is subject to taxes. This is important to a business, because the more immediate increased annual tax deductions produce more cash for working capital purposes. By availing itself of an increased deduction over a shorter time period, the newspaper defers the tax payments that would be due if it claimed smaller depreciation deductions. This tax deferral then lasts until the rapid method provides less in depreciation deductions than the slower, more conservative method would provide. This favorable tax position may be restored through purchases of new equipment down the line.

The J. K. Lasser Institute, in its informative *How to Read a Financial Statement,* provides the following example of how depreciation election affects the reporting of income:[7]

Company A and Company B are competitors, have the same amount of fixed assets, and report income of $200,000 before depreciation. Company A elects accelerated depreciation and claims depreciation of $50,000 resulting in a net income of $150,000. Company B, following a more conservative approach, takes straight line depreciation and claims depreciation of $25,000, resulting in a net income of $165,000. If only net income were compared, an observer would conclude that Company B is a more profitable company. However, a review of depreciation methods would show that there was no difference between the income-producing capacities of the two companies.

The beauty of depreciation for a company is that, once an investment is made in a depreciable asset, depreciation claimed over the useful life period does not involve any outlay of cash, unless the company chooses to set aside a certain amount of the depreciation expense for replacement costs of the machinery. These depreciated charges are accumulated on the balance sheet in an account called "accumulated depreciation," which is a direct offset to the fixed asset accounts. As the assets are periodically written off, the net value approaches zero until subsequent purchases increase the value.

This is one reason why, when a person speaks of cash flow, he generally is speaking of net profit plus depreciation. It is also why, when a potential buyer is surveying the income statement of the intended newspaper property and sees a loss on the bottom line, he should search the expense accounts to see how much depreciation is being claimed by the current publisher. If it is a large amount, there may actually be no loss at all and may even be a profit. In fact, some small, closely held newspaper companies try to show a loss so they incur no tax burden.

PLANNING: THE KEY TO SUCCESS

There is an old saying that goes, "If you aim at nothing, you're sure to hit it." Nothing could be truer in the newspaper business, and that is why the current emphasis on marketing is such good news. The reason is that effective marketing techniques couched in an overall marketing approach signify that someone is trying to find a goal to be reached and a way to reach it. Too often a newspaper publisher will say the paper has a goal, but when he is pinned down, that goal emerges as somewhat fuzzy or global. For instance, one publisher might say, "Our goal at the Daily News is to produce a quality newspaper," or, a more bottom-line publisher might say, "Our goal is to improve our revenues and dividends to our stockholders." The problem is that unless goals that contain such undefined terms as "quality" and "improved revenues" are defined, they don't mean much. Certainly one could find dictionary definitions of them without much trouble, but what is needed is operational definitions; how these ideas are defined for this particular newspaper. Is a quality editorial product more local news or more international news, or is it more celebrity news or more features? If the profit goes up from 10 to 11 percent is that improvement enough in the revenues?

Operationally defined goals are important so the staff knows exactly what they are aiming at. Further, unless there is a specific plan aimed at specific targets, no one really knows what shape the operating budget or capital budget should take. For instance, is the goal to be a newspaper that excells in investigative reporting? If so, the operating budget will need to reflect a relatively large expense for fielding an I-Team (investigative team) which will not be contributing to the daily run of news stories.

The point is that the newspaper's various budgets will be reflective of the type of newspaper the owners want to produce. You could say that if you want to know what kind of newspaper the owners want to produce, look at the operating budget. It should tell the story. The owners' vision of the newspaper is a key basis for executive planning and for budget-building. Therefore, proper planning or forecasting requires a specific vision of the kind of newspaper to be produced, an outline of various courses of action to take in producing such a product, and a decision on the best course of action for this paper to take in its quest.

A PRIMER ON DECISION MAKING

One of the things newspaper managers do every day, and which is more or less taken for granted, is to make decisions. However, decision making often requires a systematic model to help insure that all pertinent factors and alternative solutions are considered before a conclusion is reached. Various management scholars have wrestled with the process of decision making, looking for an effective model. One theorist, Henry Mintzberg, has said decision

ing is broken down into different stages. Each stage is a sub-part of the whole process. These decision making stages are:

1. The Identification Phase, in which opportunities, problems and crises are recognized and examined. This acts as a catalyst for decision making.
2. The Development Phase, in which management searches for ready-made solutions and augments them with original solutions to address the issues in Phase 1.
3. The Selection Phase, in which a large number of alternatives are reduced to a few more feasible ones. Then management reduces the few to one best choice and authorizes that course of action to be carried out.
4. The Supporting Phase, in which various implementational decisions are made with affected parties provided maximum input. This phase would also include the monitoring and self-correcting procedures which management decides upon.

In general, there are three different types of decision makers.[8] The first is the Rational Decision Maker, who considers all the alternatives as well as the consequences that would result from these possible choices, ranks these consequences on the basis of an arbitrary scale of preferences, and selects the alternative that promises the maximum benefit. Thus, the method is extremely important to the rational decision maker and provides the basis for his or her selection of the course of action.

One method the Rational Decision Maker might use is the so-called "Alternative Comparison Matrix." Using this model, the manager analyzes his company's internal and external environment, identifies problems and opportunities, selects a few criteria that must be met by any strategy chosen to address these problems, develops several alternative strategies, and then tests them against these decision criteria, asking if the alternative strategy is the one that collects the most "yes" responses.

The major benefit of the Rational Decision Maker approach is that it allows the manager to survey all the critical factors, possible solutions, and consequences of a decision before it is made. On the negative side, however, the manager is often not a unique actor but is only part of a multistage process. Also, it is impossible to exhaust all possible alternative choices and to predict all possible consequences of future decisions. We live in an age that is inundated with information, and it is impossible to digest it all, even if there were enough hours in a day to do so. Nevertheless, most observers feel this model of decision making is superior to seat-of-the-pants decisions, so it continues to find favor among managers.

The Intuitive/Emotional Decision Maker is at the opposite end of the spectrum from the Rational Decision Maker. This manager uses unsystematic methods to make decisions and instead relies on experience, meditation, and gut instinct. This manager tries to keep the overall problem in mind, continually redefining it in his mind as he goes through a series of mental and emotional exercises to reach an intuitive conclusion about the preferred course of action.

Its advantages and disadvantages would be the logical opposite of those for the Rational Decision Maker. It seems to work best when the manager making decisions has deep experience in his work and the environment in which his company operates, and when that manager is especially creative in his thinking.

The Quasi-Rational Decision Maker would be a compromise between these two other decision makers. This manager mixes experience, intuition, and emotion with the more objective and systematic tools of the Rational Decision Maker, yet he doesn't necessarily let the results of the systematic method dictate choices unless these choices make sense to him personally. This choice will usually be limited by the decision maker's values, attitudes, abilities, and experience.

DIFFERENT TYPES AND USES OF BUDGETS

Newspapers work from at least two different types of budgets, and each one is really a financial portrayal of the vision the publisher has for the newspaper. The newspaper budgets are generally the operating budget and the capital expenditures budget. Each of these budgets can be broken down into more specific budgets if necessary.

Operating Budgets

Operating budgets may include the sales revenue budget, which determines the production budget, and which in turn influences the operating expenses budget. These are, of course, forecasted budgets compiled months in advance of each fiscal year. The budgets are divided into individual monthly budgets for the upcoming fiscal year. The first of these operating budgets to be compiled is the sales revenue budget, because it provides the means for the production and operating expenses budgets. The sales revenue budget lists the various sources of revenue for the newspaper, most notably advertising. Included in the advertising portion of the sales revenue budget would be local, national, classified, and preprint advertising. Circulation sales are also included and are mapped out for each month of the upcoming year. The sales revenue budget provides the basis for the pro forma income statement, listing both sources of income and the projected expenses.

Production Budget. The production budget is made up of costs directly associated with composing and printing the newspaper. It usually includes copy processing, and press and plate expenses, and it is influenced directly by the projected circulation and number of pages per issue for the newspaper.

Operating Expenses Budget. In addition to the production budget, the operating expenses budget also flows from the sales revenue budget and covers both fixed and variable expenses associated with the items listed previously in this chapter under these headings. Usually there are separate schedules for each type of operating expense, such as payroll, taxes, insurance, utilities, and so on.

Capital Expenditures Budget. Capital expenditures reflect projected expenses for machinery, new buildings, or renovations to existing structures. These expenditures are usually projected to be amortized over several years, with the interest for these charges appearing as an expense item in the pro forma income statement, and the principal appearing on the balance sheet. It is highly important, because of the large expenses involved with capital budgets, that these expenditures be planned well ahead of time to insure that upcoming sales revenues can support both capital expenditures and the normal operating expenses.

ASSISTANCE IN BUDGET BUILDING

It is often helpful for newspaper executives to know what type of budgets newspapers of similar size have prepared. To this end, industry studies such as those mentioned earlier come in handy. There is even an organization of budget people called the Institute of Newspaper Controllers and Finance Officers (INCFO), and it publishes a monthly magazine called *The Newspaper Controller,* which discusses several budgeting trends for newspapers. Another monthly publication, produced by the American Newspaper Publishers Association, is *Presstime* magazine. It has several sections on management issues ranging from circulation to technology and newspaper education.

HOW MUCH IS A NEWSPAPER WORTH?

The answer to this question depends on so many variables that it is impossible to give one formula or rule of thumb. There are, in fact, at least two formulae, one for daily newspapers and one for weeklies, but even these are only guidelines and may vary because of several intangible factors. Another problem is that newspapers are valued according to market value and according to just how much a company wants a particular newspaper. That level of desire is extremely high these days, and some media analysts say there are hardly any daily newspapers left that are not either the target of media companies or at least the object of wishful thinking. Market value varies with the strength of the industry, changes in the local economies, and the ups and downs of the newspapers themselves. Ten years ago the *St. Louis Globe-Democrat* probably interested several potential buyers. Today that newspaper is no longer publishing. One thing is certain, however: daily newspapers are expensive, and some companies get carried away in making their purchases.

One indication of this buying fever is provided in a recent *Fortune* article entitled "Does Gannett Pay Too Much?" Focusing on the largest media company in the United States, the writers noted that, in 1981, dailies were going at an average price of less than ten times their operating cash flow. In 1986, however, the average cash-flow multiple had reached the high teens. Indeed, "acquisition mania" had taken over, and leading the charge was the Gannett Co. In just over a year, it paid $1.2 billion in cash to buy three of the largest newspaper properties in America: the *Des Moines Register, Detroit News,* and the *Louisville Courier-Journal.* Gannett's chairman Allen H. Neuharth said of these and other purchases that financial prognosticators at Gannett are expert in knowing just what a newspaper property is worth and whether its purchase is feasible. Few other companies, he said, have crystal balls as clear as Gannett's. Neuharth's trust in his executives notwithstanding, many media observers feel newspaper purchase prices have gone through the roof and that those—like Gannett—who are willing to spend so much may wind up becoming victimized by the inflated prices they help to create. Certainly the stock market plunge of 1987 showed all investors that expansion—like every other business decision— should be handled cautiously. Even so, Gannett realizes that expansion may be the only road to real profit growth. Therefore, the desire for such growth may propel what *Fortune* calls "acquisition mania" for some time to come.

Douglas H. McCorkindale, vice chairman and chief financial officer for Gannett, says he makes several calculations to size up how much and how soon an acquisition can add to the company's bottom-line profits. Offering the *Des Moines Register* as an example, he said the price was slightly under $200 million. Gannett is paying about 9 percent interest on the debt, so the company needs about $18 million pretax earnings each year to cover the interest. It sounds simple, but things quickly become more complicated, according to McCorkindale. "On a $200 million transaction . . . most of it becomes goodwill: the excess price over actual book value of the newspaper. So pick a goodwill number of say $160 million. Divide that by the 40-year amortization and you have $4 million of goodwill cost per year." However, goodwill is not tax deductible, so it takes roughly $8 million of pretax earnings to cover that. Thus, in total, Gannett needs $26 million in pretax earnings from the Des Moines paper before the acquisition starts contributing to per-share earnings. McCorkindale says the goal is to reach that level within three or four years. The Des Moines properties were earning just $8 million before taxes on revenues of $80 million before Gannett took over, which means that Gannett expects to more than triple the earnings in three or four years. Pretax earnings of $26 million would amount to a return of more than 32 percent on those $80 million in revenues, but, after factoring in the revenue-raising effect of increases in advertising and circulation sales, McCorkindale says the profit margin will have to climb only to the mid-20s to meet Gannett's goal. He said the *Register*'s pretax margin already had moved from 10 percent to the low-to-middle teens, and should reach the mid-20s on schedule.[9]

Evaluating Smaller Newspapers

Evaluating smaller dailies and weeklies is a bit simpler, but there are several plus-or-minus factors that can skew their prices as well. Marion Krehbiel, former president of Krehbiel-Bolitho Newspaper Service, Inc., a major newspaper brokerage firm, has a system that many sellers and buyers of smaller newspapers have used for some time. Basically, the system is based on answers to at least four questions.

1. What is the newspaper's last annual gross income?
2. What is the size of the community?
3. What is the newspaper's paid circulation?
4. Is the newspaper making any money and, if so, how much?

In 1978, Krehbiel cited the following figures as averages for purchase indexes of small- to medium-size daily newspaper:[10]

1. Gross Income: 210 percent of last year's gross.
2. Net Profit: 25 years' net profit after taxes.
3. City Population: $110 per person.
4. Circulation: $155 per paid subscriber.

To obtain a fair market price for the newspaper, add these four items and divide by four.

Krehbiel added a caveat to these indexes, however, when he noted in 1979 that this formula is only meant to provide purchasers with a ballpark estimate of a newspaper's worth. It is also important to note that, of the four indexes, the first two reflect percentages, and are therefore more inflation-proof than the third and fourth indexes, which use actual dollar figures.

For weeklies, Krehbiel published the following updated formula in 1980:[11]

1. Gross Income: 105 percent of gross annual income with no plant, and 130 percent with an up-to-date plant.
2. City Population: $40 per head.
3. Circulation: $45 per paid subscriber.
4. Net Profit: 12 years' net profit.

However, there are several additional factors that could increase or decrease the fair market price arrived at by applying these formulae. Some of these additional factors are:

1. Is there any competition in the town and does it carry more than half as much advertising as yours?
2. How would you describe the liveliness of the market in which the paper is located? Is the town neat in appearance? What is the number of national dealerships? What is the level of deposit in the town's banks? What is the quality of the schools? Does a state or interstate highway pass through or near the town?
3. How many owners has the newspaper had over the past several years, and why has it changed hands? What is the current reputation of the publisher who owns it now?

If it is a bad reputation, would it be easy to overcome? If it is an excellent reputation, can you match it?

4. What is the potential for expanding the paper and increasing the revenue? Could a shopper be added to turn the newspaper into a TMC product? Could special sections be added? Can the percentage of retail advertising be increased, and if so, how?

One word of caution is appropriate with regard to this business of a newspaper's potential: it is better to base the price of the newspaper on what it has done, rather than what it can do. That way, if the product does not reach its full potential, at least you have based your purchase price on the lower level of revenue generated by it.

Finally, like any other item offered for sale, there is a market value for a weekly newspaper and there is also a more personal value to the owner. Often this personal value is predicated on the blood, sweat, and tears the owner has put into the newspaper over the years and the intangible rewards he or she has received from publishing it. This second value will often result in the newspaper being overpriced as to its market value. For this reason, high offering prices should not deter the would-be buyer of a weekly newspaper, nor should they mask the newspaper's true market value. Most weekly newspapers sell for less—sometimes much less—than the initial offering price. It is important for the purchaser to exercise tact in negotiating the price down, however, because of the emotional investment the seller has in the newspaper. Many deals have gone awry because an insensitive buyer has alienated a proud seller. In addition, sellers often will listen to creative financing arrangements in which a lower-than-expected down payment can be made and offset by a balloon payment or two down the road. Normally, a seller of a weekly newspaper arranges a basic financing scheme that calls for a 29 percent down payment and the balance of the note over a 10- or 12-year period at an interest rate of anywhere between 8 and 11 percent (most commonly 10 percent).

WHY ARE NEWSPAPERS SO ATTRACTIVE?

In the summer of 1987, at least three newspaper companies were hotly in pursuit of one seemingly average, medium-size daily in New Jersey. Ingersoll Publications Co., Garden State Newspapers, and the Bergen Record Corp. were all bidding to buy the 60,000-circulation *Morristown Record,* and none of the bidders was even being actively sought, according to its then-owner, Norman B. Tomlinson, Jr. Nevertheless, Tomlinson decided to sell the newspaper to Ingersoll for a price observers feel was between $125 and $150 million, some five times its 1986 gross revenues.[12]

Why are so many investors interested in buying into newspapers in this electronic age when many studies are showing that fewer people subscribe to newspapers than ever before? What makes them so attractive? Media analysts toss out several reasons, but the overriding one seems to be that—in the overwhelming majority of cities—a daily newspaper represents a monopoly: the only show in town. As troublesome as that sounds to the idealist, it is music to the ears of investors.

The newspaper is one of the strongest performers among communications industries, and in recent years the newspaper industry has outgained other media in revenue and operating income growth, and in maintaining profit margins. Veronis, Suhler & Associates' annual *Communications Industry Report* shows that newspapers were still the communication industry's star performer in 1985 in terms of profit margins, operating income, and cash flow return on assets.[13] From 1980 to 1985, the newspaper industry's compound growth rate was 11.2 percent, while the cash flow growth rate was at 15.7 percent for the same period. Gross profit margins in 1985 were at 18 percent, while cash flow margins for that year stood at 21.4 percent.[14] The stock market crash in late 1987 may have caused newspaper stock prices to drop, but the long-term forecast is for rebound and continued growth in the industry.

Home-owned and operated newspapers are usually good candidates for purchase by media groups, because group executives feel they can provide a higher level of professional management and also a higher level of financial resources to expand the products. In addition, because of inheritance tax laws and publishing families' squabbles, it is difficult for the privately held newspaper company to stay in agreement on keeping the newspaper instead of selling it for the high asking prices being quoted today. The fact that many of these independently owned newspapers are being taken over by groups is evidenced by the dwindling number of independent newspapers. In the spring of 1987, only 434 independent dailies were still in existence, according to the ANPA. That is just over 25 percent of all dailies in the United States. About 50 U.S. dailies are sold each year, and most of them go into the fold of newspaper groups, which are about the only entities that can afford the high prices dailies are garnering in the 1980s.

SOME IDEAS ON IMPROVING INCOME

Members of the Institute of Newspaper Controllers and Finance Officers are constantly working to find new ways of improving newspaper revenues. Among some of their suggestions are the following:[15]

- Newspapers must temper rate and price increases that are beyond the inflation rate and circulation growth.
- Innovation, planning, response to change, and intelligent management must be key components in any newspaper management plan.
- Newspapers must continue to apply marketing skills to assessing what readers and advertisers want and need in a newspaper.
- Publishers may have to learn that small is beautiful, and that less is more. In other words, newspapers must become more narrowly focused in considering both their

market and their array of content. Just as general-interest magazines have given way to special-interest publications, so may the general-interest newspaper learn to become more narrowly focused.

· The real revenue growth for a newspaper may only lie in taking business away from competing media. Therefore, newspaper managers must always be alert to innovative ideas in competing with direct mail and shoppers as well as other newspapers in the area.

SOME IDEAS ON EXPENSE CONTROL

Producing revenue increases is only half of the newspaper manager's challenge. The other half is controlling expenses. Obviously, the newspaper is no better off financially in boosting revenues 10 percent if costs increase by that much or more. Unfortunately, management often has little control over two of the largest newspaper expense items: payroll and newsprint. The various unions existing at many newspapers (see Chapters 7 and 8) restrict the flexibility in adjusting the size of the payroll. No less a headache is that the price of newsprint is based on factors external to the newspaper such as industry supply and demand, wages paid at the paper mills, strikes at those mills, and so on. Still, these expense items must be addressed effectively if the newspaper is to stay on strong financial turf. Newspaper managers can deal with these troublesome expense areas in responsible—and often hard-line—contract negotiations with newspaper unions, and in lobbying efforts both with newsprint manufacturers and in Washington on matters concerning various import taxes which affect the delivered price of Canadian newsprint. Several newspaper groups even own all or part of the mills where their newsprint is made. In so doing, the newspapers can at least have more influence over the price they pay for that newsprint.

W. Marc Postlewaite, a publisher with the Chicago Tribune Co., notes that a problem in controlling expenses is using the expense budget as an index of success. Analyzing expenses in relation to the budget is only helpful if advertising, volumes, and rates are on schedule. If they are not, the expense budget is less useful and can be distorting. If, for instance, the newspaper's market will allow a 7.5 percent increase in advertising rates, yet the newspaper must absorb a 9 percent increase in the cost of goods and services, then, to retain existing profitability, the newspaper must somehow reduce expenses by 1.5 percent. The problem is also exacerbated if advertising volume declines because of a downturn in the local economy. The key may be to plan now to reduce consumption down the road and to draw up a plan showing how such a reduction can be accomplished. Otherwise, management may have to institute emergency cost-cutting measures at crisis times, and these measures may be so severe as to endanger the life of the newspaper.

One way of analyzing expenses is to compare the percent of revenue each expense category consumes by element (supplies, payroll, and so on) and by department (advertising, editorial, and so forth).[16] After finding the expense element for a particular department, one can then determine the actual expense, the budgeted expense, and the percent variance from the budget. With a system like this, the manager can pinpoint departments that are succeeding or failing in meeting the budget for various expense items. A manager can extend this analysis by showing the percent of revenue that each department is budgeted to spend in each particular expense category, and the percent of revenue actually spent. Subtracting the second percentage figure from the first will provide a look at how that expense variance affects overall profitability of the newspaper.

For instance, assume a small daily newspaper took in total revenues of $160,000 during the month of August. If the editorial department was budgeted to spend $800 on supplies during the month, yet actually spent $1,120, there was about a 30 percent variance from the budget. Assuming $1/2$ of 1 percent (.005) of the total newspaper revenue was budgeted for this editorial supplies expense, the actual expenditure represented $7/10$ of 1 percent (.007), or a deficit equaling .002 of the newspaper revenues for August.

If the newspaper comptroller goes through each expense element for each department, repeating the above procedure, he can identify which departments—and in particular which specific department expenses—are contributing to the success or failure of the newspaper's profit plan. These are the expenses that should either be left alone or brought under control, depending on the analysis and how it relates to the overall company objectives.

Two cautionary points should be made in interpreting results flowing from the above model. First, the analysis must be done on a computer or the newspaper's financial analyst will be doing nothing else with his time except adding, subtracting, and multiplying figures. Besides, the computer will do it more accurately anyway. Second, before assuming that an expense must be controlled because it is over budget, the business manager and publisher must consult with the appropriate department head to find out why the expense is over budget. There may be very good reasons why, for that particular month, the budgeted expense should have been exceeded. For instance, a major breaking news event may have required several reporters and photographers to work heavy overtime hours. The alternative would have been to trim coverage of an important news story, and that might go against one of the major organizational goals of the newspaper company.

It is thus quite possible that the decision over what to do with such budget-breaking expenses should be made by someone who is a Quasi-Rational Decision Maker as defined earlier in this chapter. Otherwise, the newspaper may be cutting off its nose to spite its face if it insists on cutting expenses that were necessary to achieve a key organizational goal.

EFFECTIVE CASH MANAGEMENT

The first asset appearing on a newspaper company's balance sheet is usually cash. The second is usually checking funds. An effective system of managing the newspaper's cash reduces the need for borrowing, improves investment earnings, and supports the financial demands of increased sales volume. This adds up to larger profits and a healthier financial statement.

Cash surpluses of financially healthy companies normally range from 2 to 10 percent of annual sales. For newspapers, however, this level is often higher. This money should be invested in short-term vehicles to maximize the company's profit potential.

The business manager, possibly with the assistance of a company cash manager, has the responsibility for maximizing this company cash. The job is three-fold:[17]

1. To increase the company's cash balance by delaying outflow.

2. To speed up cash inflow.

3. To invest cash in financial instruments that serve both the short- and long-term objectives of the company.

NOTES

1. "1986 Profits Up for Most Public Newspaper Groups," *Editor & Publisher* 28 February 1987: 16–17.

2. Inland Daily Press Association, *1986 Inland Cost and Revenue Study* (Park Ridge, Ill.: Inland Daily Press Association).

3. Gene Chamberlain, "The Business of Journalism." In *The Newspaper: Everything You Need to Know to Make It in the Newspaper Business*, ed. D. Earl Newsom (Englewood Cliffs: Prentice-Hall, 1981), pp. 147–148.

4. Mark Fitzgerald, "67th Inland Cost Study Is First In-House Effort," *Editor & Publisher*, 25 July 1987: 18.

5. Fitzgerald, "67th Inland Cost Study," p. 18.

6. J. K. Lasser Institute, *How to Read a Financial Statement* (New York: Simon & Schuster, 1984), p. 32.

7. Lasser Institute, *How to Read a Financial Statement*, p. 33.

8. William F. Glueck, *Business Policy and Strategic Management*, 3d ed. (New York: McGraw-Hill, 1980), pp. 52–54.

9. Arthur M. Louis, "Does Gannett Pay Too Much?" *Fortune* 15 September 1986: 59.

10. Marion Krehbiel, *What Your Newspaper Might Be Worth*, brochure distributed by the Missouri Press News, Columbia, Missouri, 1976.

11. Krehbiel, *What Your Newspaper Might Be Worth*.

12. Debra Gersh, "60,000–circulation Daily Sells for Over $100 Million," *Editor & Publisher* 15 August 1987: 32.

13. "Profits Slow Up, But Are Still Strong," *Editor & Publisher*, 3 January 1987: 44.

14. "Profits Slow Up, But Are Still Strong," p. 44.

15. Jerry Walker, "Straight Talk On Improving Revenues," *Editor & Publisher* 19 May 1982: 9, 16.

16. W. Marc Postlewaite, "An Analytical Approach To Expense Control," *Editor & Publisher*, 12 June 1982: 40, 48.

17. "Effective Cash Management: Maximize the Use of Company Funds," *Small Business Report* (December 1983), p. 1–4.

4

MARKETING THE NEWSPAPER

Today, companies realize that their raw material, labor, and physical-resource costs are all screwed down and that the only option for dramatic improvement will come from doing a better marketing job. As companies define marketing more clearly, they no longer confuse it with advertising, which uses media to let consumers know that a certain product or service is available. In essence, marketing means moving goods from the producer to the consumer. It starts with finding out what customers want or need, and then assessing whether the product can be made and sold at a profit.[1]

When *Business Week* writers were preparing that article for publication, they probably weren't thinking about newspapers as much as other kinds of products to be marketed. Nevertheless, the statement holds true as much for newspapers as it does for manufacturers of bath soap. There is, however, one important distinction that should be made immediately. Bath soap does not have the impact that newspapers, as purveyors of news and opinion, have on society. About the only harm a bad bar of soap can cause—assuming there are no skin irritants in it—is to leave the user smelling dirty, but a bad newspaper can cause a great deal of harm. The possibilities run from leaving the readers uninformed, to distorting the truth, to serving as a mouthpiece for a demagogue, to ruining someone's reputation. Therefore, the last sentence of this opening definition of marketing needs modifying to be applicable to newspapers:

It [marketing] starts with finding out what customers want or need, and then assessing whether the product can be made and sold at a profit *and* whether it can be made to conform to sound journalistic standards.

Other than that, the imperative of marketing holds as true for newspapers as for any other business. Lest anyone doubt this, all they must do is contact the

former publishers of the now-defunct newspapers like the *Washington Star,*
Cleveland Press, or *St. Louis Globe-Democrat,* along with several others. If
performing newspaper autopsies sounds too depressing, one can just as easily
consult executives of still-thriving newspapers to find out exactly why they are
thriving.

For instance, the 120-year-old *Minneapolis Star & Tribune* recently found
itself facing huge decreases in company earnings, administrative infighting, consumer dissatisfaction, and labor troubles.[2] Nevertheless, in an effort spear-
headed by the newspaper's marketing department, the *Star & Tribune* reshaped
itself into a newspaper better fitted to the Twin Cities market. Included in the
revitalization were increased sports and weather coverage, introduction of spot
color on the front page, and expansion of world and national news. In addition,
a commentary page, with quarter-page "advocacy" ad space facing the editorial page, was added with a revised and zoned broadsheet community section
designed for small advertisers' needs. Suburban news was expanded by a page,
a motoring section was created, and the copy desk began tightening stories to
create faster-paced reading and open up space for longer pieces.[3] Executive
Editor Joel Kramer said the rejuvenation came about to combat "a serious
image problem" that the newspaper had in Minnesota and on the national level.[4]
This was an image problem that would have probably gone unnoticed, or at
least undefined, had it not been for marketing surveys conducted to find out
how readers felt about the newspaper. Consequently, the market was assessed,
the changes made, and the product emerged in better financial and editorial
shape. Most industry observers feel the changes have also made for a much
improved newspaper serving the Twin Cities market.

PARAMETERS OF NEWSPAPER MARKETING

Any newspaper is, in reality, two different types of institutions. First, a
newspaper is a moving and sometimes explosive social force on an altruistic
mission to inform and enlighten its readers. Second, a newspaper is a business
venture in search of a healthy profit that will act as an incentive for owners to
plow even more money back into it. The greater the incoming resources, the
better the newspaper has a chance to be. Diminish either of these institutions
and you will no longer have a strong newspaper, either financially or editorially. The problem then becomes how to make the two institutions coexist in
the same company and to put both on the same mission in life. That mission is
to produce a high-quality newspaper that will reach the breadth and depth of
the geographic and demographic market. This is the Total Newspaper Concept,
discussed in Chapter 1.

Marketing helps a newspaper achieve its goal though finding out what the
readers want and need and then assessing whether the product can be made and
sold at a profit while still adhering to high journalistic standards. Involved in
this marketing process are the following tasks:

1. Engaging in preliminary research, market identification, and newspaper development.
2. Testing the revised product against accepted journalistic standards.
3. Testing reader reaction to the revised newspaper and its price.
4. Working out production capacities and costs.
5. Determining the income needed to support these changes.
6. Determining the most feasible distribution system.
7. Deciding on promotional strategies for the newspaper.

Rick Kaspar, vice president and general manager of Georgia's *Columbus Ledger,* stated recently that the new interest in marketing is the most significant and most positive development to be embraced by newspapers in decades.[5] He added that one of the most important roles of newspaper marketing has been to establish a clear set of goals and objectives that cut across department boundaries and provide a basis for integrating the department efforts in pursuit of one common purpose.

At American Press Institute seminars, participants are told that marketing involves the "Four P's." These are product, place, price, and promotion. Putting them into a meaningful statement, a newspaper is pursuing a good marketing plan by providing the right product, in the right place, at the right price, with the right promotion. If any of these marketing components goes unaddressed, the marketing plan will probably fail.

THE INDUSTRY TAKES A LOOK AT ITSELF

In 1976, the newspaper industry decided to take a look at itself and its market. The vehicle to take this view was the Newspaper Readership Project, sponsored by the American Newspaper Publishers Association (ANPA). The catalyst for the $5 million, six-year project was the realization that newspapers were losing readers and market penetration. While the twin problems still remain after the Readership Project, the data it yielded has offered newspaper publishers more insight into why those problems exist. It has also made the concept of newspaper marketing that much more important in the minds of newspaper executives and has reduced much of the tension existing between different departments in the newspaper. All departments now realize they are on the same long-term mission: to insure the survival of the newspaper.

"A concept and a method of organizing all departments in support of readership and circulation goals has been developed and found effective through the Newspaper Readership Project," according to Robert L. Burk, ANPA vice president for industry and public affairs.[6] The effort was a mammoth undertaking as four different committees examined the areas of research, promotion (including public relations and Newspaper in Education), training, and equipment and systems development. Out of the Readership Project came reports explaining the types of actions newspapers need to take to recoup readership and penetration. In addition, several ongoing efforts in the area of research and marketing were estabished and continue today to benefit the newspaper industry.

Since the end of the Readership Project, research has emerged as a central factor in such variant areas as planning editorial content, design, promotional campaigns, and long-term corporate strategy. In short, market researchers are today much more involved in the total operation of the newspaper, not just in advertising or circulation. This research is being aided tremendously by the computer revolution, which makes it possible for more newspapers to do their own market analysis in-house, or at least to do secondary analysis on data provided them by research consultants.

Kristin McGrath, former research director for the *Minneapolis Star and Tribune* and current owner of a private research consulting firm, says newspaper research is becoming much more goal-oriented than ever before. "Instead of doing a general market or readership study that sometimes is no more than a fishing expedition, they [newspapers] are deciding what their goals are in advance," she notes. "There is enough of a knowledge base built up that there are some questions people really don't need to ask anymore."[7]

In 1986, ten years after the ANPA's Readership Project was begun, the American Society of Newspaper Editors launched a survey entitled, "Love Us and Leave Us: New Subscribers, One Year Later." The point of the survey was to discover some of the reasons why many new subscribers let their subscriptions lapse within the first 12 months. The research was done by Virginia Dodge Fielder of Knight-Ridder Inc. and Beverly A. Barnum of Harte-Hanks Communications Inc., and it tracked almost 1,750 new subscribers, focusing on reader interests, content quality, circulation approaches, service, and pricing.

Results of the "Love Us and Leave Us" survey indicated that new subscribers liked the new content, but nearly half let their subscriptions lapse anyway within the first 12 months. The results, according to Dennis Dible, one of the survey's organizers, raise the question of whether editors are presenting sufficiently compelling and well-designed newspapers designed to retain reader interest. Also, he questions whether editors are really committed to doing stories addressing the everyday needs and concerns of their readers.

OBTAINING USEFUL MARKET DATA

Basically there are two types of data any newspaper can obtain about its market: primary and secondary. Primary data is that information which comes in response to original surveys or other research studies administered by the newspaper or its contracted research consultant. Companies like Scarborough and MRI conduct detailed studies of newspapers' markets and makes voluminous market profile reports available to client newspapers. Many newspapers, however, cannot afford the services of such high-powered research consultants and choose instead to do their own in-house research. Both of these options will be discussed in more detail later.

Secondary data, on the other hand, is data derived from already-existing sources. Newspapers do not have to originate any survey data, because the information is readily available in most large libraries. Some of the more common sources of secondary data about an individual newspaper market, and some of the information each provides, are as follows:

· *Editor & Publisher Market Guide.* This annual publication provides information about such market facets as the number and types of retail businesses in the market; size of bank and savings and loan (S&L) deposits; number of banks and S&Ls doing business in the market; population figures; transportation available; number of gas, electric, and water meters; and so on.

· *Sales and Marketing Management Survey of Buying Power.* This publication provides information on the market's total Effective Buying Income (EBI), the median household EBI, and the percentage of households by EBI grouping. This index also contains useful population information, broken down by age groups, for the market area.

· *Standard Rate and Data Service.* An annual publication providing newspaper advertising rates and circulation information around the country. There is also a broadcast publication giving radio and television rates. This is useful for providing a competitive checkpoint.

· *U.S. Bureau of Census.* The Census Bureau publishes a number of indexes providing general, social, and economic characteristics of each market by race and origin. For instance, for each city, census data can describe the population breakdown by sex, age, family type, educational level, employment, and income. This is a very good all-purpose research tool.

The above publications can all be located in the reference section of most large libraries. In addition, the following offices keep useful market data that newspapers can access easily.

· State Comptroller or State Tax Commission records. These can provide valuable information regarding the amount of state sales tax collected in a given city or town for the four quarters of the year. This tax collection information provides an excellent index of whether the local economy is moving upwards or downwards, and which specific retail or service business categories are doing the best.

· Local Chambers of Commerce. The Chamber of Commerce is always a good source, but most of their information probably comes from one or more of the previously listed sources. The Chamber may also arrange the data in such a way as to present the most positive view of the community, so care should be taken in interpreting it.

· State and Regional Press Associations. Most state or regional newspaper associations publish directories of member newspapers and their markets which give good cursory information about these newspapers. These directories are useful as another competitive gauge. In addition, some state press associations, like the Oklahoma Press Association, work with their state newspaper advertising bureau to do local market studies for member newspapers. These studies are usually done at or near cost and provide valuable information about local markets in the state. Press associations also publish periodic newsletters to give news of the area's newspaper industry.

This is not an exhaustive list of sources for secondary data, but if these sources are consulted regularly they will yield much useful information upon which to build a marketing plan.

Types of Primary Market Studies

Primary marketing studies, according to Dr. Maxwell E. McCombs, chairman of the University of Texas Department of Journalism, can be categorized by three types of combinations.[8]

Type A-B. This is demographic data about the newspaper's readership, and it is the most common type of newspaper market research. The 'A' represents characteristics of individuals in the market, while the 'B' represents their feelings, knowledge, and behavior related to either the entire newspaper, special sections, or specific items within the newspaper. Type A-B research thus relates the different demographics of the audience to their attitudes and behavior relating to the newspaper or parts of it. For instance, Type A-B research could discover how readers between the ages of 13 and 18 feel about the Arts and Entertainment section of the newspaper or a particular movie reviewer in that section.

Type B-C. This research relates content characteristics of the newspaper to audience beliefs, attitudes and/or responses. For instance, it might ask respondents to rate different categories of news stories as "very important," "important," or "unimportant." It looks to these content characteristics as possible *predictors* of readership.

Type B-B. This research relates one set of audience responses or attitudes to another set of audience responses or attitudes. For instance, is the individual who reads *both* a weekly and a daily newspaper more—or less—likely to believe his weekly produces credible news?

WHO COLLECTS (AND INTERPRETS) THE DATA?

Basically, the newspaper has two options for collecting and interpreting the data: do it in-house, or contract with an outside researcher to do all or part of it. There are advantages and disadvantages to each option.

The Case for Doing In-House Research

Some newspapers, especially smaller ones, may tend to forego conducting market research because of the perceived high cost associated with it. That is a mistake, because any newspaper staff can conduct its own low-cost market research. Such research can be totally based on deeper analysis of secondary data from sources like the ones cited earlier, or this secondary data can be joined with primary research done in-house, under the supervision of the marketing director.

Gerson Miller, a professor of journalism at Western Washington University, states, "Your computer expert is probably on your staff now, or advice can be easily obtained from a nearby university or community college. The time required by the person designated to coordinate the study should not exceed 100 hours during an eight-to-nine-week span and could be much less."[9] Miller points out that, exclusive of the coordinator's salary and any payment for computer advice or programming, the cost of mailing 1,000 questionnaires to current subscribers in 1985 was as low as $300 and in no cases exceeded $900. He feels a response rate of 25 to 30 percent would be normal for such a readership study.

As with any readership study, the newspaper must first state its goals and objectives and answer the question, "What exactly do we want to analyze?" This is vital, because it will affect both the questionnaire and the sample involved. for instance, if a newspaper wants to discover only whether teenagers are reading the sports section, it would not draw up a questionnaire dealing with the entire newspaper, and it would not sample anyone over the age of 19. It is always better, by the way, to have the study's focus plumb deeper than the question, "Are we being read?" It should instead ask questions like, "What features of what section are causing that section to be read in depth by a certain age, income, or educational demographic?" By isolating these predictors, the question, "How do we respond to the data?" becomes much easier to answer. True, these cause and effect relationships require more sophisticated research methodology, but the extra time spent can pay high dividends in responding correctly to the data.

After the objectives of the readership study have been determined, the next step is to decide on the type of study. If it is to be a survey, for instance, should you use the telephone, mail, or go face-to-face? Each has its advantages, but face-to-face surveys are usually too expensive for the large number of interviewers who must be paid. Therefore, for smaller papers or for papers requiring a large sample, mail or phone surveys are best.

In addition to surveys, many newspapers are moving toward using focus groups and other innovative methods. For instance, the Gallup Organization is starting to utilize a research tool that could add an entirely new dimension to the term. The tool is an "eye-tracking" technique that uses videotape cameras to record the time readers spend with each item in the newspaper.

Done properly, these in-house surveys can yield a great deal of useful information about the reading habits of the audience and how they relate to the newspaper in question. For more sophisticated testing and data, there are several newspaper consulting firms available to do more intensive and extensive market research.

Contracting With a Research Consultant

For newspapers with larger marketing budgets, contracting for market research done by professional consultants may make more sense. The reason is that newspaper marketing consultants devote their full time to the issues of who the market is, what they want in a newspaper, and whether they believe their newspaper is providing it. Consultants' research is more sophisticated in its scope and analysis, it is run through well-developed computer programs designed to ferret out predictors or cause agents that influence reading habits, and it can all be done relatively quickly. Unfortunately, it is also very expensive. Many publishers argue, however, that this expense is relative; that it may cost $100,000 to have some sophisticated market research run, but if it brings in a few thousand new subscribers and increases advertising revenues, it is worth it.

One of the newest developments in professional market research for newspapers burst upon the media scene in 1983. That was the year Simmons and Scarborough completed their first nationwide syndicated research studies of newspaper audiences. These studies, which have since been repeated annually, have begun to effect some big changes in the way advertisers and agencies evaluate and purchase newspaper advertising. Taken together, the first two studies—done in 1982 and 1983—offer one of the most far-reaching audience probes ever done in the newspaper industry. The two studies involved 125,000 respondents and a total of 225,000 interviews, all of which cost some $2 million to conduct. Many industry and advertising agency observers feel the studies also give the chance for agencies and advertisers to use newspapers as creatively as they use radio and television. In an interview with *Advertising Age,* Jonathan Swallen, vice president of media research at Ogilvy & Mathers Advertising Agency said:

These two studies have come along at a very propitious time. National advertisers, faced with rising out-of-pocket costs in network TV, are looking longer and harder at other media forms, newspapers included. The availability of audience data comparable to that for television, magazines and radio allows newspapers to be considered at the media planning level alongside those competitors. In addition there is a growing trend among advertisers toward emphasizing consumer markets that are more demographically segmented and geographically localized. These are two of newspapers' strengths. Standardized audience research facilitates quantitative analyses needed to evaluate newspapers in these terms.[10]

What the studies provide is more complete information about newspaper audiences, nationally and on a market-by-market basis in the country's top 50 media markets. The most important changes these studies have wrought include:[11]

- For the first time, media planners can include newspapers and newspaper audience data in the media planning process from the very beginning.

- Also for the first time, market lists can be developed on the basis of newspaper advertising weight goals (just as in spot and broadcast) without the need to pick specific schedules.

- Newspaper lists now can be developed on the basis of desired age, sex, or income characteristics and similar target demographics rather than on household coverage.

- Agencies and advertisers can make meaningful intermedia comparisons involving either single-market or multi-market media buying decisions. On the larger scale, of course, the syndicated studies represent a major step forward in newspapers' continuing drive to make newspaper advertising easier for national advertisers to buy and use.

By the time of the 1987 Newspaper Ratings study, some 100 newspapers, 88 advertising agencies, and two advertisers had subscribed to it. The 1987 Scarborough study was based on interviews with 61,026 respondents in the top 50 ADIs (areas of dominant influence), plus Des Moines, Iowa. The study thus reports data for 51 ADIs, 74 metropolitan statistical areas (MSAs), and 12 local newspaper markets. 1987 was the first time that at least one metro area had been reported for every ADI.[12]

It is easy to see, therefore, that the larger expenditures represented by employing a professional researcher may be intimidating at first, but could be money well spent in obtaining more sophisticated information to pass on to potential advertisers.

In addition to the large research consulting firms, which small newspapers may find prohibitively expensive, there are also several smaller firms set up to handle less extensive market research. For instance, Pulse Research of Portland, Oregon, conducts market research for small newspapers. To keep costs in line, the research firm leaves the responsibility of printing, distributing, and collecting the surveys up to the individual newspaper. Pulse submits a basic menu of questions for consideration, then analyzes the data that is collected by the newspaper. The researchers then organize a detailed report of the results and send that report to the newspaper. It is up to the newspaper to decide how it wants to use that information and to put it in a final market information kit.

One New England newspaper using Pulse Research decided to focus on three survey objectives: improving editorial content, increasing circulation, and defining readership and market strength of the newspaper. The finished market report analyzed the demographics of the paper's readership by age, education, income, home ownership, and profession. It compared the newspaper's strength in the market against competing media, and the shopping patterns of those living in the paper's circulation area. It also provided great detail on purchasing in dollars for many different aspects of the retail market, such as travel, home-related products, real estate, dining, automotive, clothing, and furniture. The results for each segment of the retail market were printed on a separate sheet, allowing for handing the presentation to different accounts. The research firm provided computer printouts of the raw market data, and the newspaper then tailored the results to its own uses. The data is expected to be relevant for two years.

Press Associations Can Also Help

There is some middle ground between the sometimes limited market research done in-house and the sometimes expensive research done by professional consultants. That compromise is the state or regional press association, several of which are actively involved in researching the media markets within their locales. Some of the more enlightened press associations—like the Oklahoma Press Association—also do low-cost market research projects for member newspapers. Using this press association data, which may be free of charge or involve minimal costs, is one way for a newspaper to avail itself of solid market research without going to the trouble of developing the data itself.

The Oklahoma Press Association, for instance, uses its subsidiary, the Oklahoma Newspaper Advertising Bureau, to provide an annual survey of Oklahoma consumers. Done in-house by the bureau's own Consumer Data service, the annual survey is based on information gathered from an extensive market research survey conducted in 72 nonmetropolitan cities and towns in Oklahoma. The survey, done jointly with the University of Oklahoma Journalism Research Center, is designed to reveal three basic findings:[13]

1. The media usage habits of consumers.
2. The shopping tendencies and frequencies of consumers at major stores.
3. The demographic characteristics of nonmetropolitan consumers in Oklahoma.

The information is based on more than 2,600 random telephone interviews with adult consumers in the 72 communities. It is a major help to member newspapers who are desirous of discovering more about their audiences and their buying habits. Other press associations provide similar services.

MARKET DATA AS THE BASIS FOR AD RATES

Of all the determinants of advertising rates to be discussed in Chapter 5, one of the most influential is market data. In fact, magazines long ago found that market data is even more important than circulation size, as they began emphasizing the quality of readership over the quantity. If a publication is reaching the target audience desired by advertisers, then advertisers will welcome the chance to enter the publication. The results of market surveys, either done in-house or by professional consultants, will tell the advertisers if the newspaper is, in fact, reaching the desired audience. It becomes the job of the newspaper marketing or advertising department, however, to promote the results of that marketing research: the market data. Earlier it was pointed out that the best market data in the world will do no good if it is not used. One chief use of that data is to provide content for sales promotion literature or videos; to promote the fact that the newspaper can deliver the kind of audience advertisers want and need.

Orange County Register Publisher R. David Threshie, Jr. feels honesty and empathy are two important principles in sales promotion.

> Tell your customer honestly that your product has what he is looking for, not what you think he should be looking for. There's a very thin line between presenting facts in the best light and distortion and misrepresentation. Advertisers are not dumb. They can spot exaggerated claims and hyped numbers. And we have competitors out there who are more than happy to point out to customers the error of our ways.[14]

Threshie adds that when newspapers are not honest in their promotions it subtracts from their reputations and it will be much tougher to sell the next promotion.

One facet of promotion should be to project a newspaper's personality, according to *Los Angeles Herald Examiner* Publisher Francis L. Dale. Dale believes most promotion should come from staff people and that a newspaper should go outside only for a special purpose or to get a fresh view. This idea of promoting a newspaper's personality is a solid one, and *Advertising Age* devoted an entire special section in 1984 to the subject of newspapers in search of a unique image.[15] Most newspapers do have a unique personality, characterized by their emphasis of certain types of news, the way they display that news, the columnists they feature, and the way the stories are written and edited. The image can range from that of the relatively staid *Wall Street Journal* to that of the racy and irreverent *New York Post*. Most of this country's newspapers fall somewhere between these two extremes, yet they still have unique perceived personalities. *USA Today,* for instance, has a definite image conjured up immediately by its lavish use of color, emphasis on upbeat stories, focus on people, and slavish attention to keeping stories short. *USA Today,* in fact, is a newspaper built largely upon market data. Extensive market research was done, and its results formed the foundation for most of what readers see in this newspaper. C. K. McClatchy, president editor of McClatchy Newspapers, noted in 1983 that ''Gannett [publishers of *USA Today*] listened to the research and responded to what it heard.''[16] McClatchy praised the newspaper and noted, ''The very things that we thought would prove to be a weakness have been determined by extensive research to be exactly what the targeted audience of *USA Today* actually wanted. They wanted short, easy-to-read items that . . . would be written to relate to readers' interests and needs rather than simply reporting an event.''[17] Gannett, which has an extensive in-house market research and promotion department, does a great job of promoting the fact that it is giving readers exactly what those readers say they want.

THE MARKET INFORMATION KIT

One result of carefully crafted market research should be an equally well-crafted market information kit. This kit should embody the best promotion available for the newspaper's research, should be aimed at current and potential advertisers, and should show the advertiser in no uncertain terms that this newspaper delivers the audience he is seeking. There are several things to keep in mind in compiling an effective market information kit, whether it is prepared in-house or by an outside consultant. The major decisions to be made involve the form the kit will take, its cost, the sources to be used, the order in which the data will be presented, the kit's emphasis, and some relatively minor details.[18]

Form of the Kit

The newspaper must first decide on the kit's exact form. Will it be an 8½ by 11 inch booklet, a multi-fold brochure, a pocket folder with drop-in sheets, or some other format? This decision will be influenced by such things as the budget allowed for the kit, the ease of updating it at desired time periods, and the ease associated with presenting it to advertisers. Color should definitely be used in every kit, even if it is only one color plus black. The reason is that color gives the kit more life and makes it stand out in the mind of the advertiser. The kit should also clearly state the location and size of the market, probably through the use of a market map on the inside front cover.

Cost

If a newspaper decides to go with the file folder and loose sheets, then the major expense should be incurred infrequently, as the file folders can be used over again. In 1986, a supply of 700 such file folders cost about $350, and the flat sheet inserts were only about 5 cents each.[19] If a newspaper is trying to impress its advertisers even more, the stapled full-color booklet may be in order, but it is much more expensive to produce and to update.

Sources

Source material may either be primary, secondary, or both. If secondary sources are used, they should be ones that the public would perceive as reliable. One source not discussed earlier is the Audit Bureau of Circulations (ABC). If the newspaper is a member of the ABC and is audited regularly by them, the ABC's data will be excellent information to include in the market information kit, as it shows exactly where the newspaper is being distributed in the market and what some of the market demographics are.

In fact, there is no reason why the ABC's annual report on the newspaper cannot be duplicated and slid into the marketing information kit. It may be better, however, to pick out attractive sections of the report and use them instead. Otherwise the advertiser will have to wade through a rather long report to find the nuggets of interest.

Presenting the Data

Putting the data into a workable order is the next step, and the goal is to have the market kit become a quick-read encyclopedia about the market and about how the newspaper can deliver the audience to the advertiser. One continual theme should run through the material: that the data is factual, well-documented, and pertinent. Remember you are selling not just the data, but also its credibility.

Pinpointing the Emphasis

Each newspaper should find out what it is best in and promote that aspect over every other. Possibly the newspaper is the oldest continuously published newspaper in the state, or serves the fastest growing county in the state. Much of the market information should go toward supporting this "Number 1" claim.

Remember Also . . .

Keep the data in the market information kit nonpersonal. In other words, don't mention names of editors, reporters, and so forth, because they can change. When they do, your kit becomes somewhat obsolete. Also, remember you are trying to sell the newspaper, so include data about the newspaper and make it appear obvious that if the reader wants to get into your market, he is going to have to advertise in your newspaper. Third, some graphic illustration is always a good idea, as long as you don't make the graphs or charts too difficult to read or understand. Fourth, continually strive to get candid opinions on the kit and improve it accordingly the next time it is updated. Finally, be sure to get competitive bids for the printing of the market kit.

MARKETING AND THE NEWSROOM

A study done at the Northeastern University School of Journalism in 1986[20] revealed that newspeople are somewhat reluctant to embrace the marketing concept when it involves possible changes in the new product. In fact, newspeople do not even like the word "product" when describing a newspaper. To them it is a service and not a commodity. Nevertheless, the Northeastern study of 52 New England newspaper editors also found some acceptance of marketing by editors, and an understanding of its need.

The survey asked editors such questions as (1) Does an editor's sense of news value correspond at all with his or her perceptions of the reader's news values? (2) If a discrepancy exists in news judgment, does it concern the editor to the point of trying to resolve it? (3) Just what do editors feel about the validity of newspaper market research data? The results of the survey indicate that differences in news judgment do exist—not just between editor and reader, but also among the editors themselves. In addition, few of the responding editors seemed overly concerned about those differences as they went about setting their daily news agendas, yet the results also showed a general similarity in judging which types of stories should be given higher news value ratings and which should be given lower ratings. It was the actual placement of stories on a 1 to 16 news-value scale, and the editor's perception of how the readers would place them, that varied many times.

The fact that most editors did not seem unduly concerned with differences between their news sense and their perception of the reader's news sense is seen in the following sample of responses to the questions of why such differences might exist and whether the editors were bothered by them:

- "Editors realize the importance of news that may not be exciting reading. I'm not worried about the differences. Some news people *want* to know; some news they *need* to know."
- "We have an obligation to report the news; not judge it by our likes and dislikes or by what we think people may or may not like."
- "Everyone perceives the importance of news differently. That's why we carry a variety of news stories."
- "I rank stories for broad appeal; and not for any specific interest group."
- "Editors should try to take a balanced look at what is interesting and meaningful. Individual readers look at only what is interesting."

Then there was this interesting observation:

- "It is a conflict of interest for me to worry about the reader's desires."

Only a few editors said the differences in news judgments bothered them. Among these, the following responses surfaced:

- "Yes, the differences concern me. We have to be in step with the readers without sacrificing traditional press responsibilities."
- "Newspapers are far too heavily weighted to male views and interests, primarily because men control most newsroom policies." (This observation, by the way, came from a male editor.)

Some of the more interesting findings of the survey are as follows:

- Editors exhibited little uniformity as a group in placement of the different types of stories on a 1 to 16 news-value rating scale. For instance, only one-fourth of the editors rated the same story as the lead story, and fewer still cast votes for any other single story as the lead story.
- Stories that most editors rated in the top 25 percent of news value differed drastically.
- Several differences appeared between male and female editors in their respective ratings of stories and in their perceptions of how readers might rate them.
- Female editors showed far more congruency between their own ratings of news stories and their perceptions of reader ratings than did male editors.
- Several differences between editors' news judgment and their perceived sense of readers' news judgment were evident.

Overall, the results indicate that the responding editors share a concern for their own rights and abilities to select their news agenda; that they feel readers want more entertaining stories than significant ones; that the editors themselves have no common idea of the exact placement of stories; that they hold several traditional stereotypes of men and women readers' tastes in news; and that women editors' news judgment is more closely related to their perception of readers' news judgment than is the case for male editors.

Finally, the results indicate editors may be difficult to convince that they should join in the overall marketing thrust of the newspaper. The job of convincing them falls to the publisher, and part of the logic that may be used follows in the next section.

TWO CASE STUDIES IN NEWSPAPER MARKETING

Earlier we saw some of the ways in which the *Minneapolis Star & Tribune* went about changing its image by finding out what readers wanted and delivering more of it to them. Other newspapers have also been drawing much marketing attention in recent years for strides they have made in reaching out to their readers. Two such newspapers are the *Christian Science Monitor* and the *Boston Herald*.

The *Monitor* caught the attention of media observers after Katherine W. Fanning took over as editor in 1983. It even caught the attention that year of the *Wall Street Journal*, which reported.[21]

The *Christian Science Monitor* has a 75-year history of prize-winning journalism and a loyal group of readers. But the median age of those readers is 60, their numbers are dwindling, and the newspaper last year had a deficit of $10 million on revenues of $30 million. That would be enough to kill many newspapers, but the *Monitor* is alive and working hard to get a bigger niche in an increasingly crowded newspaper market. It has a new manager, a new editor, and a new look. It is planning new ways to call attention to itself and attract readers.

To meet the challenges noted in the *Journal* article, the *Monitor* changed its look by moving to tabloid size; enlarged its type size; compartmentalized the news, putting international, national and business sections in the front half of the paper while turning the back half over to ideas sections covering science, education, and technology; and began an arts and leisure section as well as a home and family section. Fanning moved editorials from the back of the paper to the center, and added more complete indexes to help readers find the news more easily. The *Monitor* also began efforts to search more aggressively for national advertisers, especially corporate image advertising. To this end, it opened advertising bureaus for the first time in New York, Chicago, San Francisco, and Los Angeles.[22] It also decided to separate its front-section news content from the advertising. In 1987 the *Monitor* adopted a new system of grouping its retail and classified advertising in a back section called "Monitor Marketplace." It also consolidated its four regional editions into one national edition. In the American edition, Monitor Marketplace displays ads from different regions on a fixed daily schedule, and within each region, ads are grouped by categories, such as department stores, travel, and fashion. In addition, to boost its effort to attract national advertisers, the newspaper has decreased its ad deadline from two weeks to five days and will electronically typeset advertising copy, with no added art fees for most designs.

In addition, despite the fact that the *Monitor* was still losing money in 1987 and needing heavy subsidies from the Christian Science Church, Fanning increased the spending on news coverage because she believes this is an investment that will pay off in the long run.[23] By the way, she is joined in this judgment by newspaper analyst John Morton, who explains his logic in Chapter 10. In 1986 Fanning increased the size of the Washington Bureau from 10 to 15 staffers and opened new bureaus in Austin, Miami, Mexico City, Manila, Tokyo, Ottawa, and Paris. Two more were scheduled to be opened in 1987 in Bahrain and Nairobi. With those two bureaus, the *Monitor* has 14 foreign bureaus and 8 domestic bureaus.[24] There are few other newspapers of any size that can boast such an array of news bureaus around the world, and that kind of widespread coverage is one reason the *Monitor*'s international reporting has so long been respected by other journalists. The *Monitor* is also trying to shore up its losses by diversifying into syndicated radio and television news programs to broaden its reach and expand its revenue base.

The *Boston Herald,* perceived as the racier of the two newspapers in Boston (the other is the venerable *Boston Globe*), found itself to be a newspaper in search of an identity after Rupert Murdoch purchased it in 1982.[25] The newspaper was running a poor second to the *Globe* and was known mainly for its splash-and-dash treatment of sensational news events and personalities. Editor Joe Robinowitz said in 1984 that he felt the *Herald*'s mission was to put out a newspaper that was both entertaining and informative, with tighter, faster stories.

I think we have to produce a newspaper that informs the public, but in so doing, give them a bit of the things they *want* to know. That means entertainment. The type of publication we are appeals to the masses. I think we ought to have lots of material that appeals to an upscale audience, but not at the expense of other people.[26]

Although wanting to develop more features and sections aimed at women and youth, Robinowitz also stressed the need to continue emphasizing local news and sports, and consumer-oriented stories.[27] The *Herald* moved even deeper into gossip and advice columns, which it found to be attractive to many readers, even in what is perceived by outsiders to be a very staid city. In reality, the *Herald* seemed to prove what many Bostonians felt all along; that there is a very earthy side to residents of Beantown and that they will pay for a newspaper that entertains as well as informs them. The *Herald* also realized that, since it was competing against a newspaper that seemed to major in national and international coverage, there was room for a paper to move more strongly into local coverage. Thus, the *Herald* emphasizes coverage of local events and personalities, and has made the *Globe,* with its larger news staff, hustle even harder to keep up on the local front.

These thrusts, plus the *Herald*'s tabloid format and its use of circulation games, make the newspaper a clear alternative for Boston readers. By the look of the increased circulation numbers and street sales, the Herald seems to be on track with its marketing plan.

NOTES

1. "Marketing: The New Priority," *Business Week,* 21 November 1983: 96.
2. M. K. Guzda, "A Star Is Reborn," *Editor & Publisher,* 24 March 1984: 14
3. Guzda, "A Star Is Reborn," p. 14.
4. Guzda, "A Star Is Reborn," p. 14.
5. Rick Kaspar, "Marketing Newspapers, *"Presstime* (December, 1984), p. 20.
6. Elise Burroughs, "Readership Project: Looking Back and Ahead After Its Six-Year Run," *Presstime* (April 1983), p. 4.
7. Marcia Ruth, "Newspaper Research," *Presstime* (October 1984), p. 8.
8. Maxwell McCombs, "Using Readership Research." In *The Newspaper: Everything You Need to Know to Make it in the Newspaper Business,* ed. D. Earl Newsom (Englewood Cliffs: Prentice Hall, 1981), pp. 47–51.
9. Gerson Miller, "Conducting a Low-Cost Readership Study," *Editor & Publisher,* 12 January 1985: 26, 36.
10. James Dunaway, "Two Studies Could Boost Newspaper Advertising," *Advertising Age,* 30 January 1984: M30.
11. Dunaway, "Two Studies Could Boost Newspaper Advertising," p. M30.
12. "Scarborough Data Coming for '87," *Editor & Publisher,* 17 April 1987: 38.
13. Consumer Data Service, *A Report on the 1983 Survey of Oklahoma Consumers,* Oklahoma City: Oklahoma Newspaper Advertising Bureau (an affiliate of the Oklahoma Press Association), p.2, 1983.

14. M. L. Stein, "Better Research: The Key to Promotion," *Editor & Publisher,* 19 January 1985: 14.

15. "In Search of That Elusive Thing Called Image," *Advertising Age,* 30 January 1984: special section.

16. M. L. Stein, "Editors Urged to Listen and Respond to Research," *Editor & Publisher,* 1 October 1983: 12.

17. Stein, "Editors Urged to Listen," p. 12.

18. Elliott Brack, "Creating a Newspaper Marketing Information Kit," *Publishers Auxiliary,* 3 November 1986: 12.

19. Brack, "Creating a Newspaper Marketing Kit," p. 12.

20. Jim Willis, "Editors, Readers, and News Judgment," *Editor & Publisher,* 7 February 1987: 14.

21. William M. Bulkeley, "Staid *Christian Science Monitor* Changing its Look to Restore Readership and Profits," *Wall Street Journal* 1 October, 1983: B-1.

22. Robert Coram, "New Life at the *Monitor,*" *The Quill* (April 1987), p. 18.

23. Coram, "New Life at the *Monitor,*" p. 18.

24. Coram, "New Life at the *Monitor,*" p. 19.

25. Andrew Radolf, "In Search of the Right Formula," *Editor & Publisher* 7 April 1984: 10–11.

26. Radolf, "In Search of the Right Formula," p. 11.

27. Radolf, "In Search of the Right Formula," p. 11.

5

PRODUCING THE ADVERTISING REVENUE

The largest revenue-producing source in a newspaper is advertising. National Newspaper Foundation studies show that advertising accounts for anywhere from 53 percent for a local weekly newspaper printing on its own presses, to 79 percent for a metropolitan daily.[1] Nationally, newspapers garner more advertising than any other single medium, although television is pressing. Some of the reasons newspapers are such good advertising vehicles are the following:

1. Print advertising lends itself to explaining unique features of products instead of just presenting an image of a product as television usually does.

2. Readers can linger longer with their newspapers, and thus with their ads.

3. Newspaper advertising lends itself to a popular consumer habit: coupon shopping. Print ads can contain coupons, whereas television ads cannot.

4. Newspapers can offer partial-run advertising which goes to specific city zones. These may be the drawing areas for individual retailers who don't want to pay for advertising that goes beyond that drawing area.

5. Newspapers offer good volume and weekly performance discounts for advertising run regularly. This reduces even more the cost-per-thousand figure of newspaper advertising.

6. Many newspapers offer advertisers total market coverage by supplementing their paid-circulation product with a free-distribution shopper going to nonsubscribers.

7. Newspapers offer a vehicle for preprint advertising circulars which are popular among some large discount department stores.

8. Newspapers deliver results. The history of newspaper advertising shows that retailers who have chosen to use this medium have not been disappointed with the customers newspapers can deliver.

9. Newspapers are local. Their strong suit is local news and local advertising, and they offer national advertisers a chance to take advantage of co-op advertising plans with product makers.

10. Newspapers are published with great frequency. As a result, they can deliver advertising on a daily basis up to seven days a week.

11. Newspaper advertisements are available in a variety of sizes. The smallest advertising unit is an agate line of classified advertising, and the largest is a full-page ad. This flexibility gives newspapers an advantage over television, which can generally offer only 30- and 60-second commercial spots.

12. Newspaper readers are well-educated. Industry data shows almost 90 percent of all college and university graduates read a newspaper on a daily basis. In addition, newspaper readers have higher mean incomes than people who do not read newspapers regularly.

With the importance of advertising in mind, it is easy to see why publishers spend so much time worrying about dips in advertising revenue. Sometimes the causes of these dips can vary, and that makes the job of shoring up the erosion more difficult. Some of these causes include failing businesses in what may be a failing local economy, insufficient penetration into the market, defection of advertisers to other nontraditional media, mismanaged sales staff, inadequate sales promotion, defection of an important target reader group, a declining editorial product, poor image-building by the newspaper's marketing department, a bad fit between the market and the kind of product produced, or all of the above. One of the key jobs of the advertising director is to isolate those causes for his or her newspaper, because whatever the reason, the level of advertising revenue will influence the success or failure of every department in the newspaper.

THE AD PICTURE SEEMS BRIGHT

Predictions in 1987 from the Newspaper Advertising Bureau (NAB) about advertising expenditures in newspapers were good. The NAB projected total advertising expenditures in newspapers to grow 8 percent during the year, with a 3 percent growth in national, 8 percent in retail, and 12 percent in classified.[2] Craig Standen, ad bureau president, cautioned, however, that these were national projections, and that some pockets of the United States were still experiencing recessions and their advertising growth would be minimal. Standen also pointed out that several trends have been fueling the popularity of newspapers as an advertising medium. One is the regionalization of marketing. "There are strong indictions that the pendulum is swinging away from centralization of advertising management in companies like P&G and General Foods. Many are rediscovering the old truth that 'all business is local.' "[3] He said another trend is the opening up of new advertising categories such as health care. He said each of the current seven huge national advertising categories is worth $600 million or more to the various advertising media, and called for newspaper ad directors to go after more of that national advertising.

This chapter will explore the types and relative importance of advertising to newspapers, determinants of advertising rates, structuring and deciphering of rate cards, the reason why retailers are losing out by not using more cooperative advertising, how advertising departments can function as ad agencies, effective management of the advertising sales staff, and avoiding legal pitfalls associated with the sale of advertising.

For suburban and middle-market newspapers a report issued in 1987 also predicted a bright future but warned that advertising sales people would have to work twice as hard as in previous years to get that potential revenue. This was the crux of the 1987 annual report issued by Landon Associates, Inc., to its member newspapers.[4] Looking at national advertising, the report commented that this category needs constant maintenance and development efforts, unlike retail advertising. It noted that newspapers probably must replace from 40 to 60 percent of their national accounts annually, as well as producing large gains from year-to-year accounts just to break even. The report also predicted the newspapers will continue to experience a defection by retail advertisers from run-of-paper (ROP) to free-standing inserts.

TYPES OF NEWSPAPER ADVERTISING

Newspapers sell a variety of different kinds of advertising, targeted to different levels of clients and priced accordingly. Among the categories of advertising sold are local (retail), national (general), classified, preprints, legal, and co-op advertising.

Local

Local advertising accounts for about 60 percent of daily newspaper revenue.[5] Local advertising is sold mainly to retail merchants and service businesses located in the market area. As one advertising rate card puts it,

An advertiser is entitled to the local retail store rate when selling to the public through one or more retail stores owned and operated entirely by the advertiser. If the retailer is also territory jobber, wholesaler, distributor or dealer, the advertising will be charged at the general (national) rate.[6]

In addition, many newspapers will not change local rates if the ad copy for a local retail store bears as a signature or address, the name of a manufacturer, jobber, or distributor.[7] The importance of the distinction between local and national advertising is that local advertising rates are cheaper, as newspapers do their best to show appreciation of local retailers advertising in their paper.

The chief users of local advertising are supermarkets, department stores, and general merchandise stores.

National

This is advertising sold to manufacturers and distributors of national or regional brand products. This advertising is primarily used to promote the product rather than the local retailers. National advertising accounts for just over 7 percent of daily newspaper advertising revenue, but the percentage is slowly rising.[8] More national advertisers would probably use newspapers if the medium found a way to become more innovative in defining the demographics of readers exposed to newspaper advertising. To meet that need, many papers are bolstering the scope of their marketing/research department. Some national advertisers decry the rate differential between local and national advertising, and they are also calling for more uniform rate cards among different newspapers. Also, newspapers that offer flexibility in ad copy closing dates generally do better in attracting national advertisers. Newspapers have standardized their ad sizes with the introduction of Standard Advertising Units (SAUs), and that has helped immensely.

Classified

This is the advertising space sold both to local businesses and—even more importantly—to private parties in the newspaper's market area. Newspapers feel it is vital to get ads from private parties as well as businesses, because they draw such great reader attention. About 60 percent of all adults read classified advertising, and these ads have a very long shelf life.[9] This advertising derives its name from the fact that different types of services or sales are classified according to the category of the product or service sold or needed. In almost every newspaper there are at least four major headings: Help Wanted, Automobiles, Miscellaneous for Sale, and Real Estate. In the case of larger dailies, these classifications are further subdivided into many categories. Classified ads are the lifeblood of the newspaper, and that is especially true of private party ads. They must exist, or the commercial classifieds just won't come. Therefore, private-party classifieds are priced low, and about 80 percent of all papers offer special discounts to get them. Classified advertising brings in an average of 25 percent of all daily newspaper revenue.[10]

The 1980s have been strong years for the growth of classified advertising revenue. The *Hartford Courant* and *Boston Globe* are two metro dailies that saw their classified advertising increase greatly this decade. In 1985, the *Courant* sold a record 1.5 million classifieds, and the *Globe*'s classified ad linage increased 15 percent overall in 1986, lead by a 25 percent gain in real estate linage.[11] Nationally, advertisers spent $9.3 billion for classifieds in U.S. dailies in 1986, up 11 percent from 1985, according to the NAB.[12] That followed other years of strong classified increases. One trend is troublesome, however, and that is how closely tied classified ad revenue is to the strength of local economies. In areas where the economy is good, classifieds are way up; in hard-hit areas, the revenues are declining. Nevertheless, with some large retailers shifting to preprints, and with national advertising still hard to obtain, many analysts see classified advertising as the category that will continue to experience the largest growth.

Preprints

Preprints are newspaper advertising supplements. They are distributed by the newspaper, and the preprint advertiser is usually charged a rate based on every 1,000 copies into which the supplement is inserted. More and more preprint ads are being run by local department stores, hardware stores, supermarkets, and drug stores. They are generally in full color or at least partial color. Preprints bring in about 7 percent of a daily newspaper's revenue, ranking behind local, classified, and national as a money-maker. Still, several large department store chains have, in the recent past, switched much of their run-of-paper (ROP) advertising to preprints. Newspaper publishers would prefer to have those ads run at higher ROP rates, but they see preprints as better than not getting the accounts into the paper at all.

Legals

This is actually a form of classified advertising, but it is a special kind that is placed by city, state, and county governments required to announce official events like city council meetings, sheriff's auctions, public hearings, upcoming bond elections, and so on. Although legal advertising doesn't account for any more than 1 percent of revenue for large dailies, some weeklies—especially county-seat weeklies—can derive from 3 to 5 percent or more of their revenue from legals, and they don't even have to be solicited. Since the various governments are required to place such advertising by law, legal notices come in automatically and in a steady stream to newspapers designated as the "official" newspapers of the towns and counties.

Legal advertising not only is a source of revenue for newspapers, but it also increases their reputation as a comprehensive source of information. The ads also have a steady readership, especially among the people interested in the civic matters of their local community.

In order for a newspaper to obtain such public notice advertising, it must be designated as an "official" newspaper by the local or county government. Qualifications for this official status vary from state to state, but all states require the newspaper to show evidence of its permanence and acceptance in the appropriate region. Most states require official newspapers to carry a certain percentage of news and have a second-class mail permit.

Co-op

Co-op, or cooperative advertising, represents a cross between local and national advertising. As C. Randall Choate of the American Newspaper Representatives, Inc., notes, "Co-op advertising is of extreme importance to the newspaper and retailers in smaller communities, because it involves millions of dollars that have already been appropriated for advertising but are almost never spent." [13] As the name implies, cooperative advertising is a joint effort between a retailer and his supplier to finance the cost of advertising a product. For instance, say the manufacturers of Schwinn Bicycles set up a co-op advertising program with retailers who sell their bikes. As it so happens, Schwinn is one of the many manufacturers that do offer such advertising incentives. Schwinn will pay dealers who exclusively advertise Schwinn, in accepted media, 50 percent of the dealer's advertising costs up to an actual of $\frac{1}{2}$ percent of the dealer's total purchases from Schwinn during the designated period. [14] In other words, if Joe's Bike Shop purchases $50,000 worth of Schwinn bikes in a given period—usually a year—the Schwinn Bicycle Co. will reimburse Joe for half of $250 in advertising, or $125. If Joe's Bike Shop spent, say, $1,250 in advertising annually, that co-op sum represents 10 percent of his ad budget.

The reason co-op advertising goes unused is that many merchants don't know how to appropriate it, don't understand it, and therefore don't take advantage of it. This is an area where the ad salesperson can act as an advertising agent for the merchant, explaining the co-op system and walking him through the appropriation process.

DETERMINANTS OF ADVERTISING RATES

Just like homes for sale in competitive real estate markets, newspaper advertisements must be priced appropriately in order to be sold. Several factors influence the rates for advertisements in most newspapers. Among them are the amount of revenue the newspaper needs to cover expenses, the cost-per-thousand figure for the advertising, the category of advertising, what the competition is charging, the quality of the newspaper, the size of the advertisement, its positioning in the newspaper, whether the ad carries color, the demographics of the newspaper's readers, the depth of the newspaper's market penetration, the number of times the advertiser contracts to buy space in the newspaper over the course of a year, and the status of the local economy. An explanation of each of these determinants follows.

Revenue Needs of the Newspaper

The basic determinant of advertising rates is the amount of income the newspaper needs to cover its operating costs. If the daily newspaper publisher is projecting an operating budget of $10 million for the coming year, he knows about $7 to $8 million of it must come from ad sales, and, since local advertising makes up the largest single advertising revenue source, about $5 million must come strictly from retail display ads. This determinant sets the floor for the ad pricing. Sometimes publishers are tempted to drop their advertising rates to the competition's level, but that practice usually spells trouble if the newspaper cannot afford to meet its own costs.

The Category of Advertising

As discussed before, different categories of advertising carry different rates. Classified advertising and preprints are among the cheapest, followed by legal, local, and national. A relatively new type of advertising, developed initially by Mobil Oil Co. in the 1970s, has been called "advertorials," and features editorial messages placed over the company's logo. Since these ads are generally placed by national companies and do not promote local retailers, they are charged national rates. Still another type of advertising is political advertising, for which most newspapers require advance payment. Some newspapers even have a separate rate structure for political ads.

Cost-Per-Thousand

Sophisticated advertisers—and certainly advertising agencies—insist on having some kind of uniform standard to help them decide on their media buys. Cost-per-thousand figures are one such standard, based on the cost of reaching 1,000 readers with the advertisement. This can be a misleading standard, however, especially if the advertiser is not interested in scattering his or her advertising message across the entire city. Many advertisers choose to narrow the exposure of their ads to their store's drawing area alone. Newspapers can accommodate these demands with partial-run advertising issued in zoned editions of the newspapers. In such cases, advertisers are more concerned with the quality of their readers than the quantity. Thus, the cost-per-thousand standard loses application. Nevertheless, the cost-per-thousand standard is still used by many advertisers. Some still refer to the "milline rate," which is found by multiplying the actual cost of one agate line by 1 million and dividing by the newspaper's circulation.

The Competition

Newspaper publishers should keep an eye on what the competition is charging for advertising rates, but they should not automatically assume they must try to match those rates. There are several variables involved in pricing ad rates, as this section explains. If a publisher finds his or her competition is charging much less for advertising, there is always the possibility of cutting expenses to justify cutting the ad rates. Newspapers can get into legal trouble if the courts find they are cutting rates just to damage the competition, but a newspaper is safe in doing so if it can still prove it is covering expenses and showing a profit with the lower rates. In many cases, newspapers are justified in having much higher rates than their competition, especially if the quality of the product is obviously better or if market studies show the paper is delivering a better quality of reader to the advertiser.

Newspaper rate card information is available in the *Standard Rate and Data* Newspaper edition. In addition, *Editor & Publisher* periodically prints advertising linage data for all participating daily newspapers. State and regional press associations may also publish surveys of advertising data for member newspapers. Newspaper advertising managers are wise if they monitor all this data to see what the rate structure and advertising linage look like for similar-size newspapers, whether they are competitors or not.

The Quality of the Newspaper

Other things being equal, a quality editorial product will have greater market penetration than a poor editorial product, and so it should command higher rates for its advertising. What makes a quality newspaper? A 1981 survey of editors and journalism educators put the determinants in the following order: completeness of coverage, accuracy and ethics, design and appearance, writing and editing, community service, opinion/editorial page, aggressiveness, photography, business page, and features section.[15] Added to this list could be whether the newspaper's daily offering of news fits the demographics and psychographics of the particular market in which it is located.

Ad Size and Positioning

Newspaper advertisements are sized in a number of ways, but each way relates to the other. The smallest advertising unit that can be measured is the "line," which is a line of type set in agate (six-point) height. There are 14 lines to one column inch (one column wide by one inch deep). When one talks of "ad linage" he is speaking of the total number of lines the newspaper carries in advertisements. Most newspaper advertising contract rates are determined on the basis of volume of lines purchased, or the frequency of lines purchased, generally over a year.

Probably the most talked-about method of determining ad size, and therefore rates, is the "column inch." Many smaller newspapers will calculate their rates on the column inch, which in turn is calculated on the line rate. Say a weekly or small daily charges $4 per column inch for its ads. Then a two by five inch ad would run the merchant $40. Since there are 14 lines per inch, the line rate would be about 28 cents. The column inch is the advertising unit most retailers are familiar with, and it is the easiest for them to determine quickly. Newspapers offer discounts for full-page or half-page ads, when compared to what the total number of lines or column inches for that page would cost otherwise.

The newest method of determining ad sizes in newspapers is the Standard Advertising Unit (SAU). Again, this unit of measurement is based on the column inch rate, but the beauty of the SAU system, inaugurated industry-wide in July 1984, is that it standardizes the size of ads in all SAU newspapers, so that national or regional advertisers don't have to incur the time and expense of composing many different sizes of ads for newspapers of varying column widths and depths. Developed by the American Newspaper Publishers Association (ANPA) and the Newspaper Advertising Bureau (NAB), the basic SAU proposal established a six-column advertising format with column widths of 21/16 inches and a page width of 13 inches. There are 56 ad sizes for broadsheets with a full-depth page size of 21 inches. SAUs are also convertible to tabloid size newspapers (six columns wide by 14 inches deep). The SAU system was designed so that all broadsheet newspapers and tabloids—whether they conform to specifications for SAU newspapers or not—can accept SAUs smaller than the newspaper's normal column depth and float them in that space. Most newspapers accepting unusual ad size will require that the advertiser pay for the extra space not used. Billing for the new SAUs is in column inches instead of agate lines.[16] Adoption of the expanded SAUs also involved developing a rate card that conforms to International Newspaper Advertising and Marketing Executive standards and invoices that contain information recommended by the Institute of Newspaper Controllers and Financial Officers. An example of the new SAU System can be seen in Exhibit 5.

Display advertising is mostly ROP advertising in newspapers, meaning the advertising department can decide just where the ad is to appear in the paper, within certain bounds. For instance, if an ad is to run in the general news sections of the paper, the advertising department generally reserves the right to run it where it chooses, unless there is a special contract drawn up for its positioning. Positions can be reserved at most newspapers if advertisers want to run their ads in specific sections of the newspaper, such as the sports, television, or Sunday magazine sections. Good taste obviously comes into play when positioning ads, as well. A liquor ad should not run on an obituary page or a comics page, for example, or on the same page as a story of an automobile fatality.

Color

Printing color in ads involves extra expense for the newspaper, and that expense must be passed on directly to the advertiser in the form of higher rates for color advertising. Rate cards will give the color differential and state which sections color ads can be run in. In many newspapers, color advertising can be accepted only in the Sunday magazine section, because the cost of running

Exhibit 5
Standard Advertising Unit System

Depth In Inches	1 Column	2 Columns	3 Columns	4 Columns	5 Columns	6 Columns
FD	1-FD	2-FD	3-FD	4-FD	5-FD	6-FD
18"	1-18	2-18	3-18	4-18	5-18	6-18
15.75"	1-15.75	2-15.75	3-15.75	4-15.75	5-15.75	
14"	1-14	2-14	3-14	4-14	T 5-14	6-14
13"	1-13	2-13	3-13	4-13	5-13	
10.5"	1-10.5	2-10.5	3-10.5	4-10.5	5-10.5	6-10.5
7"	1-7	2-7	3-7	4-7	5-7	6-7
5.25"	1-5.25	2-5.25	3-5.25	4-5.25		
3.5"	1-3.5	2-3.5				
3"	1-3	2-3				
2"	1-2	2-2				
1.5"	1-1.5					
1"	1-1					

Note: 13-inch depths are for tabloid sections of broadsheet newspapers. T is a full-page size for 21.5" cut-off tabloid newspapers. It measures $14 \times 9\frac{1}{8}$. Column measures are: $1 = 2\frac{1}{16}''$; $2 = 4\frac{1}{4}''$; $3 = 6\frac{7}{16}''$; $4 = 8\frac{1}{8}''$; $5 = 10\frac{13}{16}''$; $6 = 13''$; Double Truck $= 26\frac{3}{4}''$; FD = Full Depth.

Source: Reprinted with permission of the American Newspaper Publishers Association, The Newspaper Center, 11600 Sunrise Valley Drive, Reston, Va. © American Newspaper Publishers Association.

color elsewhere in the paper would be prohibitive. With the new interest in color, based on research which shows it to have a profound drawing power, many newspapers are injecting color into their main sections and thus making it possible for advertisers to run color in them as well. In 1982, color differentials in some large dailies were running an additional $1,000 per ad insertion for process (four-color) color. Using just one or two colors is also possible, and involves lower rate differentials.

Volume Purchased or Frequency Run

Most newspapers will make annual contract (discount) rates available for local and national advertising, and encourage advertisers to sign such a contract. The annual volume contract commits an advertiser to run a certain number of ad lines or column inches over the course of a 12-month period. The rate is on a sliding scale, with the rate decreasing for the more advertising purchased. For instance, if a small advertiser signs on for a 500-line contract, he may pay $2.10 per line, or $29.40 per column inch. That rate may obligate him to purchase anywhere from 500 to 9,999 lines (or an appropriate number of column inches) over the year. If he goes over that amount and purchases, say, from 10,000 to 49,999 lines in the year, his rate will drop to something like $2.08 per line, and so on. The biggest rate break usually comes in the area of 100,000 lines per year.

The second type of advertising contract is the frequency discount contract or, as some papers call it, the weekly performance contract. Under this arrangement, an advertiser is obligated to run so many lines of advertising per week for the contract year. Many times this contract offers better rates than the annual volume contract, because newspapers like to have merchants run regular ads throughout the year.

Reader Demographics and Psychographics

Generally speaking, the more affluent the newspaper reader is, the more desirable the publication will be as an advertising medium, and advertising rates will be at a premium. However, even with zoning capabilities, newspapers do not have the luxury of being able to tailor the product to a small, select group of readers as magazines do. Newspapers are truly a mass medium, and they must serve a large and diverse audience within each market. However, with the advent of partial-run advertising, advertisers can segment that mass market to reach a particular geographic zone where their regular customers live. In addition, about 25 cities still have competing dailies, and often these competing newspapers are so vastly different in style and format that they attract different audiences and different demographics. Cities in which this is still true include New York, Boston, Chicago, Houston, San Francisco, and a few others. In each of these cases, the difference between competing newspapers (one of which is usually a broadsheet and the other a tabloid) is obvious, and it doesn't take a genius to know that each paper reaches different kinds of people within each market.

In Boston, for instance, the *Globe* boasted in 1984 that 66 percent of readers reached by one issue of the newspaper hold college degrees.[17] The *Herald,* on the other hand, stated that only about 36 percent of its Sunday readers were college–educated.[18] In addition to various demographic groups, newspaper marketers are defining various psychographic groups within the community and are trying to orient their newspaper to some of the more important such groups. The new scientific ad agency divides the general population into four target groups, each with its own most vulnerable emotions. It then structures the advertising to capitalize on those vulnerabilities. "Belongers," about a third of the population, believe in traditional values. Ads displaying nostalgia are likely to appeal to this group.

"Emulators" are the disillusioned, insecure, pessimistic post-adolescent group, and they make up about 15 percent of the population. The key to selling them is to boost self-confidence. Ads depicting a person deriving prestige from driving a snappy sports car appeal to this group.

"Emulator-Achievers" are the fairly wealthy 20 percent of the population who feel stuck just below the top rung of the economic ladder. Ads depicting status or guilt appeal to this group. For example, a computer manufacturer might warn you that your child might not get to college unless he does his homework on a personal computer.[19]

"Societally Conscious Achievers," about 20 percent of the population, are the fastest-growing and most difficult target group. William Meyers, author of *The Image Makers: Power and Persuasion on Madison Avenue,* feels that many of the recent failures emanating from Madison Avenue have resulted from advertisers' failure to win this group. These are the people who are the former malcontents of the 1960s. Part and parcel of the baby boom, they are highly individualistic in their tastes and very independent in their thinking. Nevertheless, some ad campaigns have succeeded, such as the soft-drink industry's caffeine-free campaign.

Market Penetration

A popular misconception about newspapers is that big circulations equal financial success, yet the demise of the *Washington Star* (325,000 circulation when it folded) showed that this isn't always true. In a competitive newspaper environment, it will not only be the newspaper that has the large circulation numbers, but the one that has the greatest reach or penetration into the market that will be successful. Market penetration for newspapers is defined as the number of households in the newspaper's market area divided into the newspaper's actual circulation. If a newspaper has a circulation of 300,000, and there are 600,000 households in the market area, the newspaper has a 50 percent penetration into that market. One of the reasons free-circulation weeklies have been taking advertising from metro dailies is that they can boast high levels of penetration; in some cases 100 percent. The old adage that advertisers will buy a paid-circulation paper before a free paper is quickly disappearing as the free papers are gaining greater penetration. However, a paid newspaper that can also boast a high penetration, possibly by adding a supplemental shopper, has an excellent chance of surviving and beating out these other competitors. Strategies for attaining such high penetration figures are discussed in Chapter 10. In cities where two paid daily newspapers are dueling it out, the newspaper that has the higher circulation percentage will get the lion's share of the advertising. For instance, a financier stated in the *New York Times*, "When you get 51 percent of the circulation, you get 70 percent of the advertising."

The Local Economy

E.F. Hutton Co. has cited the importance of the local economy to a newspaper's financial health. "We believe that most successful newspaper investments will be in companies that operate efficiently in strong local economies. . . . As long as the economy continues on a secular basis to produce more and more goods for more and more people to consume, we think the sellers of advertising access will remain strong."[20] It may be that the local economy is, at times, the most influential factor affecting advertising rates. A Texas newspaper publisher said recently that he had two ways to cover his expenses and produce a small profit: cut expenses or raise ad rates.

We decided to cut expenses, because it just wouldn't be fair now to our local merchants to raise ad rates, given the poor condition of the Texas economy. Besides, people remember it when you treat them well, and they also remember it when you don't. So we take the local economy into prime consideration when we are considering raising ad rates.[21]

ADVERTISING RATE CARDS

The production of an advertising rate card should be the last step in the process of setting ad rates. It should be done only after the above rate determinants have been examined and related to the newspaper in question. In addition, a look at the history of the newspaper's advertising volume, in good times and bad, will indicate how much advertising revenue the newspaper can expect in the coming period. Since newspapers must pay attention to revenue growth, however, a revision of ad rates will be called for periodically. The problem with raising rates, in addition to requiring a new rate card, is that the newspaper runs the risk of losing some advertisers who may be unable to afford the higher rates or unwilling to pay them. This risk must be measured against the opportunity for greater revenue as a result of the new rates. However often the rate cards are revised, each card should contain certain information and features. After all, the rate card, along with related market demographics, is of prime concern for potential advertisers. Aspects to the structuring of rate cards that publishers should keep in mind include the following:

1. There should be separate rate cards, or pages in rate books, for each category of advertising the newspaper offers: retail, national, classified, and preprint.
2. The rate cards should be designed for easy reading. Any possible confusing matter, such as contract or repeat rates, should be explained fully and clearly on the cards.
3. Each card should feature a ''general information'' section, detailing the advertising sales and service policies of the newspaper. For instance, how does this newspaper define retail versus national advertising, how does it handle billing of cooperative advertising, and so on.
4. Open (noncontract) rates for ROP advertising generally lead off each rate card.
5. Annual volume and frequency contract rate information should follow immediately and be explained as fully as possible.
6. Contract ROP advertising information is usually followed by special categories of advertising such as color advertising, and rates for Sunday magazines and television supplements.
7. A section is needed on each card to discuss the mechanical requirements for ads presented to the paper and stating whether the paper accepts SAU advertising. With the advent of SAU advertising, the rate card should include an SAU layout showing advertisers the sizes and types of SAUs available.
8. The rate card should close with a statement of copy, deadline, and contract regulations.

Sometimes advertisers have difficulty deciphering even the simplest rate cards. For this reason, each ad representative should be totally familiar with the card and the ways in which it can be used to find the best possible deal for each advertiser.

OFFERING CUSTOMER ADVICE

The general manager of a chain of suburban Boston newspapers commented recently that

Most local retailers really don't know what they're doing when it comes to merchandising their products. Many first-time retailers don't have any retailing background at all. They may have just inherited some money and decided to open up their own business. It is for these retailers and others like them that newspaper ad reps must also serve as advertising agents and help them in setting up annual advertising budgets. Otherwise, the retailer will just shoot from the hip in placing ads. They will advertise when the whim strikes them, and many times will pull back just when they need to advertise more.[22]

The ad manager who wants help in assisting retailers in setting up advertising budgets can find it in many places. Most trade associations and dealer associations have statistics on how much their retailers spend on advertising, and will even provide average ad expenditures (in percentage of gross revenue terms) for these retailers. For instance, the National Automobile Dealer's Association may tell you that new car franchises will spend an average of 8/10 of 1 percent of gross revenues on advertising each year. That means if an auto dealer grosses $3 million in sales annually, $24,000 of that will go for advertising. The American Booksellers Association may tell you that book stores will spend an average of 1.7 percent of gross sales on advertising. These average expenditures provide a good index in advising retailers in your city on what their peers in business are spending. Since most advertising budgets are determined on a basis of percentage of projected sales, this information is highly valuable. In addition, sources such as the U.S. Department of Commerce or State Comptroller offices can provide information showing peak and valley sales periods for different types of retail and service businesses.

Armed with this basic industry information, the ad rep can then take the inexperienced retailer through the process of setting up an advertising budget based on the merchant's projection of his coming year's sales. Once the figure is set, the space can be allocated for peak and valley periods during the year and for the best times of targeted months. This allocation means that the retailer promotes the right products at the right time, and that he allocates ad space according to the sales potential of each department or product line. The final step in setting the ad budget comes in developing an advertising schedule by putting it in writing in a calendar form for each month, working out ads by the days of the week. If this is done, the advertiser can know at a glance which ads are to be placed when for upcoming weeks, and deadlines need surprise no one.

The ad representative for the newspaper can also assist the new advertiser in translating the rate card in light of the amount of money the advertiser wishes to spend and the number of ads he would like to have placed in the year. An example of how this translation might take place is as follows:

1. Let's say the advertiser has budgeted $5,000 to spend on advertising in your newspaper for the coming year. He is interested in knowing which of the contract rates he qualifies for. Assuming the first annual volume contract rate on the card is $2.10 per line for linage between 500 and 9,999 lines, this is the rate the advertiser would qualify for. Why is this the case? To answer that, look at the next rate on the contract schedule. It could be $2.08 for linage of between 10,000 and 49,999 lines, but 10,000 lines times $2.08 equals $20,800, which is four times as much money as the advertiser wishes to spend with his $5,000 ad budget. Therefore, his contract rate will be $2.10. For this rate he can get 2,380 lines of advertising, 170 column inches, or an appropriate number of SAUs.

2. Determine exactly how many (and what size) ads that will translate to. If you and the advertiser decide that he should place two by five inch ads in the paper to ade-

quately explain his product, then since each ad comprises ten total column inches, he could get 17 of these over the course of the year. The question then becomes what products these ads will promote and at what times during the year. For that, you should consult the appropriate industry advertising averages and sales index data from the Chamber of Commerce.

The advertiser might, however, want to take advantage of the frequency discount instead of annual volume discount. Most newspapers offer such a weekly performance rate, and it is generally cheaper than the annual volume rate. Here's how it works:

Say an advertiser wants to place one two by five inch ad each week throughout the year. That would mean ten column inches per week, or 140 lines. Under the weekly performance rate, he might get that advertising for $1.80 per line, as opposed to the $2.10 annual volume rate. Therefore, for an advertiser planning to use the paper weekly, this frequency contract rate probably makes more sense.

Advertising agencies and national advertisers can receive good, useful data on advertising nationwide by subscribing to the Advertising Checking Bureau, Inc. (ACB). The ACB is a clearinghouse for newspaper publishers who want to distribute checking copies to agencies and national advertisers around the country. Advertising agencies sends copies of the newspaper insertion orders to ACB and the bureau checks for proper date, size, key number, reproduction quality, competitive ads on the same page, and so on. ACB scans almost every daily newspaper in the United States, as well as some larger weeklies. The bureau provides tear-sheet services and verification of co-op ads and they report on secondary brand mentions, as when an appliance is advertised as "powered by a Westinghouse engine." The bureau also reports on the use of material provided by the national advertiser as it is used in ads placed by retailers. These reports then tell the national advertiser which models or styles appear to be most popular with dealers.

Newspaper advertising departments can also benefit from ACB data that gives comparative data on the volume of advertising purchased in newspapers and other media by advertisers in specific business categories such as automotive, banks and financial institutions, food and grocery stores, and so on. This data can show the newspaper which categories of advertising are strong industrywide and which are weak.

APPROACHES TO SELLING ADVERTISING

Selling advertising not only involves point-of-sale activity between the ad representative and advertiser, but it also involves selling the newspaper as an advertising medium. Good sales promotion rests upon the collection of good market data, which is a subject taken up in Chapter 4. For our purposes here, we will look at a few methods and ideas that have helped others sell advertising in turbulent times. In a 1985 American Press Institute seminar on advertising sales strategies, participants discussed the following recommendations:[23]

- If newspapers are to continue their appeal as a mass medium, they must build new product lines that will attract more readers.
- Newspapers need to identify their true competition, and define it precisely to compete more effectively.
- Newspapers need to become more sensitive to the needs of the advertiser.
- Segmentation of advertising needs to be sharpened down to such a fine level as zoning the zones.
- Networking (several regional newspapers offering a multimarket buy) is a necessity to make it easier for the advertiser to buy in regional patterns.
- Newspapers must be affordable to the small advertiser.
- Advertisers want standardized market research. They are seeking national "trend information" about newspapers and their readers.
- Publishers should become more active with key advertising accounts and should occasionally accompany the newspaper's advertising salespeople to lunches or events in the local advertising community.
- Newspapers should invest in classified as a business center that will always provide an outlet for the small advertiser and that will prosper with the right promotion.
- Publishers making business trips to New York City or other major media-buying centers should build in brief visits to advertising agencies, national rep firms, or client accounts of their newspapers.

In addition to these suggestions, the following points should be observed in preparing and giving sales presentations:

- Always remember the customer. The retailer is interested in your publication for one reason only: because it may be able to deliver the kind of customers he needs. It is up to you to convince him it can.
- Don't stay too long with each customer, and don't leave too quickly. Some customers will try to engage you in protracted conversations about everything from advertising to baseball. Try to stick to advertising once the ice is broken. The advertiser himself will appreciate it, especially after you've gone and he still has work to do.
- Don't overload your presentation with statistics. Two or three charts showing the desirability of your newspaper and its readership are more than enough. When you do use figures, be sure you provide trustworthy sources.
- Tailor your presentation to each customer. This is not always possible, due to the large number of calls you have to make. However, at least for the more important customers, it is a good idea to personalize the presentation as much as possible.
- Sell quality of your paper and coverage of the desired audience first, but then tell the advertiser what it's going to cost to reach that audience. Don't try to hide this cost. Just don't commence your presentation with it.

- Think defensively. You should be able to predict what kinds of questions you will receive from the advertiser. Go over them beforehand and be prepared to deal with them at the point of selling.

- Have a strong finish in mind, and execute it at the proper time. Summarize your presentation quickly and ask for the insertion order.

- Be polite, and put the accent on the positive. Most people don't appreciate having smoke blown in their face, either literally or figuratively. It is possible, however, to structure a presentation where you emphasize the positive aspects of your newspaper and its audience without being perceived as distorting the picture.

- Know your product. In other words, read your own newspaper, front to back, every day. It is embarrasing—and may cost you a sale—if you can't react intelligently to a comment the advertiser makes about the editorial in the morning paper.

- Treat the customer as a living, breathing, feeling person. You may have a lot of people to see today, but probably none is more important than the customer you are talking to right now. Therefore, treat him as a person and not just as another notch in your sales belt. Practice good listening techniques and use them.

- Be prompt and regular with your customer calls. If you say you will drop by at 2 P.M., do so, and don't fall into the trap of regularly servicing only those retailers who buy your presentation. Make regular calls on those who don't, and one day your kind persistence will pay off.

- Be sure to provide tear sheets for advertisements. One tear sheet should be sent with the invoice, but have others available for the advertiser who may want to tape them in store windows as point-of-sale advertising. This is also an effective promotional vehicle for your newspaper.

- Have checking copies of the newspaper available for advertisers and agencies that request them. A checking copy is a copy of the entire newspaper that contains the retailer's or agency's ad. These copies are analyzed by advertisers who study the editorial climate of the paper and see what competitive products were advertised in that issue.

- If there is an error in a retailer's ad, and if that mistake was the fault of the newspaper, rerun the ad—in corrected form—in the next available issue of the newspaper. This corrected ad is called a ''make-good.'' Don't argue with the retailer; just rerun the ad with a smile.

GOING AFTER NATIONAL ADVERTISING

Since the birth of commercial television in 1945, national advertisers have seen it as the medium holding the most promise in delivering the widespread audiences they need. Television's share of national advertising has rocketed to 55 percent, while newspaper's share has declined from a high of 30 percent in 1950 to about 12 percent in 1985.[24] The newspaper industry is now pursuing several paths to try to win back some of that national advertising volume. National advertising sales divisions within newspaper advertising departments are being strengthened at many newspapers, and the industry is making more use of national advertising representatives for help in both sales and data collection about the attractiveness of newspapers for national advertisers. One large representative is American Newspaper Representatives, INC. (ANR), a national advertising sales and service organization. It represents more than 7,000 weeklies alone. In addition, the Newspaper Advertising Bureau (NAB) exists to serve newspapers, providing its members with data, training material, and ad sales help if needed. The ANR is headquartered in Detroit, and the NAB is headquartered in New York City.

The newspaper industry has seen straws in the wind that indicate television's share of national advertising may be dropping off a bit. One of the reasons for that has been the explosion of the cable television industry and the resulting fragmentation of what once was a unified national television audience for the three networks. All of a sudden, spending big bucks for fragmented network audiences doesn't make as much sense as it used to. Some industry observers feel that, with each U.S. household receiving 50 or more cable television channels and a half-dozen different magazines, the one newspaper they receive will make that medium much more attractive to advertisers.

To exploit this renewed interest in newspapers, the industry has tried to make it easier for national advertisers to use the medium. The development of SAUs, implemented industry-wide in 1984, made it less complicated for advertisers to size their ads for different newspapers. Also, to make it easier for agencies to dispatch these ads around the country, the industry developed a system called AD/SAT, allowing advertisers to expedite ad layouts to newspapers via satellites. The same system also permits electronic billing and proofing, thus bringing to national advertisers the same advantage of timeliness enjoyed by local retailers.[25] Finally, newspapers are improving the quality of reproduction by using new keyless inking procedures (see Chapter 7) and by incorporating more color into the daily newspaper. In 1984, the Newspaper Advertising Bureau launched a program to do for color—on an industry-wide basis—what was done for ad sizing with the SAUs. The NAB began working with the ANPA to show newspapers the need to produce consistent color quality throughout their press runs and to offer that quality to advertisers on an industry-wide basis. One of the complaints of national advertisers has been the inconsistency in color quality their ads receive in the various newspapers that carry them. Good color, the NAB noted, requires a strong commitment from upper management at newspapers. The reason is that new press equipment may be required for many newspapers to bring their color quality up to par with other papers. Part of the problem in developing industry-wide color standards has been that many large newspapers don't have the ability to do the job and still get their papers to readers on time. The restrictions that these newspapers face usually means they must put a limit on the number of color ads they can accept in the first place. With the various studies showing the positive influence news-

paper color has on readership in general, however, it is likely that most newspapers will continue to make this commitment to better color quality in the
years ahead.

ADVERTISING AGENCIES

Many large retailers and most national advertisers use the services of an
advertising agency to identify the media most effective for their advertising
dollars. The agencies also advise on advertising campaigns, budgets, and con-
cepts, and assist in designing ads and positioning them in various media. Ad
agencies also provide supplemental market research and can help in developing
marketing plans for their clients. In so doing, they provide a valuable service
for the clients they represent.

Most modern-day agencies charge a fixed percentage of advertising billings,
usually 15 percent, which they get from the media in which the advertisements
are placed. Agencies may add to this percentage if they perform extra services
such as conducting auxiliary market studies, but most agencies have been stick-
ing with the 15-percent commission figure. In one sense, ad agencies make it
easier for newspapers to deal with and service the large number of retailers in
a modern city, for while there are hundreds of such retailers—maybe thousands—there are only a few ad agencies, and these agencies are generally au-
thorized to make decisions on media buys for their clients. Nevertheless, these
agencies and the people who man them are extremely sophisticated in their
knowledge of media effectiveness, so it is incumbent upon newspaper ad salespeople to know their own product well and be able to state how that product
can deliver the desired audience for the advertiser.

A large agency, like Young & Rubicam or Ogilvy & Mather Intl. employs
three different kinds of professionals to assist retailing clients. One type handles creative services, which include artists and advertising production people.
Developing the ad campaign and preparing the theme usually are jobs falling
to this group, which also creates the actual ads. The second group is the client
services group, where the advertising account executives work. Account executives are the interface people with the agency's clientele. They must decipher
the clients' needs—and in some cases help define those needs—and translate
those needs back to creative services for effective advertising to be created.
The third group in the large ad agency is the marketing services group, which
is responsible for all media and market research needs the client may have.[26]

Much of the local advertising run in newspapers is done without the mediat-
ing services of a full-service ad agency. After all, only the larger retailers can
even justify the cost of such an agency. Nevertheless, ad representatives will—
at one time or another—come into contact with such agencies and should bring
their own high degree of sophistication to this information exchange.

MANAGING THE SALES STAFF

The newspaper's advertising manager, along with his or her divisional managers in charge of retail, national, and classified advertising, must remember that they have important management functions to perform. Among these are the following:

1. Know the market and amount of potential advertising money available in that market. One rule of thumb commonly used to ascertain the potential advertising revenue available in the market is to take 2 percent of the annual retail sales in the market. That is the average percentage all businesses spend on advertising. The retail sales figures can be obtained from the *Sales and Marketing Management Survey of Buying Power,* or from the State Comptroller's Office. Once the estimated advertising allocation is found, subtracting the amount received by your newspaper and the competition will give you the untapped potential. That, then, becomes the target to shoot for.

2. Set quarterly goals. It is imperative to have annual sales projections to shoot for, but a newspaper cannot afford to wait until the end of the year to find out if it has hit these marks. Consequently, quarterly projections and goals are needed so the ad director can measure the newspaper's progress toward its advertising revenue goals for the year. Mid-course corrections may be called for so the remainder of the year can be more beneficial.

3. Transmit this market knowledge and these quarterly goals to the sales staff. This information should be part of the initial orientation program provided each new sales rep, and the information should be updated as often as necessary in sales staff meetings.

4. Obtain standard sales reports regularly from each salesperson. Some sales managers will take weekly sales reports from their salespeople, while others will take monthly reports. Either way, it is important to have first-hand, up-to-date knowledge of how your sales reps are doing so you can praise them on exemplary efforts and coach them on efforts missing the sales mark. In addition to these sales reports, which show the businesses actually purchasing advertising, sales managers should also obtain call sheets from each ad rep. These call sheets show the number and kinds of sales calls made on prospects each day of the week. If trouble is occurring in the form of a low sales quota, it can often be diagnosed by analyzing these call sheets to see if enough calls are being made, if the appropriate amount of time is taken with each call, and if follow-up or service calls are sufficient.

5. Plan sales strategy with the ad reps. This is especially important with new salespeople or with those who tend to shoot from the hip too much and, as a result, produce sporadic sales results. Often these strategy sessions between sales manager and sales rep are one-on-one coaching sessions, and they probably take the most time of many sales managers' days. The temptation is always there for a sales manager to get out and produce the sale himself if he finds a particular ad rep is not doing the job, but sales managers must realize they can multiply their efforts if they will just take the needed time with their sales staff to coach them on the best strategies for selling difficult customers.

6. Having said that, there is nothing wrong with the sales manager occasionally tagging along with a sales rep to see a hard-sell advertising prospect. Sometimes it does help to have at least the presence of the ad manager at the point of sale to increase the clout of the ad rep. It also offers a good chance for the sales manager to see his sales reps in action and to make comments about the selling tactics of the staffer.

7. Hold regular staff meetings with the sales crew. Part of the reason for these meetings is obviously to pass on information and to receive information from the field on the problems and opportunities existing in the market, but another vital function of these staff meetings is to make each of the ad reps, who is many times out working on his own, feel a part of the newspaper's total sales effort. People naturally work better and feel better about their work when they know it is contributing to the larger goals of the company. Also, hearing success and failure stories from other sales team staff members lets them know others are experiencing the same kinds of situations they are.

8. Make sure the sales reps know the newspaper as well as the territory. Sales managers must insist that their reps read the newspaper regularly so they can carry on intelligent conversations with clients about the contents of the newspaper.

9. Make sure the sales staff knows buyers' traffic patterns in prospective client stores; what is selling and what isn't, and which days are important to retailers and buyers. This data can form the basis for an intelligent advertising schedule for the retailer, who may be too busy running the store to check these indicators.

10. Know the media competition, understand the nature of it, and look out for possible antitrust abuses. For a further discussion of such abuses, see Chapter 10.

11. Look for the competitive strengths of your newspaper and promote them in graphic form, making use of market research surveys.

12. Instill in the sales staff the idea that they should sell benefits of your newspaper as an advertising medium; not space or results.

SALES COMPENSATION PLANS

A recent session for advertising managers at a New England Press Association Convention addressed the question, "What is the best sales compensation plan for ad sales people?" The responding consensus was that there is no best plan, for although there are a variety of ways of paying ad reps, each leaves something to be desired, especially when trying to apply one particular plan to several different media workplaces. Some ad reps need the kind of motivation and incentive commissions can provide; others will work long hours because they enjoy what they are doing. For them, straight salary may be best. Still others may need a combination of the two plans. If there was one area of agreement among the New England ad managers, it was that the most effective plan will involve commissions in some way.

Media consultant James B. Kobak believes the basic objective of any compensation arrangement is to develop the most sales at the least cost, but, he adds, that definition is not good enough. A better one is this: to develop the most profitable sales at the least cost.[27] This means that the first step is to determine which really are the most profitable pages in both the short and long run. Kobak says any effective sale compensation plan must result in a living wage, be equitable to all, give a fair value for the services rendered, result in competitive pay scales, steer salespeople to the most desirable type of sales, not result in overcompensation, and be simple to understand and administer. It is not easy to get all this into one pay plan.

What are the various pay plans used by newspapers to compensate their ad salespeople? They range from straight commission to straight salary, and include several gradations in between.

Straight Commission

This is probably the best known of the compensation plans for ad sales reps. For a newspaper, it is based on the sales in a territory or for designated retail accounts. The obvious advantage of the plan, from a management standpoint, is that it pays only for sales produced. As such, it is very cost efficient and acts as a good incentive for the sales rep to produce as many sales as possible. It is also fairly simple to administer, with the sales rep getting a cut of the sales, usually once the advertiser has paid.

On the down side, the equity of a straight commission plan assumes that all reps' sales territories are created equal. This is seldom the case. Some territories are better than others. One of the most difficult managerial duties of the ad manager is to help insure equity among the different sales territories, especially if his people are being paid on straight commission. Another problem is that, once an ad rep gets a major account or two hooked, he may feel he can skate in future years by resting on the continued commission of the accounts he netted years ago. To combat this problem, one New England publisher adopted a system of a sliding scale commission that goes like this: if an ad rep nets a large account this year, the commission will be higher than normal, but next near the commission on this account will drop a few percent, and the third year it will drop even lower. This encourages the ad rep to keep on going after large accounts instead of resting on his laurels.

Still other problems pertain to sales reps becoming too independent of management by feeling they are working for themselves, and a final problem is that straight commission, while good for some personalities, frightens other would-be super-sellers away because there is no guaranteed base income. Furthermore, if the local economy goes sour and retailers cut back on advertising, the ad rep's salary will be cut through no fault of his own.

Straight Salary

A Texas newspaper publisher recently told of hiring an inexperienced ad rep whom he felt had the capability of being a good salesperson despite her insecurity about those abilities. To ease her mind and allow her to focus on the task at hand, the publisher put her on straight salary for the first few months. It worked. The publisher's prediction was correct, and the woman did become an excellent sales rep. At that time, he discussed with her the possibility of going on straight commission, and she jumped at the chance. This pattern repeats itself at many newspapers. The straight salary option seems best for new, and especially inexperienced, sales reps. The straight salary plan also acts as a hedge against situations when ad sales are more the result of group effort than individual effort. If there is too great an inequity in sales territories, there may also be a need for a straight salary plan in those territories deemed tougher— at least for awhile.

One of the key aspects of the straight salary plan is that there should be a regular readjustment of the salary. Most sales reps should only be on straight salary for a limited time, and there should be a good reason to change from that plan. Those reasons usually have to do with increased sales results on the part of the ad rep.

Draw Against Commission

This is a middle-of-the-road plan that allows a sales rep to obtain a draw against expected commission earnings. Anything over that draw is a bonus for the ad rep, but any sales under the draw mean that the remainder of the draw should be repaid to the newspaper at a later date. In point of fact, many publishers using a draw against commission plan don't require the repayment of the unearned draw. If this sales condition persists, however, the ad rep with the poor record will probably be looking for a new job before long.

Salary Plus Commission

In this plan, an ad manager may pay about 75 percent of the ad rep's expected intake in salary form, and the rest must come by way of commission. Commissions would be paid for sales over a preset amount—or quota—and there are various ways for determining what that quota should be, based on past sales history of the territory, and so on. If a large amount of a newspaper's advertising seems to come flowing in by itself—as in the case of a newspaper that has established and maintained a large group of regular advertisers—this combination plan might work best, since no new ad rep is going to deserve credit for originating old business, yet still needs a spur for originating new business.

Salary Plus Year-End Bonus

This is a modification of the salary-plus-commission plan, although the commission comes in the form of a year-end bonus, determined on sales over a set quota. The problem is that it may cause some ad reps to work harder toward the end of the bonus year and work less hard during the rest of the year. That situation can be remedied, however, in the way the bonus criteria are established by the ad director.

Group Commission

This plan is used in some cases, but not many. How can you reward strong and weak performance alike just becasue the ad reps work for the same organization? Selling is usually more of an individual effort than a team effort; in the latter, someone usually gets paid for something they didn't do or gets paid the same amount for producing great results as another ad rep who didn't produce at all.

LEADERSHIP STYLES IN THE AD DEPARTMENT

The advertising manager is no less a people manager than the managing editor in the newsroom. As such, ad managers must realize the importance of human resources to the effective selling of advertising. For a detailed analysis of which leadership styles are more likely to produce results than others, see Chapter 9 and its discussion of motivational techniques and leadership theories X, Y, and Z. Since ad reps also consider themselves professionals, and since ad reps work fairly independent of each other, Chapter 9's analysis applies as much to what might work in the advertising department as the news department.

ADVERTISING'S LEGAL PITFALLS

Much of the advertising profession is regulated by its own code of ethics, since there are few laws that pertain to advertising. The American Association of Advertising Agencies (AAAA) developed a Creative Code in 1962 which states that advertising professionals will adhere to an ethical foundation as well as existing laws. This ethical foundation, according to the AAAA, is based on the following considerations, and states that advertising people will not knowingly produce advertising which contains:[28]

1. False or misleading statements or exaggerations, visual or verbal.
2. Testimonials that do not reflect the real choice of a competent witness.
3. Price claims that are misleading.
4. Comparisons that unfairly disparage a competitive product or service.
5. Claims insufficiently documented, or that exaggerate the truth or application of statements made by professional or scientific authority.
6. Statements, suggestions, or pictures offensive to public decency.

As is the problem with all codes, however, the 4-A's code is ambiguous in places. For instance, what is the meaning of "unfairly disparage a competitive product" or "Claims insufficiently documented"?

As David Aaker and John Myers point out, deceptive advertising exists

"when an advertisement is introduced into the perceptual process of some audience, and the output of that perceptual process (1) differs from the reality of the situation, and (2) affects buying behavior to the detriment of the consumer. The input itself may be determined to contain falsehoods. The more difficult and perhaps more common case, is when the input [the advertisement] is not obviously false, but the perceptual process generates an *impression* that is deceptive. [29]

The Federal Trade Commission (FTC), in 1983, delivered its definition of deception on a 3–2 vote, stating:

The Commission will find deception if there is a misrepresentation, omission or practice that is likely to mislead the consumer acting responsibly (or reasonably) in the circumstances, to the consumer's detriment . . . [that is the act or practice is] likely to affect the consumer's conduct or decision with regard to a product or service. If so the practice is material, and consumer injury is likely because consumers are likely to have chosen differently but for the deception. [30]

It is important to note also that the FTC judges an advertisement by its general impression. In other words, the entire ad can be literally true, yet leave an erroneous impression. An advertisement can be seen as being deceptive if the reader or viewer can perceive it in at least two ways, one of which would be deceptive.

What remedies exist if the FTC finds an advertiser guilty of deceptive advertising? For one, the FTC can issue a cease-and-desist order preventing the company from engaging in future deceptive practices. Complying with the ordered remedies may be easy in comparison with trying to regain readers' trust, and once that trust is gone, so may purchasers of the product. Therefore, it is incumbent upon newspaper advertising departments to try, to the best of their ability, to insure that deception does not creep into advertisements it carries. After all, deceptive ads can deplete the reader's trust in the newspaper as well as the deceptive advertiser.

NOTES

1. Gene Chamberlain, "The Business of Journalism." In *The Newspaper: Everything You Need to Know to Make It in the Newspaper Business*, ed. D. Earl Newsom (Englewood Cliffs: Prentice Hall, 1981), p. 147.

2. Debra Gersh, "The Ad Picture Brightens," *Editor & Publisher* 18 July 1987: 9.

3. Gersh, "The Ad Picture Brightens," p. 9.

4. Debra Gersh, "Landon Issues Annual Report to its Newspapers," *Editor & Publisher,* 24 January 1987: 27.

5. Chamberlain, "The Newspaper," p. 147.

6. *Boston Herald-American,* rate card, Boston, Mass. 1981.

7. *Boston Herald-American,* rate card, Boston, Mass. 1981.

8. Chamberlain, "The Newspaper," p. 147.

9. Christopher Eddings, "Management of the Weekly Newspaper," seminar, American Press Institute, January 22, 1983, Reston, Virginia.

10. Eddings, "Management of the Weekly Newspaper."

11. Margaret Genovese, "There Is a Boom in Classifieds. The Question Is: How Long Will it Last?" *Presstime* (April 1987), p. 22.

12. Genovese, "There Is a Boom in Classifieds," p. 22.

13. C. Randall Choate, *The Newspaper; Everything You Need to Know to Make It in the Newspaper Business,* ed. D. Earl Newsom (Englewood Cliffs: Prentice Hall, 1981), p. 116.

14. New England Press Association, *Co-Op Advertising: Sources for More Advertising Revenue* (Boston: New England Press Association, 1984), p. 25.

15. "What Makes a Quality Newspaper?" *Editor & Publisher* 17 October 1981: 48.

16. Andrew Radolf, "Publishers Gearing Up for Ad Standardization," *Editor & Publisher,* 27 August 1983: 10.

17. *1984 Scarborough Report for the Boston Market,* Boston, Mass. p. 17.

18. *1982 Simmons Study, Boston ADI,* Boston, Mass. p. 20.

19. Nick Overduin, "Psychographics: Ad Alley's Wonder Tool," *Journalism Research Report: The Newsletter for Newsroom Executives,* 26 February 1985: 1–2.

20. Patrick O'Donnell, *The Business of Newspapers: An Essay for Investors,"* E.F. Hutton, February 12, 1982, pp. 1–2.

21. Gary Burford, interview with author, March 2, 1987.

22. Joe Bergeron, interview with author, November 15, 1985.

23. *New Strategies for Advertising Sales* (Reston, Va.: American Press Institute, 1985), pp. 7–8.

24. John M. Lavine and Daniel B. Wackman, *Managing Media Organizations: Effective Leadership of the Media* (New York: Longman, 1987), p. 26.

25. John Morton, "Smoothing the Way for National Ads," *WJR* (October 1986), p. 52.

26. David A. Aaker and John G. Myers, *Advertising Management,* 3d ed. (Englewood Cliffs: Prentice-Hall, 1987), pp. 14–15.

27. James B. Kobak, "Sales Compensation: Designing the Right Plan," *Folio* (April 1981), p. 58.

28. Aaker and Myers, *Advertising Management,* pp. 533–536.

29. Aaker and Myers, *Advertising Management,* pp. 535–536.

30. Aaker and Myers, *Advertising Management,* pp. 535–536.

6

PRODUCING THE CIRCULATION REVENUE

The circulation department is a key link in the production chain that leads to fulfillment of the newspaper's overall mission. The circulation department must get the newspaper into the hands of the readers who otherwise would be left uninformed—or at least underinformed—about the day's events. A favorite admonishment of the city editor to a slow reporter approaching deadline is, "The best story in the world will do us no good if we can't get it to the reader's doorstep."

The circulation department must, in many cases, work extremely fast to overcome blown deadlines in the newsroom. Circulation is the last link in the production chain, and a deadline missed by 10 minutes in the newsroom may be extended to a 30-minute delay or more in getting the papers out of the pressroom and onto the circulation docks. The irony is that, given the importance of the circulation department to the newspaper's overall mission of informing the public, this department is still sometimes treated as a stepchild or given little thought at all.

CIRCULATION TRENDS

The circulation trends for newspapers in the United States suggest a good-news, bad-news scenario. The good news is that newspaper circulation is up since 1946. The bad news is that population growth has occurred at an even faster rate, and newspaper circulation growth is not keeping pace with it. For instance, daily newspaper circulation was 62,490,000 in 1986, but that was only 90,000 above the 1981 figure and about 275,000 less than the 1985 total.[1] Taking the longer view, daily newspaper circulation rose from about 51 million in 1946 to about 62 million in 1980, yet that represents only a 20 percent growth over three and a half decades, while the United States population soared during that same period. You have to look to the category of small- to medium-size dailies before you find strong growth among U.S. newspapers. For instance, during the decade of 1965–1975, while large dailies (circulation 100,000 and above) were decreasing in circulation by 8 percent, small- and medium-size dailies increased 12.4 percent.[2] Much of the decline in circulation among large dailies was registered by afternoon dailies, which have lost 3 million subscribers since 1950. This has forced many evening newspapers to either suspend publication, convert to morning distribution, or become folded in with their morning counterparts to one newspaper published by the same company.

In 1983, one interesting readership sign was detected by a Scarborough Research Corp. survey that showed daily newspapers averaging 2.77 readers per copy—about the same as the 2.73 readers per copy reported earlier in the year by Simmons Market Research Bureau.[3] The figures in both studies were up about 20 percent from the 2.2 average that had been recorded in previous years. That finding, although not totally understood by consultants, has both positive and negative connotations for newspapers. For one thing, it should make advertisers happy because more people are exposed to their messages, but for another, it may mean fewer people are buying their own copy of the newspaper, choosing instead to borrow someone else's.

On an international level, it might surprise some people that, in spite of the high standard of living and education level in the United States, it nevertheless ranks only 19th in daily per capita newspaper circulation around the world.[4] Ranking above the United States in higher newspaper circulation figures are such countries as Japan (which ranks first), East and West Germany, Great Britain, the Scandinavian countries, Singapore, Iceland, and even the Soviet Union. The 1986 UNESCO Statistical Yearbook states that U.S. daily newspaper circulation per each 1,000 inhabitants was 268 in 1984, the latest year for which figures were available. The book also reported that there were 1,687 U.S. dailies in that year. While that is far more than Japan's 125 dailies, it is less than half of Japan's ratio of 562 copies per 1,000 people. Many observers see this as a sad commentary on the apparent lack of hunger many U.S. citizens display for knowing what is happening in the world. It should also be noted, however, that they—unlike Russians for instance—have many more ways of getting at least the headlines of world news via television and radio.

Another way of looking at daily newspaper circulation trends in the United States is to compare them with the increase in the number of U.S. households. Between 1970 and 1980, the number of U.S. households rose from about 65 million to 80 million, while daily newspaper circulation remained relatively stable at about 63 million.

Overall, these circulation statistics serve as a solid warning that newspapers desperately need to find new ways of attracting more readers. Al Gollin, vice president and associate director of research for the Newspaper Advertising Bureau, notes that penetration has declined, largely due to the growth of new

households—especially single and female-headed—as the baby boom genera-
tion has matured over the past ten years. Gollin explains that the most discon-
certing part of the problem is frequency of readership, noting that on a weekly
basis five of six adults read a newspaper, 62 percent read it frequently, and 28
percent only read it once in a while. Gollin says

Occasional readers are the best potential target. . . . One key is to develop the reading habit early, when reading begins, and to do that, newspapers should get both parents
and children involved. A powerful boost comes from Newspaper in Education programs, especially in cases where the newspaper is not received at home.[5]

CIRCULATION, ADVERTISING, AND NEWS

There are strong links and dependencies between the circulation, advertising,
and news functions of the newspaper. Obviously, the larger the circulation a
newspaper has, the more advertising it will attract (assuming the demographics
of its readership interest advertisers). However, what happens when you have
two competing newspapers in the same city, each with large circulations? The
fact that only about 25 of the nation's cities experience this situation is a commentary on the danger awaiting the uncompeting newspaper that ranks second
in circulation. Most of these secondary newspapers have simply had to cease
publication for lack of advertising support. Every one of the metro dailies that
folded during the first half of the 1980s was a secondary newspaper (in terms
of circulation) within its market.

How far behind must a competing daily be before it finds itself in trouble
with advertisers? Newspaper analyst John Morton asserts that if one of the two
dailies has a significant circulation lead it can charge higher advertising rates
than its competitor and still offer advertisers a lower cost-per-thousand figure.

Advertisers respond to these circumstances by placing a disproportionate share of
their spending with the larger paper. The paper with 60 percent of the circulation in the
market might get 70 to 75 percent of the advertising. Thus the newspaper with 40
percent of the circulation gets a small share of the advertising, and this . . . often
means that not enough revenue comes in to cover operating costs. The small paper's
operating costs will be less than the big paper's, but not greatly so. The small paper
does not skimp on staff and news hole if it hopes to remain competitive.[6]

The circulation department's relationship to the news function, and vice versa,
is no less important. A close working relationship between editors and circulation personnel is vital to maintaining readership. Many editors fear continuing
losses of duplicate readership unless metro newspapers give suburban subscribers heavy doses of news in their areas, as well as news of a larger scope.
Often the newspaper personnel who know these suburbs and the issues they
face best are circulation department employees or independent contractors who
deliver the newspaper. Certainly even metro dailies don't have the money to
send forth legions of reporters into these important suburbs, but there are le-

gions of newspaper carriers servicing them every day. Editors are missing out on a vital contact with the people in these areas if they fail to consult regularly with people from the circulation department. Some newspapers feel so strongly about this link, in fact, that they put the executive director in charge of circulation as well as news. One such newspaper is the *Philadelphia Inquirer*.

"When is the last time you, as an editor, took a district [circulation] manager to lunch?" asks the *Inquirer*'s executive editor, Eugene Roberts. "They will tell you what it's really like in the trenches. If you are losing circulation in a particular area, a talk with a district manager may be vital."[7] Roberts adds that newspapers are not responsive enough to complaints from readers about content, complaints that newspaper carriers hear on a regular basis.

DIFFERENT CIRCULATION SYSTEMS

Newspapers are well-known for their reluctance to do things in uniform fashion. Even group-owned newspapers pride themselves on a certain degree of independence and—at times—eccentricity. This holds true for circulation systems as well, because there are several types in existence at daily and weekly newspapers. Basically, however, they fall into one of a few patterns as follows:

Mail-Based Systems

Most weeklies and many small dailies (indeed even a few large dailies like the *Wall Street Journal* and *USA Today*) distribute most of their papers through the United States Postal Service under second-class mailing permits. Free-circulation papers go via third-class mail, although that may change if publishers of shoppers win their argument for going second-class. Newspapers circulating by mail find the system more feasible than carrier delivery, but they must have excellent relationships with the Postal Service.

Employee-Based Systems

Some newspapers not only field a circulation management staff, but they also employ the individual carriers themselves. In such cases, the carriers work for the newspaper directly and draw salaries from it for delivering the newspaper and, possibly, collecting for it. In such cases, the newspaper has the greatest control over the distribution system, the way the paper is delivered, the price charged for it, and the people who deliver it. Only about 9 percent of daily newspapers use this employee-based system,[8] however, because of the expense and wide-ranging management headaches resulting from it.

Independent Contractors

The independent contractor may be an adult or youth. In fact, about 85 percent of these carriers were youth carriers in 1987.[9] The independent contractor is, by definition, an independent businessperson who is in charge of motivating himself or herself, delivering the papers, and collecting for them. The contractor buys papers from the newspaper company at wholesale and sells them at retail. The contractor—not the newspaper company—sets the price to subscribers for home delivery. Gross earnings of carriers generally vary from about 23 percent to about 33 percent of the actual subscription price.[10] A youth carrier throwing papers from a bike or shoulder bag could make about $35 weekly in 1987, but an adult carrier, serving a larger route, could make about $185 part-time, or up to $37,000, according to some circulation managers.[11] Newspapers have embraced this type of "little merchant" or independent contractor system, as is evidenced by the fact that about 70 percent of daily newspapers use this system.[12] The newspaper company does employ district managers to interface with these independent carriers.

Circulation Agencies

An agency system is a cross between the employee-based system and the independent contractor delivery system. Under this system, the newspaper contracts with an agent or agents who, in turn, make their own agreements with other people to deliver the papers. The newspaper company can control the price charged for the paper and can handle the collections, usually by mail. About 20 percent of all daily newspapers use this agency system.

METHOD OF PAYMENT

Newspapers also differ in the way they bill customers and collect payment for subscriptions. For instance, about half the newspapers collect monthly, and most newspapers collect after the delivery has been made rather than before. Most of the other half of the nation's newspapers collect on a weekly basis, although some prefer collecting on a three- or six-month basis. This practice is discouraged by many circulation experts. Newspapers are also divided over whether to have their carriers collect in person or send subscribers bills through the mail. The percentage of paid-up subscribers may be higher when the bills go through the mail, but the carrier misses the opportunity to collect a tip for his or her work by not collecting in person. Also, in-person collection means the subscriber has a chance to either personally praise or criticize the carrier for the way the paper is being delivered to the doorstep. There is a variation of this collection system, and that occurs when the carrier inserts a small collection envelope within an issue of the newspaper each month and asks the subscriber to put the payment in the envelope and leave it to be picked up the next day. Some observers see this as somewhat impersonal, however, and it also means the carrier will be walking around in the early morning hours with a pocketful of money. This increases the carrier's chances of being mugged. Also, some subscribers are reluctant to put money out on their doorstep for fear of having the wind—or a thief—steal it.

A further variation on collection methods has some newspapers allowing payment to be charged to a VISA or MasterCard. The customer can simply submit a credit card number to the circulation official, and the newspaper can send the bill directly to the issuer of the credit card.

ADULT OR YOUTH CARRIERS?

Should a newspaper use the services of adult or youth carriers to deliver its papers? This is a growing area of concern in the newspaper industry, and there are advantages and disadvantages to both adults and youths. Champions of the little merchant system argue that this provides youths an opportunity to learn responsibility and function as independent businesspeople. They point to illustrious former newspaper carriers such as Bob Hope, Herbert Hoover, and John Wayne, and declare that they all got their start by throwing newspapers. Other defenders of this system assert that youths are better salespeople for newspapers than are adults and are easier to manage.

On the other hand, there is a growing number of circulation executives who feel adult carriers represent a more reasonable choice. Defenders of the adult carrier system say it is difficult to get a 12-year-old out of bed at 3:30 A.M. just to make $25 or $35 per week. Society has become too affluent, and youths can find easier and more profitable work by mowing lawns, cleaning out swimming pools, or caddying. In addition, the early morning hours can be dangerous for youths to be on the street. Many youth carriers have been victims of attack and robbery over the years, especially in and around large cities. Defenders of the adult system also point out that the turnover rate of adult carriers is much lower than for youth carriers, and that adults can deliver more newspapers from cars or trucks then youths can on foot or bicycle.

Whichever side is more correct, the fact is that, while youths still make up about 85 percent of the carrier force for daily newspapers, the percentage has eroded from almost 94 percent at the start of the 1980s. Some newspapers, like the *St. Louis Post-Dispatch,* rely almost entirely on adult carriers. "The route is the adult's responsibility," Circulation Director Roger Ruhe told *Presstime* magazine in 1987. "We will not run that route for them." On the other hand, Ruhe added, if a youth gets up and doesn't feel well, the mother will tell him to stay home, and often the district manager winds up delivering the newspapers instead.[13]

Another daily met some parental opposition when it decided to drop youth carriers in favor of adult carriers. California's *Santa Rosa Press Democrat* had used both youths and adults as deliverers, but its publisher decided in 1987 to convert to an all-adult force. Former Publisher James C. Weeks said he made the decision after two readership studies showed the major complaint readers had was late delivery of their newspaper.[14] California state law bans youths from beginning their newspaper routes prior to 5 A.M., although adults can begin their routes as early as 3:30 A.M. Weeks also pointed out that turnover among its youth carriers had been much higher than among adults, especially during the summer months. He added that the newspaper could reduce the number of routes from 700 youth-carrier routes to about 325 adult routes.

Some newspapers are trying hard to maintain a mix of adult and youth carriers and feel that this is the optimum solution.

SINGLE-COPY SALES

Although the bulk of circulation revenue comes from paid subscriptions and this is the kind of circulation that most interests advertisers, newspaper publishers are still concerned about single-copy sales of their newspaper.

An important aspect of single-copy sales is pricing, and the cover price of newspapers is going up around the country. A recent ANPA survey of daily newspapers showed that, while most dailies still cost a quarter a copy, many are shifting to a price of 35 cents or more. In fact, the number of papers in the 35-cent range increased from 202 dailies in 1985 to 344 in 1986.[15] Some dailies, such as *USA Today,* have even gone as high as 50 cents per copy. Prices for Sunday newspapers are up to $1 or higher per copy around the country. This all indicates that newspaper executives are realizing that their single copies have been underpriced, and they have decided to become more aggressive in those pricing policies. In a speech to the 64th Annual Sales Conference of the Cal Western Circulation Managers Association, J. Scott Schmidt, president of the *Los Angeles Daily News,* declared that publishers will have to depend more on circulation departments and single-copy sales to help reach their profit margins in the future. Schmidt said single-copy sales eliminate carrier costs, while still meeting readers' needs.[16]

COMPETITION FORCES CHANGES

In addition to some of the changes already noted, circulation departments have been required to modify and experiment in other ways because of new competitive forces from the electronic media and from shoppers, direct mail, and suburban newspapers. As a result, the role of the circulation manager is changing and becoming more complicated. Leo Bogart, executive vice president and general manager of the Newspaper Advertising Bureau, said recently:

When newspaper readership dropped in the 1970s, retail advertisers insisted that their advertising coverage levels be maintained within specific zones or in the entire market. As a result, newspapers with falling circulation-to-household ratios have faced sharp competition from radio and TV advertising, from shoppers, doorknobbers and direct mail. The diversion of newspaper retail advertising to these other media has had a profound effect on newspaper economics. But it also affects circulation directly, because advertising is a major service and attraction to readers.[17]

Some of the observations the NAB made, following trips to 15 daily newspapers in 1982, were the following:[18]

- Circulation management is shifting its focus from the handling of the physical product to the handling of information, with the computer at the center of the change.
- There is a striking absence of women and minorities in circulation management, although both the need and opportunity for greater involvement are evident.
- Rather little of the research that has been done to serve the needs of the advertising and editorial departments has been turned in the direction of defining and solving circulation problems.
- Circulation training does not appear to have been taken seriously by many circulation departments, and there has been insufficient use of the materials and programs produced by the Newspaper Readership Project.
- There is a basic dilemma as to whether circulation is to be seen as an independent profit center within the newspaper organization, operating at the lowest possible cost, or whether its primary job is to maximize the numbers that the advertising department can sell to advertisers at a profit. In achieving this latter objective, circulation departments have found that they really must operate at a deficit, especially when factoring in all the circulation contests and gimmickry associated with such loose circulation operations. These newspapers believe they can achieve almost any level of circulation they desire, but it will be at a price.
- Circulation managers have changed their thinking by accepting and embracing the marketing concept and recognizing the part they play in meeting the newspaper's overall objective of serving the community and advertisers.

Certainly a major change brought about by the introduction of shoppers and direct mail is that so many dailies and weeklies have gone to produce some type of TMC product, and that has brought about a direct impact on the circulation department's activities. One such impetus for change has occurred because of the rise of advertising inserts. The newspaper industry carried 16 billion preprints in 1975, and that figure grew to some 49 billion in 1987. In addition, advertisers are increasingly wanting to zone those inserts, which causes even more headaches for the newspaper's mailroom where these inserts are stuffed into the newspaper. Labor costs in the mailroom are growing throughout the industry, while payroll in other areas has declined. As a result, more and more newspapers are moving toward automated mailrooms to handle the growing number of inserts and to moderate the payroll costs.[19]

PLAYING GAMES WITH READERS

One of the controversies in the field of circulation management is how far to go to attract subscribers to the newspaper. Those who believe in tight circulation operations feel you should not give the newspaper away at a ridiculously low discount or entice readers with gimmickry that usually includes games like "Wingo" or "Portfolio." Those who believe in looser operations argue that the main goal is to boost circulation numbers to draw in more advertising. In many ways, the ends justify the means in getting those numbers, they say, even if the means are circulation games. Those newspapers playing games with readers say business is good; those who don't play games say, "Okay, but at what journalistic price?"

Many games are designed not for the reader, but for the nonreader of the newspaper. The reasoning is that, while in-newspaper games do a good job of attracting more interest in the newspaper among readers, they don't do much for attracting nonreaders. William F. Girling, president of Girling Wade Marketing of Toronto, Canada, distributes computerized Bingo cards to all households in the targeted market area. The cards go out via mail or in a TMC product doing business in the area. Bingo numbers to use in the cards are printed daily in the newspaper along with a "lucky number." The game is designed to bring in more nonreaders to the newspaper.

Critics of such out-of-paper games point out that the problem in building circulation is not to attract the nonreader so much as the infrequent reader. They believe going after the nonreader may not be as fruitful as trying to get a reader to go from purchasing single copies of the paper once or twice a week to becoming a daily reader through taking out a subscription to the paper. Catching the attention of such infrequent readers can be done using in-paper games, these observers assert.

An extremely popular game in the United States has been Wingo, used by several newspapers owned by Rupert Murdoch's News America Corp. Murdoch introduced Wingo into his newspapers in Boston, New York, San Antonio, and Chicago (a newspaper he has since sold). In all cases, his company reported circulation gains after the games were introduced. The price for such gains has not been cheap, however. The first 20 weeks of Wingo at the *Chicago Sun-Times* in 1984 reportedly cost $2.5 million in operation and promotion.

Daily newspapers in states that have lotteries, such as Massachusetts and New York, get many of the benefits of games without bearing the cost of buying and distributing them. These newspapers simply run the winning lottery numbers in each issue, thereby creating reader interest for those people who did not catch the numbers on television the night before.

POSTAL RELATIONS ARE VITAL

Whether a newspaper circulates the majority of its copies through the mails or not, every newspaper has an important stake in the United States Postal Service (USPS). In the 1980s newspapers find themselves lobbying on at least two fronts with the Postal Service. On the one hand, newspapers are seeking continued federal subsidy of second-class rates, while on the other they are seeking even higher third-class rates. This is because their strongest competitors—shoppers and direct mail—travel via third-class, and newspaper executives feel those rates are unfairly low. A special report in a 1986 issue of *Presstime* noted that, in effect, newspapers and the USPS are now competitors in the business of delivering free-standing advertising materials. Even though they are competitors, however, newspaper executives realize they must worry about developments that could undermine the Postal Service's ability to remain a viable department, because if the USPS goes under, so will the delivery system that many newspapers depend on.

For these reasons, a major lobbying effort of the ANPA has centered on the issue of postal affairs. Early in the 1980s the ANPA addressed the threat to newspapers posed by telecommunications carriers, especially AT&T, that were eyeing electronic publishing. By the middle of the decade, the ANPA was spending about $450,000 a year on postal lobbying efforts. Much of that effort has centered on the following issues:[20]

- Whether the rate for bulk third-class pieces that are presorted to the carrier route level is unfairly low, and whether "detachable labels" used in conjunction with third-class advertising packages get an unfair "free ride" because they do not pay full postage independently.
- The degree to which lawmakers will continue to vote subsidies for "preferred" second-class mailing categories, such as the mailing of newspapers within the county of publication.
- Some daily newspapers' controversial use of second-class mail as part of their TMC programs. Shoppers are an integral part of TMC programs, and shoppers generally are required to go third-class. Some newspapers have found a loophole in that postal regulation, however, and are sending out their regular paper plus their shopper via second-class mail. That may be threatening the integrity and continued subsidy of second-class mailings.
- Whether free-distribution papers, which now must use third-class mail, should have the right to use the cheaper second-class rates in-county.

At the heart of newspapers' concerns are the status and future of second- and third-class mailing rates. Included in the second-class rate structure are Regular rates, used for mailings of 5,000 or more copies outside the county of publication; Limited Circulation rates, for fewer than 5,000 copies outside the county; and In-County rates. The latter two are subsidized by the federal government. In-County and Limited Circulation rates are used mainly by small- and medium-size newspapers that mail a hefty portion of their total circulation in the immediate market area, usually in the county of publication. Regular rates apply chiefly to larger dailies that mail relatively few copies. Large newspapers often mail less than 5 percent of total circulation, and those mainly are to pockets of light penetration in the market area, or to far-flung subscribers. A big question is what to expect in terms of continuation of the second-class subsidy. Robert Brinkmann, general counsel of the National Newspaper Association, believes Congress recognizes the importance of small newspapers and that the funding will continue. Brinkmann also believes the USPS will stay committed to serving the newspaper business, because it wants their business.[21]

However, as newspapers survey the third-class rates, many publishers feel the rates are unfairly low and result in higher-than-needed first-class rates. This causes first-class to subsidize unsolicited third-class "junk mail." Sandry Hardy, chairman of the ANPA Postal Committee, has found that third-class mail represents 39 percent of total mail volume, but only 20 percent of mail revenue. First-class mail, on the other hand, accounts for 50 percent of volume and 58 percent of revenue. USPS argues that first- and third-class mail "each covers its own costs and makes a suitable contribution to fixed costs. The main reason that third-class rates are lower is that its costs are lower," USPS says.[22]

REQUIREMENTS FOR SECOND-CLASS NEWSPAPERS

In order to obtain and maintain a second-class mail permit from the United States Postal Service, newspapers must meet several requirements including the following. Violations of these requirements can—at best—result in poor relations with the local post office and—at worst—result in the newspaper's losing its privilege to mail second class. The requirements are:

1. The publication must have at least 51 percent of its circulation paid. If not, it falls into the controlled circulation class, and it is subject to higher mailing costs.
2. The newspaper must provide an up-to-date subscription list as proof of its paid circulation.
3. The advertising portion of any one issue may exceed 75 percent, but it must not exceed 75 percent during six consecutive months' issues.
4. The publication must be regularly issued at stated intervals.
5. Each issue must bear a date of issue, be numbered consecutively, and issued from a known office of publication.
6. Each copy must publish certain information "conspicuously printed" on one of the first five pages. Included should be title of publication, date of issue, regular period of issue, serial number, known office of publication, subscription price, and notice that it has been entered as second-class matter.
7. A statement showing the number of second-class copies mailed is filed with the post office at the time of each mailing. At least once every six months, the post office will verify the paid subscription list.
8. Address labels must be affixed to the front cover or back cover of the publication, and must contain zip codes.
9. The newspaper must file an annual statement giving information required by the post office. This information includes the names and post office addresses of the editor, managing editor, publisher, business managers, and owners. If it is owned by a corporation, then it must include a list of all stockholders owning more than 1 percent of the capital stock or owning at least 1 percent; the names of all bondholders, mortgagees, or other security holders owning 1 percent or more of such bonds, mortgages, or securities; and a statement of the average number of copies of each issue of each publication sold or distributed to paid subscribers during the preceding 12 months. Many smaller newspapers, which are not members of the Audit Bureau

of Circulations, will use this annual statement to provide proof to advertisers of the newspaper's circulation claims. Most knowledgeable advertisers, however, would prefer to have the results of an independently audited circulation.

MARRIAGE MAIL

A recent phenomenon in delivering advertising to the public has been the introduction of "marriage mail" or "shared mail." Under this system, two or more advertisers go together to insert their advertisements—often coupons—into the same envelope with a detached mailing label, and share the costs of going third-class. In so doing, such advertisers get their advertising out in a TMC vehicle and pay only a small portion of the mailing bill. Shared mail began actively in 1981, and the largest of the direct-mail companies that has emerged has been AdvoSystems Inc. Many observers feel the meteoric successes of Advo have leveled off, however, and partly for that reason the third-class mail volume overall has been growing at a slower rate.[23] An adjunct to the third-class rates issue is the controversy over detached labels—the postcard-like address cards that accompany shared-mail packages. The Postal Service in 1980 approved use of the separate labels to "increase efficiency." Users of detached labels, most frequently direct mailers, do not pay separate postage even though the labels are handled by mail carriers as separate pieces of mail. Instead, the slight weight of the card is added to the weight of the shared-mail piece, and only a charge for the total package is paid. In 1983 the ANPA filed a complaint with the Postal Rate Commission over the labels, arguing that the Postal Service is losing vital revenue by not charging separately for them.

SAMPLING REGULATIONS

Sampling is a way many hometown newspapers with second-class mail permits can solicit new subscribers by delivering free sample copies of the newspaper. Sampling is especially good in attracting rural-route families who live out in the county yet still in the retail trading zone. A sampling program for both in-town and rural-route residents is easy to formulate, but the main thing is to give would-be subscribers a long enough look at the newspaper. To do that, circulation consultants suggest about four weeks' issues of the weekly paper should be delivered, or five days' issues of a daily.

Setting up a selective sampling program on a route-by-route basis can be done by compiling a list of all families who live on all rural routes. These numbers can be obtained from the Postal Service. Sampling ideally should focus on a single route or two at the start. These routes should be some of the weaker ones for the paper where subscriptions have been hard to sell. Along with each issue of the newspaper, a subscription card should be sent, inserted into the paper. Some type of house ad in the newspaper announcing the benefits of subscribing should also be part of the sampling issues.

The USPS allows newspapers that hold second-class mail permits to mail sample copies of the newspaper at any time during the calendar year to the extent of 10 percent of the total estimated weight of copies to be mailed to subscribers during the calendar year.[24] That means if the total estimated weight of all newspapers in a year is 20,000 pounds, for instance, 2,000 pounds of newspapers can be sent out as samples free to subscribers without violating the provisions of the second-class mailing permit. The circulation manager can keep a running tally of the estimated total weight of the sample copies mailed out. The Postal Service does require that newspapers going out as sample copies be labeled as such, with the words "Sample Copy" appearing at the top of Page 1 in the flag area.

The idea behind selective sampling is to send out sample copies to the non-subscribers on a particular route. Therefore, if there are 500 families on a route, and if 300 of them take the paper by subscription, then sample copies go to the other 200 families.

If a newspaper wishes to sample would-be subscribers who live in the city, it must follow another set of guidelines. Most newspapers find it best to connect this in-city sampling program with a telephone solicitation program after the families have received their sample copies and have had a chance to look them over. For sampling in-city families, the circulation manager needs to obtain a list of nonsubscribers or at least a list of street addresses. The Postal Service frowns on newspapers blanketing a city carrier route as it might do a rural route. Some circulation managers base their sampling routes on a "non-served" list, using the town's phone book. By comparing names in the phone book with the newspaper's own mailing list, the newspaper can come up with a pretty accurate list of families which do not subscribe. Sometimes newspaper publishers can also obtain a list of utility hookups from the city power or water company and proceed in similar fashion from that list. Either way, once the lists are compiled with street addresses, the sample papers can be mailed out and followed up with a phone call asking the recipients to subscribe to the paper and taking their order. To answer any reader questions before they arise, the circulation manager can always send out a letter before the sample papers go out to explain that the family will be receiving several free issues of the paper in hopes they will like it and subscribe.

VERIFYING CIRCULATION FIGURES

Advertisers require more than the word of the publisher that their newspaper has so many subscribers and so much penetration into the city and outlying retail trading zone. That demand is not unreasonable, because advertisers are buying exposure, and they want a guaranteee on how wide that exposure will be. For that reason, various circulation auditing agencies have arisen over the past several decades to provide such verification. The most important such auditing agency for daily and weekly newspapers is the Audit Bureau of Circulations (ABC). The ABC is the oldest of the circulation auditing services, although there are others now on the scene as well. The CAC, or Certified Audit of Circulations, exists to verify circulation figures for some weeklies and free-distribution papers. Some weeklies also use Postal Service receipts or annual statements to the post office of the number of copies mailed, but the ABC is the grandfather of circulation agencies, and the best known and trusted among advertisers and ad agencies.

The ABC: Its Strengths and Challenges

In 1914, advertisers, advertising agencies, and publishers joined to establish ground rules for circulation accounting and to give birth to an independent referee to enforce those rules and provide reports of verified circulation data. This referee became the Audit Bureau of Circulations. Today an estimated 5,000 dues-paying advertisers, agencies, and publishers of daily and weekly newspapers and other publications support the ABC in the United States, Canada, and Central and South America. About 90 percent of these ABC members are publishing companies, represented by their circulation executives. Essentially a self-regulating bureau, the ABC exists for three stated purposes:[25]

1. To issue standardized statements of the circulation or other data reported by members.
2. To verify the figures shown in these statements by auditors' examination of any and all records considered by ABC to be necessary.
3. To disseminate these data, without opinion, to be reported.

The bureau notes that about 75 percent of all print media circulation available to advertisers in the United States and Canada today is reported and verified in accordance with ABC standards.[26]

Members of the ABC's 33-member board of directors are elected by members at an annual meeting held each fall. These board members develop standards and guidelines for the bureau's work and they act on appeals to rulings made by the president and managing director. Representation on the board generally includes eleven advertisers; seven advertising agencies; eight newspapers; three magazines; two business publications; one farm publication; and one (Canadian) periodical director-at-large. Further, ABC bylaws provide that the chair of the board shall always be a representative of either advertisers or ad agencies, and that the buyers of advertising will always have majority representation.[27]

Day-to-day operations are managed by a president and managing director. A 175-person staff carries out the activities from headquarters in Chicago and member service offices in New York and Toronto. The core of the staff is about 80 trained circulation field auditors, backed up by house auditors and specialists who review and process field reports and Publisher's Statements.

The ABC reports circulation facts in standardized reports consisting of ABC Publisher's Statements, issued twice a year, and audit reports, issued annually for all but smaller publications. Also, the bureau issues two FAS-FAX reports, appearing every six months and containing unaudited readership claims taken from statements submitted by publishers. The ABC reports identical circulation breakdowns for competing publications, permitting direct comparison with other ABC-audited publications.

The ABC will audit only paid publications, not shoppers. At least 70 percent of a paper's circulation must be paid to be audited by the ABC. A basic rule of the agency is that audited paid circulation includes only copies of a publication that have been paid for by the consumer at not less than 50 percent of the basic price. This limits the scope of some circulation gimmickry at newspapers which offer discount subscriptions.

The ABC also reports facts concerning specific market areas covered by the member newspaper. For instance, the ABC provides facts on circulation by population-size groups; county, states, or provinces; local market zones or areas; cities; businesses or occupational groups; and rural and urban distribution.

Despite its prominence in the world of circulation auditing, the ABC is not without its challengers. The most outspoken of these has been the Gannett Co. which, by the end of 1985, was locked in a war of nerves with the ABC. Gannett has disagreed with the ABC for several years over the bureau's handling of *USA Today*'s so-called "blue-chip" sales. These are the newspapers sold at half-price to hotels, motels, and airlines that distribute them free to their patrons. These sales amount to about 13 percent[28] of the newspaper's circulation, but the ABC will not tally them in its "average net daily paid circulation" figures reported in its audit statements. Starting in late 1985, as a result, about a dozen individual Gannett newspapers withdrew temporarily from the ABC, each protesting what they termed "old-fashioned and outdated methods" of auditing on the part of the ABC.[29] Among those leaving the ABC fold were the *Des Moines Register,* and New York's *Rochester Times-Union* and *Democrat & Chronicle.* *USA Today* itself did not join the ranks of those leaving the bureau.

Gannett has not been alone in challenging the ABC. Before the Gannett papers started to withdraw, the *Toronto Globe and Mail* withdrew, complaining about the ABC's refusal to include readership studies in its audit statements. The outcome of these challenges remains unclear. However, in late 1987, it looked as though the long battle over how to count bulk sales of newspapers was drawing to an end. A compromise whereby the ABC would report the bulk sales number in the first paragraph of its audit report and Publisher's Statement seemed to meet everyone's approval on both sides of the controversy. Under the compromise, bulk sales would still not be reported in the first paragraph of the ABC's FAS-FAX reports, but farther down instead. That bulk sales number would be known as "Average Paid Circulation (by Individuals and for Designated Recipients)." It would continue also to be the number supplied to such reference sources as Standard Rate and Data Service and American Newspaper Markets. Also under the compromise, newspapers would not be allowed to utilize the bulk sales figure when comparing their circulation to other newspapers, but bulk sales data can be included if a newspaper is promoting only its own circulation. With that smoke cleared, it is likely the ABC will continue to exert the circulation auditing power it has had for the past 70-plus years.

NOTES

1. "A Year of Ups and Downs," *Presstime* (May 1987), p. 124.
2. "83 Facts About Newspapers," *Presstime* (May 1983), insert.
3. David Astor, "20% Higher Reader per Copy Figure Found in Second Study," *Editor & Publisher* 2 July 1983: 7.
4. Marion Lewenstein, "Global Readership," *Presstime* (September 1987), p. 10.
5. Debra Gersh, "Circulation Must Stay at Top of Newspapers' Agendas," *Editor & Publisher* 17 January 1987: 28.
6. John Morton, "Singleton: Hedging the Risks," *WJR* (November 1987), p. 52.
7. M. L. Stein, "Editors Told to Interact with Circulators, Carriers," *Editor & Publisher* 24 October 1987: 28.
8. C. David Rambo, "Adult or Youth Carriers?" *Presstime* (February 1987), p. 25.
9. Ibid.
10. Ibid.
11. Ibid.
12. Ibid.
13. Ibid.
14. "Youth Carriers Dropped; Parents Protest," *Presstime* (April 1987), p. 57.
15. "Most Dailies Still Cost a Quarter, But Many Are Shifting to 35 Cents or More," *Presstime* (April 1987), p. 56.
16. M. L. Stein, "Circulation Urged to Try for More Single-Copy Sales," *Editor & Publisher* 6 November 1982: 16.
17. "Competition Brings Change to Circulation Departments," *Editor & Publisher* 26 June 1982: 58.
18. "Competition Brings Change to Circulation Departments," p. 58.
19. Mark Fitzgerald, "Borrowing Technologies," *Editor & Publisher* 28 March 1987: 30.
20. C. David Rambo, "Newspapers and the Postal Service," *Presstime* (January 1986), p. 21.
21. Rambo, "Newspapers and the Postal Service," p. 21.
22. Rambo, "Newspapers and the Postal Service," p. 22.
23. Rambo, "Newspapers and the Postal Service," p. 22.
24. George W. Trotter, "Marketing the Newspaper." In *The Newspaper: Everything You Need to Know to Make It in the Newspaper Business,* ed. D. Earl Newsom (Englewood Cliffs: Prentice Hall, 1981), p. 154.
25. Audit Bureau of Circulations, *This is the ABC,* brochure, Schaumburg, Ill.
26. Ibid.
27. Ibid.
28. Mark Fitzgerald, "An Active Year for Newspapers," *Editor & Publisher* 4 January 1986: 38, 55.
29. Fitzgerald, "An Active Year," pp. 38, 55.

7

PRODUCING THE PHYSICAL PRODUCT

Many changes have occurred over the past two decades in the way newspapers are produced. Contrary to other industries where changes have evolved over the past 100 years, most of the major changes in newspaper production have occurred since the 1960s. A typesetter retiring from the newspaper business as recently as 10 years ago would probably not recognize the backshop of a newspaper today if he were to enter it. Not only have cumbersome and slow composing procedures given way to the cut-and-paste artistry of offset printing, but offset printing has moved aside for electronic pagination where the composing is actually done out in the newsroom. The lines between the newsroom and the backshop have thus become blurred, as reporters and editors have taken over some of the functions that compositors and typesetters used to fulfill. In addition, the cost of printing the newspaper has fluctuated and will continue to do so as newsprint prices refuse to stabilize. This chapter will discuss some of the aspects of the production process and their implications to the newspaper of the 1980s and beyond.

FROM HOT LEAD TO COMPUTER CHIPS

Until the 1960s, most newspapers in this country followed a production process that went something like this:

Reporters in the newsroom would produce their copy on manual typewriters, and editors would scrawl editing marks and instructions to typesetters on the hard copy with editing pencils. The copy would be sent to the backshop, often in pneumatic air tubes, and it would then encounter one of two processes. Either it would be set into type on metal "slugs" by one of several linotype machines, or it would go to a typesetter working on a machine that produced a perforated tape to automatically drive the linotype. The metal slugs would then be encased in a frame called a "chase" by skilled compositors. Each chase would then be rolled to a page-casting machine where a papier-mâché mat of the page would be cast. Then the mat would be converted into a semi-circular lead plate where the letters would stand out in relief. Areas on the page for photographs would be blank. Into them would be stripped engravings of photos which had been prepared in another part of the backshop. The entire lead plate, complete with engravings, would then go to the pressroom and be placed on letterpresses that would print the newspaper. The process seemed cumbersome and painstaking to the casual observer, but highly skilled production people kept things going in an efficient manner.

With the introduction of photographic typesetting and the offset printing process, however, things began to change fast. The first victim of that change was the linotype machine, which—even with an experienced hand—could churn out only five or six lines of lead type per minute. The renewed production process went something like this:

Copy in the newsroom was prepared in the same way, but this time it encountered a typesetter in the backshop who produced a perforated tape that was fed into an electronic typesetting machine that produced justified, typeset copy at whatever width was ordered. This copy was then pasted down on a paper page, and black cutouts were pasted down in positions to be occupied by "halftone" photographs. That page then went to the reproduction camera room where a large camera shot a page-size negative of it. The photo areas came up transparent, and into them were stripped halftone negatives of photos shot by news cameramen. A halftone negative is one which results from having the reproduction camera reshoot the original photo overlaid with a screen of dots to keep the proper contrast when the page goes to press. The completed page negative was then touched up and placed over a light-sensitive aluminum plate. The plate was exposed to an intensive light and rubbed down with a developing solution to produce a positive image. The aluminum plate was then put on an offset press which uses a combination of oil and water going to sensitized and nonsensitized areas on each plate. The presses, faster than the older letterpresses, then printed the paper more quickly and with clearer imagery.

This process was updated at many newspapers in the early 1970s when manual typewriters in the newsroom were replaced with electric typewriters featuring removal typing balls. These typewriters were matched with electronic copy readers or "scanners" in the backshop. The copy, typed onto white bond paper instead of the older newsprint, was coded by reporters and editors with instructions for the scanners. Editing marks were made with typed corrections between the lines on the copy. Headlines were also written onto the top of the first page of each story and were coded as to size and type font. Upon reaching the backshop, the pages were fed, one at a time, into the Optical Character Reader (OCR) machine, or scanner. The process was similar to feeding sheets of paper into a large copying machine. There was no retyping of the copy.

Instead, the scanner produced typeset, justified copy that was ready for the paste-up process. The OCR process had its good and bad features. On the good side, it eliminated the retyping of stories in the backshop, and thus significantly reduced the chance for new errors to be typed in. On the negative side, these scanners were very sensitive. If letters on the reporter's typing ball became smudged, if a command were written inaccurately, or if the copy were wrinkled or contained smudge marks, the scanner had a tendency to go haywire and the process either came to a halt or produced some very strange-looking copy. In some cases the scanner would break down completely, and technicians would have to be called in—sometimes from great distances—to repair the machines.

As a result, the OCR process became only a short, intermediate step before the introduction of total electronic editing and word processing. Under this newest system, the typewriters are replaced altogether in the newsroom by VDTs (video display terminals). Now the reporters not only produce their stories but also produce the final typeset copy in one stroke. After the stories are input to the terminals, editors call them up electronically on their screens, make changes, assign headlines, and send the stories to the backshop electronically with the touch of a button. There a computer produces typeset, justified copy. The process is still being updated, as many newsrooms are trading in their large, front-end systems for personal computers (PCs). Some observers feel PCs can give a lot more output for a lot less money. For instance, a PC-based editorial system can cost 60 percent of the cost of a comparable front-end system. However, difficulties arise when various users choose their own formats and software options. Also, the maintenance record of PCs has yet to be proven. In addition to using computers to edit copy, the electronic editing process is being expanded to include electronic designing of pages through the process known as pagination, to be discussed later.

The evolution in production techniques has produced several positive changes for the newspaper. First, the process is now extremely fast. Not only are intermediate steps of retyping and galley proofreading eliminated, but computers produce thousands of lines of type in a minute as compared to the linotype's six lines. Copy is cleaner, and typographical errors are rare. Funds that were once spent on typesetters and compositors in the backshop have been released to go to other newspaper departments. Progress has also produced its problems, however, as the rugged glamour of the old backshop is no more. Many skilled typesetters and compositors, who could read lead type upside down and backwards with ease, have given way to computerized typesetters and have been retrained for other duties. Computer programmers in white coats are prime fixtures in the backshop and, somehow, the whole process is much more sanitized now. Indeed, if sanitary conditions are not present in the backshop, the computers will simply refuse to function properly.

ELECTRONIC PAGE DESIGNING

Designing pages electronically is an idea that began to take hold as newspapers entered the computer age several years back. The process, called "pagination," has now come of age, and many newspapers—both dailies and weeklies—have begun purchasing and integrating pagination systems into their production operations. "Pagination technology has finally come together," according to Brac Tucker, marketing systems manager for Hastech, a manufacturer of pagination systems.[1] Tucker's firm, for instance, has a system that allows editors to move photos and other graphics around on an electronic page dummy. In addition to blowing up and cropping graphics, users can electronically "airbrush" any defects in pictures. Several pagination companies make entire systems that can do everything: scan graphics, store editorial text, electronically design pages, and produce offset printing plates. Furthermore, while paginating news pages is one phase of the revolutionary process, paginating display ads is newer and possibly more complex technically, yet newspapers are now applying pagination to the production of ads as well as news pages.

A REVOLUTION IN PRINTING

At the start of the 1980s, about 75 percent of all U.S. daily newspapers were printed by the offset process, but most of these newspapers were medium- and small-size dailies and, in fact, offset dailies accounted for only about 42 percent of total newspaper circulation in the United States.[2] In 1987, with the demise of some of the newspapers represented in the 1980 figure, the ANPA estimated the number of dailies in both the United States and Canada still using some form of the letterpress system at 35 percent. The rush that had begun in the new offset process in the late 1960s and 1970s slowed a bit as large dailies wondered what to do with their huge investments in letterpresses. Also slowing the move to offset was the growing realization that this new printing process, while producing better imagery, left a lot of ink on the hands of readers and resulted in some newsprint waste.

Newspapers still using letterpresses represent a lucrative market for manufacturers of new presses, most notably flexography presses. For one reason, many newspapers using letterpress equipment cannot afford to junk their multimillion dollar press investments, and there is no demand for old letterpresses in today's printing environment. Flexography is a process that can be achieved by simply modifying those existing letterpresses. For those newspapers printing on offset presses, it is too early to sell those presses, many of which were just installed 10 to 15 years ago. However, flexography printing has proven itself in testing to be cleaner, simpler to operate, and cheaper than other printing methods. In 1987, 16 percent of all printing done in the United States was done on flexographic press units. Just what is this new method in printing, and does it represent a revolution in newspaper production?

First, although offset printing dominates the newspaper market and probably will for the foreseeable future, many observers see flexography as the wave of the future. Simply defined, flexography is a direct-relief printing process that uses photopolymer plastic plates on web presses. The flexibility of the plates, which can be wrapped around a cylinder, gives the process its name.[3] The "flexo" process also uses far fewer components than does offset printing. Flexo presses utilize an "anilox" roller, a plate cylinder, an impression cylinder, and a "doctor blade." The anilox roller is engraved mechanically or with lasers to produce thousands of microscopic cells of various shapes, sizes, and depths. The roller is fed ink from a trough, and the cells on the roller transfer ink to the plate. The doctor blade in the troughs scrapes excess ink from the roller that contacts the plate. The shallow relief plate is buffered by a foam cushion. Although letterpress printing is also direct-relief printing, flexo's shallow relief plates and the cushioning produce a "light kiss" printing impression that yields sharper imagery than letterpresses. However, unlike offset, which can be used with extremely fine screens in excess of 85 lines per inch, flexo performs best in the 65- to 85-line screen range and does not produce well on coated paper stocks as one might find in magazines. Newsprint, however, poses no problem. The result of all this is printing quality that is better than letterpress, but not quite as good as offset.

Some distinction exists between what is called true flexography and modified flexography. The latter means that only a a few alterations are made to letterpress units, while the former involves entirely new presses or new units slid into existing press networks. The anilox system is common to both. It works well because it is "keyless," or does not require fine-tuning during the press run to keep ink amounts constant and proper. That has been a problem with traditional offset printing and has resulted in some newsprint waste.

Among the positive features of flexo printing are the fact that newsprint waste is kept to a minimum due to the keyless inking feature; the inks are water-based and do not rub off on readers' hands, yet make clearer impressions; there is less run-through to the opposite side of the page; presses are easier to maintain; and printing seems to be more consistent throughout the press run. The biggest disadvantage comes in comparing flexography to offset reproduction quality. Offset produces clearer images. That, however, could change with continued technological advances in the flexo process.

Many newspapers, including the *Miami Herald* and the *Washington Post,* were still in the process of testing flexo presses in 1987, but others had finished their tests and concluded that flexo works. As a result, papers like the *San Francisco Examiner* and *San Francisco Chronicle* began purchasing flexo presses and were joined by smaller dailies such as Georgia's *Macon Telegraph* and *News,* and Indiana's *Evansville Courier,* which agreed to buy two flexo presses as the centerpiece of its new $26 million downtown headquarters.[4]

"Flexo's about to explode," says George Cashua, ANPA director of technical research. "There's no doubt it's come of age, and a great many newspapers are on the verge of either purchasing it outright or testing it. It won't be until the 1990s that you see widespread use, but it's coming."[5]

What is happening is that the variety of printing processes and printing press manufacturers is making the 1980s a good time for newspapers to consider purchasing new presses. This decade is a far cry from the 1970s when newspapers generally looked to only one printing process—offset, and one pressmaker—Goss. Now, several pressmakers are marketing press units that can print via offset, keyless offset, flexography, and keyless letterpress processes. Obviously, the keyless feature is becoming very popular. Ed Padilla, head of the newspaper press division of M.A.N.-Roland USA Inc., a large pressmaker, has predicted that by the start of the 1990s most U.S. newspapers will move to keyless inking. In fact, he says that feature will have as much effect in the pressroom as computers had in the composing rooms. He also feels that, by the year 2000, the standard news ink will be water-based.[6]

Among the vendors for presses printing via the above methods are Goss, Koenig & Bauer/Egenolf, M.A.N.-Roland, M.L.P., Motter Printing Press Co., North American Cerutti Corp., Publishers Equipment Corp., Taft Equipment Sales Corp., and Windmoeeler and Hoelscher Corp. Other companies manufacture flexo equipment that can be used to modify existing letterpress plants, turning them into flexo presses.

Beyond offset and flexography, some printing analysts are predicting that electronics will move the heavy iron presses now used in pressrooms into museums, instead.

Currently, newspapers use an iron monster weighing 400 tons to put one-fifth of an ounce on 64 pages of paper. Such complex press systems severely limit the flexibility of a newspaper to zone its ROP advertising and news content. Today, newspapers can zone preprinted advertising inserts with precision, yet they cannot offer the same flexibility with their mainstay ROP product. What's more, newspaper ROP reproduction can't compete with that of many preprints. Current press technology also prevents distribution of news of special interest to subscribers. One news package must fit all. The electronic press technology of the 21st century will allow a newspaper to customize each subscriber's news copy and allow advertisers to reach target zones or even particular subscribers. Electronic press technology will enable newspapers to print high-quality ROP and to run preprints on coated stock as part of the subscriber's newspaper. Instead of receiving preprints by truck from a commercial printer, the newspaper will receive an advertiser's prepared copy on a delivered electronic compact disc or from a satellite transmission directly into electronic ad storage. The electronic newspaper of tomorrow won't have to share preprint expenditures with a commercial printer and a trucker.[7]

Electronic newspaper imaging will be made practical, forecasters say, because of the development of a product called the erasable laser optical-storage disc. Its addition will enable newspapers to serve advertisers and readers better by giving newspapers complete flexibility to customize copies. The initial electronic imaging will probably take the form of add-on units to existing presses, but as the technology improves, the iron presses could be replaced entirely by the new electronic imaging systems.

NEWSPRINT

After the payroll, newsprint is the largest single expense a newspaper faces. Altogether, printing costs amount to about 22 percent of all newspaper expenses,[8] and newsprint represents most of these production costs. The unfortunate thing for the newspaper industry is that newsprint pricing is highly volatile and has been for many years. With only a couple of exceptions, those prices have been going way up since 1970. For instance, in 1970, one metric ton of Eastern U.S. newsprint cost about $175, but in 1987, that price was up to about $650.[9] Some industry analysts predicted the prices would go to $700 a ton within another year or two.

One of the chief impacts of higher newsprint prices is that more newspapers have begun stringent cost-cutting measures. Not only is more attention being paid to conserving newsprint (thus making printing processes like keyless inking more attractive), but cost-cutting strategies are spreading throughout the newspaper. Since the largest expense item a newspaper has is its payroll, many newspapers have been making staffing cuts across the board to offset the higher newsprint costs. In addition, smaller news holes are the order of the day at many newspapers as are shorter stories occupying those news holes. If this wasn't true a few years ago, it is definitely true in the 1980s, especially with the loss of many ROP ads to preprinted inserts. In addition to cost cutting, some newspapers are being forced to raise advertising and subscription rates, although there is doubt that these can be raised enough to cover higher costs and still maintain the number of advertisers the newspaper currently has. "In these low inflationary times, it will be more difficult to pass those kinds of increases on to the reader or advertiser," according to Douglas H. McCorkindale, vice chairman of the Gannett Co.[10]

Pushing newsprint prices up is the fact that there is no new supply, while demand has been increasing steadily at about 2 percent per year.[11] In fact, U.S. consumption of newsprint was at an all-time high in 1987, at 12.3 million metric tons that year, up from 11.9 million metric tons in 1986. U.S. mills produced about 5.2 million tons of newsprint in 1987, while Canadian mills produced about 10.2 million tons.[12]

One positive sign in this escalation of newsprint prices is that research is proceeding on a new type of newsprint that can be manufactured in the United States and will add to the existing overall newsprint supply. This new type of newsprint is made from kenaf, a fast-growing fiber that has been in development for about a decade. Traditional newsprint is made from pine. In the summer of 1987, both Florida's *St. Petersburg Times* and California's *Bakersfield Californian* reported very positive results from some of the most extensive live tests of printing on kenaf to date. If kenaf is found to be feasible for large-scale newsprint use, it has the potential of boosting newsprint supplies for all U.S. newspapers. That is good news to publishers who realize that two-thirds of all newsprint in use in the United States comes from Canada, that this northern neighbor has a tight supply of it, and that Congress looked in 1987 as if it would impose important taxes on that Canadian newsprint. In all, that import tax could cost U.S. newspapers $40 million, based on current imported newsprint usage.

LABOR UNIONS IN THE BACKSHOP

Organized labor is a prevalent sight in the backshops of many newspapers. In fact, about 300 of the nation's 1,660 dailies, or about 40 percent of total circulation, have one or more unions represented.[13] For publishers, unions represent constraints on management style and may mean higher payroll costs. For employees, unions represent a level of security and possible higher pay but also annual dues. Few publishers want employees represented by a union at their newspaper. Most publishers don't even see the need for unions. Nevertheless, especially in the backshop, unions are a fact of life for many management teams. Three unions that management has encountered most often on the production side are the International Typographers Union (ITU), International Printing and Graphic Communications Union (IP&GCU), and the International Mailers Union (IMU). Recently the ITU was absorbed by the Communications Workers of America (CWA). After adding some 40,000 ITU workers to its ranks, the CWU rose to about 700,000 workers.[14] One of the first things the CWU did after adding the ITU was to announce its intention of unifying traditional ITU craft workers with office and other newspaper and publishing employees in a "front-to-back" organizing effort under one union: the Printing, Publishing and Media Sector of the CWA, or what used to be the ITU. The CWA did, however, say that newspapers where the Guild is organized will be exempted from their attack, because it did not want to compete with the Guild.[15]

The IP&GCU, more commonly known as the Pressmen's Union, has been active in collective bargaining at newspapers and has caused production headaches during strikes at such powerful papers as the *St. Louis Post-Dispatch, Philadelphia Inquirer,* and *Dallas Morning News,* as well as others. At times the union locals have not stopped with striking, but have also resorted to press sabotage at such papers as the *Washington Post,*[16] even though such tactics are not sanctioned by union officials. The threat of strikes by the Pressmen's Union, as well as other unions, has become so severe that a special production training program for newspaper management has been underway in Oklahoma City for many years. Supported by member newspapers, the program features short-term, hands-on production training sessions for managers who may have to direct the production process during a prolonged strike.[17]

The primary issue for pressmen at many dailies has been the manning level of the presses, or the number of employees hired to work the equipment. Reduced manning levels have been a direct result of new pressroom technology and higher-speed presses. Striving to reverse this trend of cutting pressroom staffs, the union passed a resolution for local negotiating committees to attempt to increase the number of men per press wherever and whenever possible. Many of the strikes brought about by the pressmen have focused on this issue of manning levels.

The IMU is the newest of the large newspaper unions and also the smallest. An offshoot of the ITU, it nevertheless has kept its ties to the ITU at the national level for greater bargaining clout.

To newspaper management, unions represent a threat in a day when cost-cutting strategies are the norm. Union contracts act as an obstacle to such cost-cutting, and may prevent it entirely. When Rupert Murdoch was negotiating to purchase the *Buffalo Courier and Express,* a condition of his purchase was that staff levels be cut. It was on that point that the pressmen balked. In the end, the deal fell through, and the newspaper folded for good.

The ANPA's Human Resource Committee is committed to the stated goal of "wherever applicable, a union-free environment."[18] The association points out that the union movement is declining at newspapers and that, from 1979 to 1985, the percentage of union members working at U.S. newspapers dropped from 21.4 percent to 19.2. Also, from 1975 to 1985 the number of elections for union representation at newspapers dropped from almost 65 to fewer than 20 percent.[19] Charles Cole, ANPA labor relations manager, said publishers are more alert and responsive to employee needs than in the past, and that government regulation and court decisions have afforded workers more protection. He also says many employers at nonunion shops pay close to, or better than, area union scale.[20]

The existence of such volatile unions in the backshop makes it imperative that production department managers be adept not only at their trade, but also at understanding the workings, history, and philosophy of the unions involved in their department. As is the case with all departmental managers, production department supervisors must have good people skills and be able to mediate informally when labor problems arise in the backshop.

NOTES

1. ANPA Research Institute, "Daily Newspapers Printed by Offset," *Special Report of the ANPA Research Institute,* Reston, Va.: 29 August 1980: 1.

2. Mark Fitzgerald, "Pagination Comes of Age," *Editor & Publisher,* 16 June 1984: 10.

3. Rosalind C. Truitt, "Flexo on a Roll at Newspapers," *Presstime* (December 1986), p. 37.

4. Truitt, "Flexo on a Roll," p. 37.

5. Truitt, "Flexo on a Roll," p. 38.

6. Truitt, "Flexo on a Roll," p. 38.

7. William D. Rinehart, "Presses May Be Museum Pieces by the Turn of the Century," *Presstime*, p. 66.

8. Gene Chamberlain, *The Newspaper: Everything You Need to Know to Make It in the Newspaper Business*, ed. D. Earl Newsom (Englewood Cliffs: Prentice Hall, 1981), p. 146.

9. Rosalind C. Truitt, "Newspapers Brace as Newsprint Prices Continue to Spiral Rapidly Upward," *Presstime* (September 1987), p. 68.

10. Truitt, "Newspapers Brace," p. 68.

11. Truitt, "Newspapers Brace," p. 69.

12. Truitt, "Newspapers Brace," p. 69.

13. George Garneau, "Labor Unions Get Tough," *Editor & Publisher*, 14 February 1987: 40.

14. Garneau, "Labor Unions Get Tough," p. 40.

15. Garneau, "Labor Unions Get Tough," p. 40.

16. F. Robert Livernash and William E. Fulmer, "The Washington Post (A)," in Harvard Business School, *Harvard Business School Case Study No. 677-076*, (Cambridge, Mass. Harvard Business School, 1976, pp. 6–7.

17. Livernash and Fulmer, "The Washington Post (A)," pp. 6–7.

18. Garneau, "Labor Unions Get Tough," p. 40.

19. Garneau, "Labor Unions Get Tough," p. 40.

20. Garneau, "Labor Unions Get Tough," p. 40.

8

PRODUCING THE NEWS

When you strip away all the fiscal matters, the main justification for a newspaper's existence and for the special place it occupies in the Constitution is to produce the news. If a newspaper does a good job of that, it usually will be well-read. If it is well-read, advertisers will flock in, and the newspaper will have the resources needed to do an even better job of producing the news. This theory is, of course, predicated on the assumption that the newspaper's owners will not get too greedy when it comes to profit taking. A discussion of this problem can be found in Chapter 10.

The responsibility for producing the news falls to the newspaper's editors who oversee their staff of reporters, copy editors, and photographers. As discussed in Chapter 2, the key editors at any newspaper include the editor-in-chief, executive editor, managing editor, news editor, and the various desk editors. Jobs they face include developing an overall philosophy of news for the paper and implementing it; planning for the needs of the newsroom; recruiting and orienting news staffers; maintaining newsroom budgets; developing and maintaining effective systems of news coverage; providing effective management of people in the newsroom; and insuring that an accurate, well-edited news product emerges. Thus, running an effective, efficient, modern-day newsroom requires more than the technical editing skills one ordinarily thinks of when considering the editor's job.

"WHAT EDITORS DO ALL DAY"

University of Maryland Journalism Professor Carl Sessions Stepp gives some idea of the breadth and depth of the editor's daily job. "Editors are teachers, counselors, negotiators, schedulers, taskmasters, disciplinarians, ethicists, motivators, ombudsmen and referees,'' Stepp says. ''They are also managers and judges, facing the daily idiosyncracies of human relations and newsgathering . . . and the inflammatory task of deciding where the new furniture goes. More than anything else, editing is decision-making under pressure.''[1] However, Stepp notes that these tasks are not exactly what editors had in mind when they accepted their jobs.

Too often, we teach them [would-be editors] the mechanics and trust they will absorb the more subtle skills elsewhere. In newsrooms, we have a tendency to make people editors because they were good reporters, when—as anyone who has done both jobs can testify—the required talents aren't the same. As a result, too many editors are forced to learn on the job, haphazardly, relying on hunch and guesswork to make the hair-splitting judgments required day after day after day.[2]

Stepp's points are well taken. Anyone who has served as an editor knows a typical day at the office may consist of deciding how to handle a story whose central figure has just called and threatened suicide if it is published; how to tell your star education reporter he can't be rotated off his beat yet because you don't have anyone with his kind of moxie to do the job; how to handle letters to the editor around local election time and how to discern which letters were written as part of a political action committee campaign; how to advise a reporter who shows she has been treated unprofessionally by your own superior in the newsroom; and what to tell a reporter when she encounters a story that the publisher—because of political reasons—simply does not want in the paper.

Obviously, not all these problems are going to arise on the same day, although at times it seems they do just that, but over the course of a few weeks or months, most editors will come into contact with just about all these—and more—newsroom dilemmas.

DEVELOPING A NEWS PHILOSOPHY

One of the primary functions of the newsroom management team is to develop an overall philosophy of news for the newspaper that is specific, yet broad enough to cover most of the situations the news staff will confront. Such a philosophy, conspicuously absent in many newsrooms, serves several functions. First, it provides a common goal toward which editors, reporters, and photographers strive. With such a philosophy in place, assuming it is communicated to the entire staff and is in writing, the editor and reporter should be talking about the same thing when they refer to an excellent news product. This news philosophy should be relatively short, possibly under 200 words; it should be clear and unambiguous; yet it should leave room for the always-arising exception to the rule. An example of such a philosophy of news could be:

To the *Daily Bugle,* 'news' is defined as an event, issue, or personality that is of timely interest to the people in our market. To be of utmost interest to our readers, the news must signal an event or issue which will impact on them. This means the *Daily Bugle* will shy away from mere titilating events and pseudo-news. Entertainment will have its place in this newspaper, but that place represents only a small proportion of the average daily news offering. Further, every effort will be made to do issue-oriented reporting rather than the easier—but generally less significant—event-oriented reporting.

The above sample news philosophy at least draws parameters around the idea this newspaper has about news. It could be followed by a statement of means which may point out that, to do this issue-oriented reporting, the newspaper will make use of "precision journalism" techniques such as content analysis and random sample surveys. It may also have a statement of some constraints which will have to be addressed in carrying out the news philosophy. For instance, it should realistically address the issue of whether out-of-state travel will be provided for stories or if the reporter should plan on resorting to the telephone instead for out-of-state sources.

The second thing a philosophy of news does is to provide a reference point for what is considered a good edition of the newspaper and what is considered a bad edition. If one edition of the *Daily Bugle,* for instance, devotes 70 percent of its front page to automobile accidents, celebrities, and convenience store robberies, then it would not be considered consistent with the paper's philosophy of news expressed earlier.

Third, a news philosophy—especially one that results from the input of the news staff—provides the basis for an atmosphere of trust and consensus. These are necessary for more enlightened styles of management. Participative management, to be discussed in Chapter 9, is growing in importance and popularity because of studies that have shown that workers contribute more and work better in a workplace where they have input.

Fourth, a philosophy of news provides the basis for budget building. If issues are more important to a newspaper than events, then budgets should reflect the need for a larger news staff. If an editor has a large enough news staff he will be able to let several reporters have time to develop longer and more thought-provoking pieces while still having enough reporters to cover the daily beat and general assignment pieces.

Fifth, a news philosophy provides the basis for staffing and recruiting requirements. An issue-oriented newspaper, for example, will probably be looking for more reporters with advanced degrees in specific fields such as law, science, or economics, instead of filling the staff with young B.A.s from journalism schools.

Some of this discussion may seem idealistic to the veteran editor who complains that his newspaper's news philosophy is set by the owner, and that there is never enough money to do the job right anyway. To be sure, the owner's philosophy of news may in fact influence the managing editor's definition, but it doesn't have to be the most important determinant, and part of the editor's job is to convince the owner or publisher why a particular news philosophy is good or bad. After all, an editor's job is not complete just because he serves as a "yes man" for the publisher. Most owners and publishers want their editors to formulate and implement an appropriate news philosophy and strategy of news coverage. Media groups like Gannett pride themselves on the concept of one ownership, but "a world of different voices."[3] Editorial autonomy is a real thing in most daily newsrooms. If there is a problem, it is usually with budgetary restrictions. That is when it takes an editor with creative talents and a sense of efficiency to produce a newspaper that supports the adopted news philosophy.

Determinants of a News Philosophy

What are the criteria upon which a sound news philosophy is built? The following are some of the more important determinants that the newsroom management team must take into consideration:

Market Needs and Conditions. Chapters 1 and 4 detail the kinds of problems that can arise when a newspaper's readers are ignored in the formulation of a news agenda. This determinant is perhaps most important when it comes to the issue of the newspaper's survival in the market.

Accepted Journalistic Principles. These are principles such as truth, accuracy, and fair play, as set forth in such codes as the Sigma Delta Chi Code of Ethics, and the ASNE Canons of Good Journalism. They are also principles like fulfilling the First Amendment mission of offering a public forum for important issues and events of the day. These principles must balance the newspaper's market ethic.

The Newspaper's Own Editorial Mission. How does the newspaper conceive of its editorial mission? There are, for instance, newspapers that conceive of themselves as being more entertainment-oriented. Others see themselves as investigative journals. Still others see their main mission to be covering national and international affairs, and some see themselves as locally oriented first and last. It is important for newspaper executives to avoid the trap of assuming that every newspaper sees its mission as being identical and believing that everyone even on their own newspaper sees the newspaper's mission similarly. As discussed in Chapter 3, a concept of the newspaper's editorial mission is needed before a budget can be formulated with various areas of emphasis.

The Owner's Philosophy of News. To be certain, the newspaper's owner or publisher can have a strong influence in determining which news philosophy the paper adopts, but his or her ideas should not necessarily overshadow the ideas of everyone else in the newsroom. It is the editor's job to stand up for the philosophy he or she feels is best.

The Editor's Idea of News. This is probably where most news philosophies originate, but only the most arrogant editor would try to ramrod a news philosophy that few others in the newsroom supported or saw value in.

The News Staff's Ideas of News. The more enlightened newsroom management team will ask for and receive maximum input from the news staff as to what should be included in the newspaper's news philosophy. This can be done through staff surveys, informal meetings with editors, or more formalized Quality Circles, as discussed in Chapter 9. A key advantage of getting others to contribute to the philosophy is that such input leads to greater trust and consensus-building, and once consensus is present, the staff will generally support and contribute to a news philosophy better than if their ideas went unheard in the first place.

Events of the Day. Any news philosophy must place a large emphasis on the comprehensive coverage of the day's news events. Although some planning can be done for these events, inasmuch as editors can predict that certain types of news will happen every so often, the events themselves are usually spontaneous and require even the best daily news agenda to be modified occasionally. The important thing about event-oriented reporting, however, is to not believe the staff must wait for something to happen before doing any reporting. This type of reaction reporting syndrome has struck too many newsrooms over the years and has caused some editions of the paper to be very good and others very bad. If something happens, it's a "good news day"; if nothing happens, it's a "bad news day." This is not true. The best newspapers are those which seek out and monitor trends by using various social indicators, which will be discussed later. The events of the day make up a healthy part of the newspaper, certainly, but the other stories that put events into context become the foundation of the newspaper.

"Hot" Topics. For better or worse, the public seems from one year to the next to latch on to particular topics or issues as being singularly important. The news media assists in this process by providing saturation coverage of the subject matter. Many say the agenda is set by the media itself; the public merely reads or tunes in, and their attention becomes even more heightened. Others say this doesn't give the educated public much credit, and it is they who determine the media's agenda. Whichever position is correct, everyone in the news business knows that, whereas world hunger may be the overriding issue one year, some dreaded disease like AIDS may be the issue the next year, homelessness the next, and so on. Sometimes the public's attention seems to fix on a particular problem industry like airlines, or on some age group such as children or the elderly. A newspaper's philosophy of news must make room for these timely topics when they arise and accommodate them.

Taste. There has probably never been an adequate definition of the term "sensationalism" when applied to the media. Like beauty, it is generally in the eye of the beholder. Some in the media distinguish between a sensational event and sensational treatment of that event. That is probably not a bad distinction to make. The mayor of the city dying in a fire at a gay bar is a sensational event, yet few would deny it should be reported. The question of taste arises in how it is reported, and so taste becomes at least an influence on the news philosophy.

The Competition's Idea of News. Most newspapers are affected by how their competition defines news. More than one newspaper has chased a story it might otherwise ignore just because its competitor—either another newspaper or a television station—is also chasing the story. It is easy to analyze any medium's news philosophy by doing a simple content analysis of a few weeks' worth of news stories from that station or newspaper. Then it is up to the news executives to see how far they want to go in trying to cover the same bases as the competition.

The Wire Services' Ideas of News. The Associated Press and United Press International probably set more news agendas for daily newspapers than any other of the determinants listed here. This is not always a good thing, as Timothy Crouse points out in *The Boys on the Bus.*[4] Crouse says that more than one exclusive story has been spiked by an overly cautious editor who couldn't find a similar story on the wires. The argument from the enterprising reporter that the story is an exclusive and therefore not reported by other media many times has little weight as editors seem to trust the wires at times more than their own reporters. Anyone who has worked in the business very long, however, knows that the AP and UPI are staffed with reporters as fallible as any newspaper reporter. The wire services have no lock on the truth, and they do not define the boundaries of what is happening on any given day, yet the wire services seem to offer a certain safety that a newspaper will not be too far out of line if it goes along with the wire's budget of stories for that day. Unfortunately, this can lead to lazy and stifling reporting.

Newspaper Finances. Editors wish this determinant did not exist, but every editor knows it does. "Champagne tastes on a beer budget" is a phrase that has great applicability here. Dreaming about fielding a two-person investigative team is one thing, but affording it is something else. That is why an editor should be adept at finding money where none seems to exist and in controlling costs elsewhere so a more important resource can be added. Most reporters would rather work in an older newsroom that features outdated VDTs yet which has the funds to staff the newspaper as it should be staffed.

Classic Criteria of News. Once more, for all the graduates of Reporting 101, here they are: conflict, uniqueness, prominence, human interest, significance, proximity (geographical and psychological), timeliness, and so on. Any editor who is unaware of these should go back to journalism school, because these do characterize events as newsworthy or dull.

"Enduring Values." Credit Columbia University's Herbert Gans with interpreting a host of news stories in light of the values they seem to address.[5] These "enduring values" help us to see how editors and news directors attach the idea of newsworthiness to events and people. These enduring values include ethnocentrism, responsible capitalism, rugged individualism, small-town pas-

toralism, order, altruistic democracy, leadership, and moderatism. Thus, a story about a blind sailor crossing the Atlantic addresses rugged individualism; a story about a mayor using city funds to remodel his home bathroom is a story addressing (the violation of) altruistic democracy and leadership. A story about a chemical company dumping pollutants into a stream is a story addressing the issue of responsible capitalism. This is not a bad way of looking at what news is.

Instinct and Experience. So many times the decision on whether to classify an event as newsworthy comes down to these twin criteria. In close-call situations, they are good determinants to rely on, especially when a veteran editor is at the helm. One of the chief tenets of this book, however, is that instinct and experience are not the only bases on which editors should make decisions—they should be supplemented with other tools such as market research and editorial staff input.

A POSTSCRIPT TO THE NEWS PHILOSOPHY

In all cases, however the news philosophy is determined and enacted into policy, it should be written out, delivering the overall goals in one paragraph and having specifics follow. Further, if this philosophy originates from a Quality Circle, it must still be agreed to by the editor and publisher, and in all cases should contain positive answers to the following questions:

1. Is it appropriate to the newspaper's size and market?
2. Is it consistent with sound journalistic principles?
3. Is it financially feasible?

PLANNING FOR NEWSROOM NEEDS

One of the editor's primary functions is to plan for newsroom needs. The main need the newsroom has is for qualified personnel to act as editors, reporters, photographers, and copy editors. According to William Glueck, every coordinated hiring system should include the following components: employment planning, recruiting, selection, and orientation.[6] The major reasons for formal planning are to achieve:[7]

1. More effective and efficient use of the human resources.
2. More satisfied and more developed employees.
3. More effective equal employment opportunity planning.

For our purposes we might also state that another major reason is to bring in employees who are trustworthy and who will be able to place confidence in—and have confidence placed in them by—the editors who are staffing the newsroom. As in the other phases of newsroom management, the operating manager (departmental editors in our case) should have a large role in employment planning for his or her department.

Since departmental editors are so besieged with other daily duties, however, a simple projection technique seems called for. The Unit Demand Forecasting Technique is such a procedure and basically calls for the editor to analyze his department's person-by-person, job-by-job needs in the present as well as the future. By analyzing present and future requirements of the job, and the skills of the incumbents, this method focuses on the quality of the workers. Usually the department editor can start with a current census of reporters compiled on a list called a "manning table." Manning tables list the jobs in a department by name and number and record the number of jobholders for each entry. The resulting tables can be evaluated by both numbers and skills of the present personnel. Consideration must be given the effects of expected losses through retirement, promotion, or other reasons. Whether those losses will require replacement and what the projected growth needs, if any, will be are questions the planner must answer. These answers are then projected into his or her calculations in determining net employment needs.

Whatever his system, the editor should know the current and probable future status (as far as he can determine it) of each employee in his or her department. In analyzing current and future needs of the department, the editor should look at two points: what are the department's needs, and what will be the needs of the replacements coming into the department. The first question indicates the type of person needed to fill the opening (which may be current or anticipated); the second question is an effort to match the offerings of this department to the anticipated needs of the qualified candidate. If a current position is to be staffed by someone else within the newsroom, a detailed position replacement chart can be used like the one in Exhibit 6.

A key ingredient in employment planning is the job analysis. If the editor makes an effort to match the right candidate to the right job, then job analysis is a vital part of that effort. Basically, job analysis concerns itself with defining the aspects of each job such as the work activities, the tools needed, the context of the job (working conditions), and the knowledge, skills, experience, and personal attributes needed for the job.[8] More than ever, employers are taking a hard look at this last requirement to make sure the applicant has the personality and traits needed for the available opening. This is very important in judging applicants for reporting jobs, given the special traits required to do the job.

However, job analysis is done for other reasons as well, including: to provide information for the preparation of job descriptions and specifications; to help in the hiring, orientation, and training of employees; as an aid in job evaluation for pay purposes; for collective bargaining reasons; for safety purposes; and as a requirement in equal employment opportunity planning and analysis. From the data gathered in the job analysis, job descriptions can be formed and can then be sent to the personnel office, which can do the original

Exhibit 6
Position Replacement Chart

Position			
Reporter, City Hall			
Performance **Incumbent**		**Salary**	**May Move**
Outstanding Mel Murray		$32,000	1 year
Replacement 1		**Salary**	**Age**
Earl Renfraw		$27,000	29
Present Position	**Employed:**		
Reporter, General Assignment	**Present Job**	**Company**	
	3 years	10 years	
Training Needed		**When Ready**	
At least one week on the city hall beat with Murray; orientation to the process of city government.		2 weeks	
Replacement 2		**Salary**	**Age**
Bernard Storey		$22,000	33
Present Position	**Employed:**		
Reporter, Science Beat	**Present Job**	**Company**	
	1 year	2 years	
Training Needed		**When Ready**	
Same as Renfraw		1 year	

screening of candidates. To be a valid and useful job description, it must be behaviorally based. The following steps can be taken to insure it is.

1. Decide upon job objectives and state them in the form of terminal behaviors (what the job candidate actually does).
2. List the tasks required for desired performance.
3. Differentiate between routine and critical task performance.
4. List alternative methods of performing the tasks.
5. Specify criteria used to determine if terminal behavior has been evidenced and thus if the job has been done right.

6. Specify favorable and unfavorable conditions for the attainment of the objectives.

7. Specify other general information regarding the job, such as title, salary, supervisor, and so on.

8. List work qualifications, education, and experience levels required.

The planning phase will obviously take some work on the part of the departmental editor, but it is a process which should have to be updated only once or twice a year unless turnover is a big problem with the newspaper. The main benefit of planning is that it can help insure that whatever personnel problems are present now will not be carried into the future with new employees.

RECRUITING AND SELECTION

For the editor looking for new staffers, it is important that the process is not just seen as one whereby the applicant shows his best side. The newspaper must also show its best side if it expects to interest the best candidates.

In large newspapers with fully developed personnel departments, personnel may do the initial recruiting, using as a guide the employment forecasts, current needs, and job analyses supplied them by the departmental editors. In smaller newsrooms, the editors themselves may have to do the recruiting. Whoever does it, however, must rely on the forecasts and the job analyses, or else finding a good match will be based only on chance. This is true whether the editor is looking at current employees to fill a vacancy or going outside. Furthermore, whoever the recruiter is, he or she is the filter and the matcher, the one who is actually seen by the applicants and is studied as a representative of the company. The recruiter, Glueck points out, is not just an employee, but is also viewed as an example of the kind of person the organization employs and wants.

What of the applicant? Is it possible for an editor or personnel manager to screen out incompetent or otherwise unattractive workers before they are hired? At least one editor for a large publishing group thinks so. Ruth Stidger, editorial director for the International Group of the Technical Publishing Co., says her definition of a competent worker is one who is able to do a job well and who is willing to put in the effort required to complete a high volume of quality work.[9] She says it is possible to locate and identify such employees, and she conducted a survey to find out some of the characteristics of competent workers. Some of her results are:[10]

1. Top-rated workers put family or love first in order of what's important to them.

2. Top-rated workers take the most pride in their work.

3. Top rated workers work long weeks.

4. Top-rated workers think money is important, but not nearly as important as the satisfaction of doing a job well.

5. Top-rated workers think accuracy is the most important element of a job well done.

According to several editors and managers Stidger interviewed, the portion
of the job application which became their best tool for screening out incompe-
tents was the employment history section. They feel the most useful information in this section is the following:

1. Beginning and ending dates of the job. These should tally with ex-employers' records.

2. Company name, address, and phone number of employers. The phone number will
   save time in checking references.

3. Immediate supervisor's name. This is used when checking references, even though
   the supervisor may not be contacted directly.

4. Summary of job skills and responsibilities.

5. Salary when beginning and leaving the job.

In addition to the application, the job interview affords the recruiter a chance
to see if the person actually has the qualities needed for the job. Some of the
qualities editors should look for in candidates are a high degree of professionalism; an alert, interested, serious attitude; neat appearance during the interview; a firm handshake; and punctuality. In addition, the resume and clip file
of stories should be neatly prepared. If the candidate follows up the interview
with a letter of thanks and additional work samples, that is also an indication
of his or her interest in the job.

Another guide to competency may be various skills tests, such as an editing
or spelling test. Editors must be careful, however, because their state may have
laws regarding such screening tests. Laws concerning aptitude tests vary from
state to state, but the federal government requires that all job candidates be
treated fairly and equally. Therefore, if one candidate is administered a test, all
candidates must get it as well.

While on the subject of laws relating to hiring of employees, it might be
wise to take a look at some current trends in discrimination law. Whitman S.
Browne, Jr., of R.J. Carroll and Associates, has counseled many newspaper
editors on discrimination laws. In summary, Browne feels that editors can stay
on the safe side of the law if they treat all applicants for positions equally and
don't ask questions in the interview stage that mix an applicant's personal and
professional lives. Two attorneys, Richard Perras and Alvin Glazerman explain, for instance, that at the applicant stage there are two basic discriminatory
employment practices involving "disparate treatment" and "disparate impact."
Disparate treatment involves the intention to discriminate on the basis of race,
sex, color, national origin, or some other outlawed criterion. In order for an
applicant to prove such disparate treatment, he or she must prove that the employer was guided by a motivation of discrimination. Disparate impact, however, involves not the motivation, but the effect of the treatment. For instance,
a "facially neutral" decision or business practice, such as questioning a person's marital or family status, may be illegally discriminatory if it has a signif-

icant discriminatory impact on an individual or group because of race, sex, color, national origin, religion, or some other prohibited factor. For example, it is illegal to screen out women because they are married, mothers, or potential mothers on the grounds that they have greater attendance problems, unless the same standards are applied to married men and fathers. In similar fashion, it is illegal to discriminate on the basis of things like height, weight, having relatives or friends in the workplace, education, experience, and recent work requirements if the employer cannot prove a business necessity was justified in the denial of employment.[11]

Two other guides to a person's competency for the job are reference checks and try-out periods, both of which are legal if used in the correct manner. In checking references, it is important to phrase questions specifically enough so that the answers shed some real light on the person's qualifications. For instance, instead of simply asking, "How is this person as a worker," an editor might instead ask, "What percentage of the time does this person meet his deadlines?" or "Roughly how many errors does this person make in his reporting throughout a month or year?" Editors must realize that ex-employers will think twice before giving a bad report on an individual, because the law frowns on ex-employers who deliberately and falsely malign employees, or who file reports that they cannot substantiate. However, the person who gives an honest evaluation of work performed, and says it is just his or her opinion and not necessarily fact, violates no laws.

Try-out periods are probably the best way to judge a candidate's abilities for the job, but most applicants resent them—and do so justifiably, by the way. In order for an applicant to try out for say, a two-week period, he must somehow get release time from his current job, and his current editor is unlikely to provide it if he knows his employee is using it to try out elsewhere. Consequently, the employee must use vacation time for this purpose, and that probably will not make him feel good about the job. Possibly a better way of handling this would be for the newspaper to assign the applicant some freelance or consulting work and then assess it prior to hiring him. This freelance work will not require the candidate to either give up his current job to try out or give up his vacation time.

Before leaving this section, it should be noted that small dailies and weeklies have a special problem in attracting quality talent, generally because of low pay and the lackluster nature of smaller cities. Still, editors at these papers need not despair. They can attract quality beginners if they involve themselves in an aggressive recruiting program whereby they visit college campuses, set up networks with journalism faculty members to locate promising talent, step up their internship programs, and generally show pride in their news operations. Promotion of news awards is a great way of showing young talent that good reporting is not the sole possession of larger dailies.

One shining example of quality journalism in a small-city setting is Missouri's *Columbia Daily Tribune* (circulation 18,000). The *Tribune* is among the nation's 1400 or so daily newspapers with circulations under 50,000, yet the *Tribune,* under its publisher Henry J. Waters III, chooses not to base its potential for greatness on circulation size. Instead, it pursues an aggressive policy of investigative reporting and of pumping money into the newsroom. For instance, in 1985, Waters spent $800,000 a year on his newsroom budget, or about 16 percent of total revenue.[12] That is about $135,000 more than the average comparable daily was spending on its newsroom operation, according to the Inland Daily Press Association. That year, the *Tribune* had 34 full-time employees and 11 part-timers in the newsroom. That compares to a national average for papers of that size of 22 full-time and 6 part-time newsroom employees.

The *Tribune* also pays higher-than-average salaries and, because of its commitment to quality news coverage and presentation, it attracts some of the best young reporting and editing talent. After a few years, many of these journalists move on to other papers. In recent years, *Tribune* graduates have wound up at such prestigious places as *The Philadelphia Inquirer, Miami Herald, Kansas City Times, Seattle Post-Intelligencer, Hartford Courant,* and even *Rolling Stone* magazine. Applicants for vacancies on the *Tribune* understand the possibilities of working for this newspaper, and that makes the prospect even more appealing to them. Meanwhile, Waters accepts this state of affairs and has resigned himself to the turnover problem. "We can pay competitively for people with a few years' experience, but after two or three years here, we have trouble keeping up," he notes. "They can go elsewhere for $25,000 instead of the $18,000 we can pay. We try to keep a cadre of three or four who provide continuity."[13] If more newspapers followed the example of the *Columbia Daily Tribune,* editors in smaller towns would have much less problem attracting quality editorial talent.

ORIENTATION OF NEW STAFF MEMBERS

A common complaint heard around many newsrooms is that a reporter or copy editor wasn't given any orientation to a new job he or she was assigned to. Therefore, the first few weeks may have been wasted and bad mistakes made before the employee found out what the job was all about. To cut down on this problem, some type of formal orientation program is called for.

The newsrooms that make the best use of their new talent offer formal orientation programs which include opening-week interviews with the managing editor, the departmental editor, and the assistant editor to which the staffer is assigned; a meeting with the employee relations officer to discuss the company benefits and the employee handbook in detail; introductions to other staff members in the new employee's department; and a great deal of time for the new staffer to ask questions and have them answered. One newspaper, in fact (the *Lawrence Eagle-Tribune* in Lawrence, Massachusetts) has prepared a list of the hundred most asked questions by new employees over the years and has published the list as part of an orientation handbook for new employees. Questions covered include everything from "Can I get Christmas Day off," to "Am I expected to eat on the job, or do I have a dinner period built in to my schedule?"

In truth, every orientation program has both its formal and informal halves. The formal part of the program, interviews with managers for instance, is meaningful, but perhaps not as meaningful to the new staffer as the informal half where he or she gets a chance to discuss the job with peers in the department. Editors should realize this informal orientation will be taking place, and try not to get upset about it or rely on its taking the place of the formal half.

Howard Rausch, editorial director of Gralla Publications, feels the orientation process should be carefully coordinated to give the new employee—or a reassigned one—everything he needs to know about the company and the job to help him succeed and see how he fits into the overall picture. Rausch believes the orientation of new staffers should come in two parts: orientation toward the newspaper company (usually done by the personnel department), and orientation toward the newsroom (done by the managing editor and departmental editor).[14] The managing editor may take part in the overall orientation process, but most of it is devoted to discussion between the personnel manager and the new employee. If he does take part in the overall orientation, the managing editor should:[15]

1. Stress the productivity standards of the publication.

2. Discuss the importance of personal organization.

3. Discuss the importance of accuracy.

4. Discuss all major policies of the newsroom.

5. Discuss writing styles and the "Fog Index."

6. Discuss the business expense/voucher policy.

7. Advocate writing notes of thanks to sources on stories and stress the importance of keeping up with sources.

8. Discuss the realities of the news business such as rewritten copy and last-minute editing.

This discussion must go both ways, with the new staffer getting an adequate chance to make input and ask questions.

In the second half of the orientation—toward the newsroom—the new staffer should be able to meet all the reporters and editors and be required to read a certain number of back issues of the newspaper to find out what issues are ongoing and get more of an idea of the paper's style. He should be given a chance to work with an experienced hand for the first few days on his new job assignment; be told how the scheduling works; and be given any information possible about quirks of the job and so forth.

In most cases, the whole orientation process should be finished within a week, and it will be the best-spent week the publication ever had, because it will pay off in employee motivation and quality of work produced down the line.

PAYING ATTENTION TO MINORITY HIRING

One area of recruiting that requires special attention in the 1980s is the hiring of minorities in the newsroom. Even a casual glance at most newsrooms in the United States shows a shamefully low number of Black and Hispanic reporters and editors. Even though many newspapers and newspaper groups are making strong efforts at attracting minority journalists, the problem still exists in large measure. There is no one best way of attracting and hiring qualified minority candidates to the newsroom, but that just leaves the door open for different newspapers to be innovative in their efforts.

One way is simply to keep track of promising minority journalists around the country. Newspapers can network with each other in this effort and start a file of minority candidates. That network can reach out to include journalism schools as well, as editors ask journalism professors to refer their minorities to them while still in school for discussion about future openings.

Hosting job fairs for minority journalists and journalism students is another excellent way of discovering talent. Several cities, including Boston and New York, host such minority job fairs regularly. Editors find them to be a good source for finding out who the current and future job prospects are.

Beverly Richardson, personnel director of the San Bernardino *Sun,* says her newspaper's success in introducing minorities into the staff has had a tremendous effect on recruiting other minority talent. ''Now that we have substantial minority employment here, people are *aware* that opportunities exist,'' she says.[16] The *Sun* also features its own minority staff members in its newspaper promotions. Richardson feels that probably affects the number of minority job candidates the newspaper gets.

Among the resource organizations helping newspapers to find qualified minority candidates are the Institute for Journalism Education, the American Newspaper Publishers Association, the Conference on Minorities in the Newspaper Business, and the National Association of Hispanic Journalists.

WOMEN IN NEWSPAPERS

In 1985, Jean Gaddy Wilson, a faculty member of the School of Journalism at the University of Missouri, conducted an exhaustive survey on the status of women in newspapers. Some of her more interesting findings were as follows.[17]

1. The overwhelming majority of management jobs on the most influential papers continued to be held by men.
2. The overwhelming majority of management jobs on mid-size and small newspapers also continue to be held by men.

3. Women's salaries lag behind men's in almost every newspaper job, in almost every circulation category.

4. Even when women and men with the same length of service are compared, women's salaries in a majority of cases lag behind those of their male counterparts in the same job at newspapers of similar size.

5. Although the number of women employed at newspapers is still below the number of men, there appears to have been a steady increase of women in management and professional positions in the past two decades.

6. Only 7 percent of publishers and general managers are women. Fewer than 20 percent of managers of the news, advertising, and circulation departments are female.

Clearly, the newspaper industry needs to wake up to the need of moving more women into management positions. Many observers feel that, like the situation with minority hiring, the only way to bring more women into newspaper management is to position women in key managerial positions with the authority to hire managers in positions below theirs. There are indications that women are making a strong bid for getting those management jobs. For instance, there are more women in the newsroom today than ever before with about half the reporting corps of newspapers made up of women. In addition, journalism schools are reporting that more women are entering their programs than men.

NEWSROOM BUDGET PLANNING

Some of the key tasks of the editor are to plan for, prepare, implement, and control newsroom budgets. The degree of control the editor has over the size of his or her newsroom's budget may vary from paper to paper, but most top editors at least have control over the shape of that budget. The degree to which this editor, in turn, shares budget setting responsibility with editors under him also varies, but the best newsrooms are those in which the individual desk editors can contribute to the formation and implementation of the budget. Chapter 3 discussed the types and roles of budgets in the planning process. A budget is a tool to help editors set priorities in the newsroom. It involves both planning the budget and controlling it. Some edtiors choose to start the budget-planning process by forming a "wish list" with no thought given to cost. Then the winnowing down process begins as available financial resources come into play. Others choose to go from a "zero-based budget," with editors starting from a zero point and needing to justify every item they add to that baseline.

A typical budget-planning process might involve the following:

1. Looking at the current year's budget and comparing it with upcoming needs.

2. Analyzing areas of over- and under-spending. If this year's budgeted spending and actual spending have actually matched, why not use the same budget again this year? If wide variations exist, something has changed, and it needs attention before the next budget is finalized.

3. Getting as much input as possible from the various newsroom divisions on the budget. Certainly the editor of the lifestyle desk knows his or her division's needs and opportunities better than the managing editor or executive editor.

4. Looking at the salary expense in relation to the rest of the newsroom budget. In most newsrooms, for example, payroll accounts for about 75 to 80 percent of the budget. If the payroll expense is much higher or lower, attention should be paid to it. Experience has shown most editors that this payroll allocation is not going to change that much from year to year, barring any major expansion or retrenchment effort on the part of the newspaper's management. Thus it is important to use the newsroom staff wisely, and editors can't know if they are being deployed wisely unless they look at each position and assess its overall benefit to the news hole and mission of the newspaper.

5. Reviewing any union contracts and seeing what salary increases are mandated under them.

6. Paying close attention to overtime, which is the source of much overspending at newspapers. If it has advanced dramatically, it may be time to institute new rules regarding how overtime is permitted and used in the newsroom.

7. Turning attention to other expense items and assessing their increased or decreased cost.

In general, a typical budget for a large daily newsroom might look like this:

I.   Payroll (including overtime): 75%

II. Other Operating Expenses: 25%
     These include:
         wire services 30%
         other features 18%
         travel 12%
         phone charges 20%
         business mileage 8%
         stringers 4%
         supplies 3%
         subscriptions 1%
         bureau rental 2%
         misc 2%

COST-CONTROL MEASURES

Some measures editors can take for controlling expenses include buying supplies in bulk to achieve quantity discounts from suppliers; paying as many bills in advance as possible, because some suppliers offer cash discounts; using budget surpluses to help fund projects for the coming year; taking bids on supplies and services (even though this will add time to the requisition process); and making reservations for airlines and hotels well in advance to take advantage of lower fares and rates. In addition, it might be a good idea to appoint an assistant managing editor as cost-control officer for the newsroom.

DETERMINING SALARY LEVELS

For various reasons, the executive editor may not have as much flexibility as he or she would like in setting salary levels in the newsroom. For one thing, the publisher may take the payroll expense under his or her wing, due to the large cost it represents. For another, the newsroom may be represented by a union such as the Newspaper Guild, so the salary levels may arise out of labor negotiations which the editor may not even be a party to. Then, once the contract is agreed to, the salaries are something the editor will have to live with.

Nevertheless, some editors do have quite a bit of flexibility in setting salaries, and there are a few guidelines that are helpful. For one, the Newspaper Guild periodically lists the salaries for reporters, copy editors, and photographers at member newspapers. Excerpts from one such listing are contained in Exhibit 7. In addition, state and regional press associations will periodically poll member newspapers to get an average salary for the area. Other press agencies, like the Inland Daily Press Association, also report salary averages. Editors and publishers at conventions like the ones the American Society of Newspaper Editors (ASNE) and Associated Press Managing Editors (APME) host also exchange salary information. One guideline that seems to have general acceptance is that the city's superintendent of schools and the newspaper's top editor should be making about the same salary.[18] That means if the superintendent is making $75,000 annually, all but one salary in the newsroom will fall below that level, if the newspaper is using this guideline.

A never-ending job of any editor is to fight with the publisher for higher salaries for the newsroom staff. The fact that newspaper reporters are generally underpaid, when compared to other college-educated professionals, is no secret. Many observers feel if something isn't done to increase the level of pay, the newspaper industry will lose its best potential talent to other fields.

NEWSROOM UNIONS

Journalists in many large daily newsrooms are represented by a union. The national union representing most organized journalists is the Newspaper Guild. Large as it is with its 31,500 members,[19] the Guild is still a stranger to the majority of U.S. newsrooms and to the 200,000 editorial and commercial employees it counts as eligible for membership. Still, the staffs of such prestigious news organizations as *The New York Times, The Washington Post,* The Associated Press, United Press International, *Time,* and *Newsweek* are covered by

Exhibit 7
Some Top Minimum Salaries in 20 Guild Newsrooms

	Minimum	After
New York Times	$ 929.16	2 years
Chicago Sun-Times	866.03	5 years
Minneapolis Star & Tribune	792.00	5 years
Philadelphia Inquirer	743.59	5 years
Denver Post	738.00	5 years
San Francisco Chronicle	733.86	6 years
Cleveland Plain Dealer	680.00	4 years
Washington Post	664.35	4 years
Boston Herald	589.81	4 years
Indianapolis Star	583.95	6 years
Portland Press Herald	559.00	4 years
Lowell (Ma.) Sun	543.00	4 years
Scranton Times	519.46	5 years
Sioux City Journal	447.20	4 years
Lexington Herald-Leader	425.00	4 years
Yakima Herald-Republic	414.00	4 years
Rochester Democrat & Chronicle	380.00	4 years
Newport News	340.00	2 years
Utica Observer-Dispatch	335.00	5 years
Chattanooga Times	280.00	4 years

Note: The average top minimum for reporters and photographers on 20 of the 121 Newspaper Guild Contracts as of October 1, 1987. The average top minimum for all Guild papers on that date was $595.94. This table is excerpted from information provided by *The Guild Reporter.*

the Guild. Other papers, like the *Boston Globe,* have resisted Guild overtures, but some of these papers have their own independent union instead.

Membership has not been increasing for the Guild, and many observers feel it is losing some of its clout and is beset by internal problems.[20]

The most immediate font of trouble for the Guild is the rapid-fire abandonment by their publishers of dailies with proud traditions, leaving one metropolitan center after another with only one paper of city-wide importance. No amount of Guild cooperation in cost-cutting has proved to be much of a life-extender, nor has any serious attempt been made at reviving the casualties under employment ownership. . . . The Guild's problem is that the industry moves increasingly under the command of giant communications conglomerates, with whose ever-expanding scope and power it is utterly unequipped to cope. The Guild has never developed any counterpart of the industrywide or companywide bargaining structures that enabled other unions born in the Great Depression to establish some measure of parity in negotiations with the behemoths of the mass production industries.[21]

Some observers also feel the Guild needs to pay more attention to issues affecting the quality of journalism rather than economic issues.

Despite the speculation about the Guild, it still is a formidable bargaining force at many newspapers. Included in Guild contracts are provisions detailing the Guild's jurisdiction at the newspaper; the wages paid its members; the hours worked by its members; the overtime rate; dismissal pay; vacations; sick leave; military service; job security; leaves of absence; insurance and welfare; and pensions. Obviously, in newsrooms where the Guild is present, the editors in charge face several restrictions in their management authority.

BUDGETING THE NEWS HOLE

Keep in mind that the second largest expense item for the whole newspaper is newsprint, and you realize how imperative it is that the newsroom not waste space in the newspaper. Most metro dailies run an advertising-to-editorial ratio of about 65 to 35 percent. There isn't a large daily in existence that wouldn't like to open up more space in its news hole, and most will do it if news conditions warrant it, but it would be fiscally irresponsible for an editor to ask for more news space than he or she really needs. The larger the news hole, the more pages must be added to the paper; the more pages added to the paper, the larger that second-biggest expense item becomes. Part of the editor's job is to convince the publisher of the need for more news space if it is in fact needed. However, that editor had better go armed with good reasons, because a smart publisher will not waste newsprint.

One technique some editors use in planning out the year's general news hole is to keep in mind the times of the year that will require more (or less) of a news hole. Christmas is traditionally a slow time, as are the summer months. October and November, however, are big news months, especially in state and national election years. Editors must also project the timing of upcoming in-depth news features and series and request space ahead of time. The editor must remember that his is only one department—even though he might consider it the most important—in the entire newspaper. As such, he is competing with all the other newspaper departments for resources.

GOOD COMMUNICATIONS ARE VITAL

Good communications are vital in the daily process of getting out the newspaper. Most newsroom veterans have asked themselves at one time or another, "If we're supposed to be in the business of communicating, why do we do such a poor job of it in the newsroom?" Possibly because reporting and editing are seen as such individualistic jobs, it is hard to convince the newsroom staff there must be more of a team effort unlocked by good staff communications. If, for instance, an assignment editor wants a particular story focus, he must communicate that desire to the reporter who is sent to cover the event, and if that communication has not taken place, the editor should not be surprised when the story comes back with a different focus. Likewise, if the dayside city editor expects to see a story on the metro page the next morning, he should communicate that wish to the nightside city editor before leaving, or if a reporter on the city desk happens to be working on the same story as a reporter on the lifestyle desk, the editors of these two desks had better be in regular communication to see the stories don't duplicate each other.

These and many other newsroom situations call for effective communications. Even standards and ethical policies must be communicated so the reporters are not operating in the dark, only to come back to a fire-breathing editor who now tells them, "We don't do it that way around here!" For instance, if the paper has a certain policy on handling off-the-record comments, the editor cannot assume the reporter knows what the policy is if he hasn't been told. One sad commentary on bad newsroom communications surfaced in a Dallas newsroom several years ago when a reporter was bemoaning the lack of newsroom communications between editor and reporter. "The policy around here seems to be, 'Use your own judgment, except in cases where it doesn't apply'." The problem is, no one was ever told what those inapplicable cases were.

Management communications is at the heart of performance in a newsroom. The newsroom is like a dry prairie waiting for a spark to ignite a sweeping fire of rumors, and this is especially true for a news staff who is not being told what management is up to. Certainly if a newspaper wants to conduct business under a more participative management style, good two-way communications are essential, and it is up to management to set them in motion. Trust is a key ingredient in well-managed newsrooms, and it is up to management to foster that trust by taking input from the news staff and passing information along to them.

One reason the Total Newspaper Concept (discussed in Chapter 1) is such a good management model is that it tears down the barriers between newspaper departments and fosters more communication across departmental boundaries. Such should also be the case in the newsroom itself. There needs to be more communication between, for instance, the copy desk and city desk; the city desk and lifestyle desk; the state desk and the city desk; and so on.

As in most undertakings, there are two aspects to a newspaper's internal communications system: structure and performance. On the structural side, most newspapers have the following internal communications systems in place: a management committee or some top-level interdepartmental group; intradepartmental meetings; an employee newsletter; a suggestion box; bulletin boards; and a routing system for professional publications and correspondence. These components, although vital, only represent the means by which communication can be achieved, however. The degree to which they are actually used is the performance side of the equation. Two main reasons these structural systems no longer suffice in and of themselves are that most newspaper jobs now re-

quire greater knowledge and coordination than in the past, and, as never before, employees not only insist on being kept informed, but they also want to
provide feedback to management.

To be sure, a paradox exists in newsroom communications. Journalists are
hard-pressed just to handle their daily tasks, let alone become involved in a
sophisticated system of internal communications requiring commitment and time.
Therefore, although journalists want more input into decisions affecting their
jobs, they don't want to be saddled with more meetings and assignments to
input their ideas to the system. That paradox is the editor's challenge: to find
a way of getting the staff's input while not overloading them with too many
additional chores related to that input.

Excellent communications at upper levels can be misleading, causing executives to believe that it exists down through the ranks. Consequently, more
newspapers are building in feedback systems through which managers can de-
tect communication failures. Publisher John H. McMillan of Oregon's *Salem
Statesman-Journal* uses the following system, for instance.[22] The publisher and
top editors move around frequently in the newsroom just to talk to and listen
to reporters; there is a weekly meeting with the top 25 supervisors; there are
postings on all the bulletin boards of the minutes of intradepartmental meetings,
and there are weekly meetings of the 7 division heads; there is a monthly house
organ; letters from the publisher are inserted into paycheck envelopes every
two weeks; an orientation for new employees that permits them to talk with all
division heads is provided; and a weekly meeting is held with night supervisors—on their time—as are weekly meetings of all staffs with division heads.

The Vancouver Sun came up with some 25 recommendations for improving
internal communications at their newspaper.[23] These were then issued in a 30-
page summary and distributed by immediate supervisors to all newsroom staff.
Some of the barriers to effective communications that were found are the following:

- Information often does not flow in an organization because it has value as currency,
  particularly as currency related to power. Superiors can hold power by not filling in
  subordinates on needed information. Subordinates can undermine the power base of a
  superior by not passing on needed information.

- The increasing need for more information increases as work becomes more complex
  and interdependent between different units in the newsroom and the different divisions
  in the newspaper. Ironically, information overdose can occur. Then the recipient starts
  filtering information out of front-line consciousness.

- Complexity of the message versus complexity of the receiver can be a barrier. The
  sophistication of the receiver of information must be equal to the sophistication of the
  message, otherwise the message will not be received.

- Generalized messages that try to reach everybody but instead reach nobody are also a
  problem. Sometimes the message is too hard for half, and too easy for the other half
  of the recipients. In a differentiated organization, the need is for different messages
  for different receivers.

• Inadequate attention to feedback is also a barrier. Communications must be a two-way street.

COVERING THE NEWS

The main job of the news staff is, of course, to cover the news. To complete this task, editors are responsible for organizing an effective system of beat coverage, in addition to covering the bases on current issues and investigative projects. This section will discuss three variations of the traditional beat system, a modification of that system known as Module or Cluster reporting, and a third system utilizing social indicators. This third system can actually be integrated into any of the other systems.

The Traditional Beat Systems

Geographical Coverage. Smaller dailies and weeklies are generally restricted in how they map out their coverage of the town's news center by the small number of reporters at their disposal. This number is as small as one or two on some weeklies, or maybe as large as eight on a small daily. Newspapers that field such small staffs generally deploy their reporters on a geographical basis around town for the most efficient coverage. Since one idea of the beat system of reporting is to have a reporter cover the same beat, meeting with key sources, day after day, it is not a bad idea to group these beats by geographical location in town so reporters can cover one, two, or even three news centers in the same sweep, then return to the newsroom to write the stories.

One Beat, One Reporter. This is the most commonly used system at medium-size dailies and even some large ones. The idea is, again, simple: decide which beats you want covered and assign one reporter per beat. Standard beats at most dailies include City Hall, Police and Fire, Criminal and Civil Courts, Country Government, Education, Politics, and the Statehouse if it is in the area or if the paper is large enough to report on statehouse activities. Other beats are many and varied, depending on the location of the newspaper and the kind of market it serves. For instance, the *Kansas City Star* would have an Agri-Business beat, while the *Boston Globe* has a strong higher education beat. If there is a federal courthouse in town, there will also be a Federal beat. In most cases, the above beats will be staffed by reporters from the city desk and possibly the state desk if the paper has one. Other news beats, like Business, Features, Sports, Travel, and Food are so diverse that entire staff divisions are assigned to cover them. They are not part of the city desk operation.

One news beat that is of relatively recent origin and that has been drawing a lot of attention lately is the Science and High Technology (some papers call it the Sci-Tech) beat. Papers like the *Boston Globe* put out an entire weekly section on science, high tech, and medical research matters. Still other important beats these days are Business, Arts & Entertainment, and—in many papers—Religion.

Team Coverage. This is simply a sophisticated version of the One Beat, One Reporter method. Sometimes standard beats like Police or City Hall become so diverse in and of themselves that two or more reporters are assigned to cover each of them. This is a good practice, but it is also a luxury only larger dailies can afford. *The Dallas Morning News,* for instance, has often assigned two or more reporters to cover police at the same time. Sometimes one of these reporters will cover external police activity, while the other reporter might cover internal police activity. This is especially true when the particular department has itself become the source of regular stories because of its unusual way of doing things, or if there is conflict present in the ranks.

At City Hall, one reporter might be responsible for the Mayor's Office, while another might cover the City Council, and still another might cover the various administrative departments in City Hall. Of course, teams can be constituted at any time, and usually are when there is more news than usual coming out of a particular beat. However, these are usually reactionary practices, and some newspapers prefer to anticipate such coverage in advance and set up beats accordingly. Two beat systems that lend themselves to anticipatory reporting are Module Reporting and Social Indicator Reporting.

Module Reporting

It is difficult to tell when or where this system of beat coverage began or who is responsible for it. Several newspapers have probably experimented with it in some form or another. One such paper was the *Dallas Times Herald,* which tried the system on its city desk several years ago. Under this system of coverage, the editors develop modules or clusters to cover. These modules are large news centers around the city which produce news in the areas of Government, Law Enforcement, Education, Politics, Courts, and Suburbs. Thus, general subject areas like these become the modules into which are assigned groups of reporters. The size of these groups can vary, but should be at least five or six reporters to each module for best use of the system. There should also be a General Assignment Module to catch the everyday news and features that inevitably fall between the cracks of the other modules or that don't really fit their spheres of interest.

After reporters are assigned to the modules, the modules elect leaders or captains. These module leaders then confer weekly with each other and with editors from the city desk. The leaders then assign reporters in their module to the appropriate news center for that day. The leaders also report in addition to directing coverage of their modules. By assigning reporters to general subject areas like Government or Education, the modules have a chance to concentrate their coverage on a particular news center within that subject area on any given day. For instance, if news at City Hall is dry, the Government team could be dispatched to the County Courthouse instead where the events are more interesting.

A "Saturation Day" can also be a part of this system, wherein most of one module could converge on one specific story in one news center. Saturation Days can arise as needed by the day's events or issues.

Another feature of the Module System is the "loaner" where a reporter from one module can be loaned to another module for a specific story that might require specific credentials not possessed by members of that module. For instance, a story on a new type of civics class at the high school might benefit from having a local government reporter cover it instead of someone from the Education Module.

The advantages and disadvantages of this system are fairly obvious. One big advantage is the flexibility it gives editors to assign reporters to different beats while still keeping them within the arena of their knowledge. It also allows flexibility to move beat reporters to the hottest beats of the day, thereby overpowering the competition and going deeper on stories. A disadvantage with the Module System is that it puts more links in the supervisory chain between reporter and editor. This can inject more of a possibility for misunderstood communications or for communication that doesn't quite filter down from editor to reporter. On the other hand, better communication between divisions of the city desk could result, as module leaders and editors meet weekly to share ideas and discuss current story projects.

Social Indicator Reporting

In their book, *Handbook of Reporting Methods,* McCombs, Shaw and Grey introduced what they term "social indicators." These are indices that can guide reporters and editors in their coverage of news.[24] Social indicators are all forms of evidence—but primarily statistical evidence—that enable a community to assess where it stands, and where it is going with respect to its values and goals. Social indicators also help in evaluating specific programs and determining their impact.

Every governmental office, from the town level up to the federal government, develops and maintains such social indicators. A partial list of some simple indicators kept by a local community, for instance, is as follows:

• City Clerk's Office: Statistics on business licenses issued, dog licenses issued, fishing and hunting licenses issued, birth and death certificates, number and types of ambulance calls, number and types of fire calls, number and types of police calls, and building and zoning permits applied for and issued.

• Planning Commission Office: Statistics on population trends for the city, age distribution for city residents, age-sex distributions, comparison of median ages for city residents, comparison of median school years completed, annexation trends, population projections for the city, unemployment trends for the city, and occupation trends for city residents.

- Public Works Department: Statistics on daily water pumped, water levels, comparisons of usage on particular days and months, and comparisons of what units need servicing most frequently.

- District Court Clerk: Statistics on number of arrests for a given period, number of convictions for a given period, kinds of crime per specific time period and per area of the city, demographics of victims and criminals, average time of incarceration before trial, kinds of weapons used, number and types of cases plea-bargained, numbers of first-time and repeat offenders, and average time of trial.

- School Administration Office: Statistics on attendance, truancy, enrollment, cost of education per pupil, percentage of juniors taking the SAT test, percentage of seniors going on to college, average SAT scores, budgets for each school, demographics of students at each school, and teacher salary levels.

Any editor or reporter with any kind of creativity and a good nose for news can see the possible in-depth pieces that could be done by tracking any of these statistics, using that data to form questions for public officials, and then interviewing people impacted by these trends.

The beauty of social indicators is that they look at both the social ills and assets within a community. Social indicators can track divorces, and they can track new construction of homes equally well. Social indicators also look behind the structure the government has established to meet problems, to the performance of that structure. For instance, they can look behind the city's new Rape Hotline for women who have been attacked, to the number of hours it is actually staffed, and the number of calls handled on a weekly or monthly basis.

Social indicator reporting can also be woven into any system of beat coverage as an adjunct to that system. Beat reporters are just trained to monitor the important social indicators on their beat. In this way, a small number of observers can monitor vast segments of the community by tracking a few statistics that have already been kept by someone else. The productivity per reporter is higher because they have more to observe and more from which to draw stories.

The goals of Social Indicator reporting are to anticipate trends and issues, and to form "social mosaics"[25] out of otherwise seemingly isolated events. Therefore, social indicators offer a grand strategy for a broad orientation toward community reporting. The best tactics available for transforming this strategy into effective stories are the principles of quality journalism, buttressed by techniques borrowed from behavioral scientists: observation, content analysis, and random sample surveys.[26]

FACING THE LIBEL THREAT

An ever-present and, some would say, ever-changing threat to covering the news is the specter of libel suits. Editors and reporters have used the phrase "chilling effect" often in recent years to describe the impact of some recent libel rulings. Indeed, the mere threat of libel has been enough to cause some newspapers to moderate their reporting on certain sensitive stories. Publishers realize that, even if a newspaper winds up winning a libel case, it can still spend hundreds of thousands of dollars and waste months—and maybe even years—in defense of its position. "First Amendment Insurance," as libel insurance is sometimes called, moderates the heavy impact of such libel suits, but libel insurance premiums are expensive, especially if the coverage is large enough to do the job, and some smaller newspapers find it difficult to justify that expense.

A full discussion of libel is beyond the scope of this book, but most editors understand that a statement is actionable at law if it is false and damaging to an identifiable person or persons, and if that statement was made with "reckless disregard" as to its truth. This latter part of the general libel definition is the malice issue. A newspaper will have little defense if it prints a false and damaging story about an identifiable individual and does so on the basis of shoddy and incomplete reporting. Good sources come into play here, and if a plaintiff can show the reporter should have known better than to trust this particular source, he can prove the newspaper guilty of libel with malice. On the opposite side of the courtroom, however, a newspaper may be in good shape even if its statement is found to be false and damaging. That could occur if it can show it had good reason to trust this source who had knowledge of the issue and who had proven trustworthy in the past. The best newspapers will choose, however, not to rely on absence of malice. Instead they will insist that their reporters come up with a fair and truthful story.

GOING FOR THE GOLD: ACCURACY AND FAIRNESS

In 1986, the Newsroom Management Committee of the Associated Press Managing Editors Association issued a report on handling errors in the newsroom. In it were results of interviews with several editors on how they handle errors in their newspapers. A sampling of opinion follows.[27]

• Jim Willis, (not the author of this book) managing editor of the *Birmingham Post-Herald,* said, "After the correction is printed I send a clipping of it to the reporter or copy editor and ask them to report back to me on how it happened and how we can keep it from happening in the future."

• Marcia McQuern, managing editor for news of the *Riverside Press-Enterprise* in California, has a similar system. "The person who has made the error has to write me a note explaining how it happened and how it could be avoided. And we file those in their personnel files. When times comes up to review for merit, we look at how many there have been and . . . if they've got a pattern going we start looking at what we can do."

• Paul Reynolds, managing editor of Maine's *Bangor Daily News,* said, "We have a weekly meeting on Monday afternoon at 3 which is called the desk-head meeting. If somebody makes a mistake . . . we all discuss it. That's the primary way of communication. When a reporter makes an error, the managing editor, city editor and reporter meet privately and we discuss it, how it happened, and we just decide if there was a lesson to be learned.''

Of course, the frequency of mistakes can be lessened if quality people are hired in the first place and work under good supervision (not necessarily tight supervision, though). One of the most important areas an editor can concentrate on when hiring a person is that candidate's commitment to accuracy and fairness in their reporting. Clips can go only so far in showing that commitment; how the candidate addresses the issue in the face-to-face interview, and references from former editors, are the best ways of assessing that commitment.

Many editors do not believe in tying the concept of accuracy to punishment, however. They feel that the threat of punishment is no way of raising the level of accuracy in the newsroom. Indeed, editors must begin with the idea that the reporters they hire crave accuracy and fairness in their reporting, and let the reporters prove them wrong. What most reporters need are encouragement and coaching on how to overcome problems of errors, and coaching is one key responsibility of the editor.

NOTES

1. Carl Sessions Stepp, "What Editors Do All Day," *Quill* (February 1985), p. 27.

2. Stepp, "What Editors Do," p. 27.

3. *Gannetteer* (March 1982), Inside front cover.

4. Timothy Crouse, *The Boys on the Bus* (New York: Balantine, 1973), pp. 20–23.

5. Herbert J. Gans, *Deciding What's News* (New York: Random House, 1980), p. 42.

6. William F. Glueck, *Personnel: A Diagnostic Approach* (Dallas: Business Publications, Inc., 1978), chapters 4–8.

7. Glueck, *Personnel*, p. 89.

8. Glueck, *Personnel*, pp. 104–106.

9. Ruth W. Stidger, *The Competence Game: How to Find, Use and Keep Competent Employees* (New York: Thomond Press, 1980), p. 2.

10. Stidger, *The Competence Game*, pp. 5–6.

11. M. K. Guzda, "Complexities in Labor Law," *Editor & Publisher*, 6 April, 1985: 18.

12. Steve Weinberg, "The *Columbia Daily Tribune:* What's Right with Small-Time Journalism," *WJR* (May 1985) pp. 39–40.

13. Weinberg, "The *Columbia Daily Tribune*," pp. 39–40.

14. Howard Rausch, presentation Magazine Publishing Week, New York City: 6 May 1981.

15. Rausch, presentation.

16. "Developing Newspaper Minorities," *Minorities in the Newspaper Business* (November-December 1986), pp. 1–2.

17. Jean Gaddy Wilson, "Women in the Newspaper Business," *Presstime* (October 1986), pp. 31–37.

18. Tom Blount, "Setting Salaries," *Newsroom Management Handbook* (Washington: ASNE, 1985), Chap. 24, p. 1.

19. A. H. Raskin, "The Once and Future Newspaper Guild," *Columbia Journalism Review* (September-October 1982), p. 26.

20. Raskin, "The Once and Future Newspaper Guild," p. 28.

21. Raskin, "The Once and Future Newspaper Guild," p. 28.

22. Malcolm F. Mallette, *How Newspapers Communicate Internally,* (Reston, Va.: American Press Institute, 1981), pp. 8–12.

23. Mallette, *How Newspapers Communicate,* pp. 4–11.

24. McCombs, Maxwell, Donald Lewis Shaw, and David Grey. *Handbook of Reporting Methods.* (Englewood Cliffs: Prentice-Hall, 1978), pp. 18–32.

25. McCombs, Grey, and Shaw, pp. 18–32.

26. McCombs, Grey, and Shaw, pp. 18–32.

27. John Vormittag, "Handling Errors," *Managing the Newsroom.* Report from the 1986 Newsroom Management Committee of the APME Association Convention, October 21–24, 1986, Cincinnati, Ohio, pp. 32–34.

9

THE EDITOR AS A PEOPLE MANAGER

Newsroom leadership is a thorny problem that many editors have been trying to solve for years. Perhaps Walker Lundy, executive editor of the *Tallahassee Democrat,* captured the feelings of many editors when he noted in an article that

> We are not your pointy-headed, button-downed corporate managers—we are newspapermen and women. *Editors,* by God . . . we are not executives. We're reporters who've gotten one promotion too many. We're paid too much money to go back now where the fun is. But we'll be damned if we'll be managers.[1]

Having expressed these feelings, however, Lundy quickly assumes a more practical bent and warns editors that, tantalizing as this philosophy is, it will unfortunately not work in newsrooms anymore. He warns editors to discard it and acknowledges that, really, it never has worked. It was just easier before to get away with avoiding being a manager in the newsroom.

Many editors still find themselves trying to make Lundy's caricature work, however, and too many newsrooms still evidence this lack of management ability. As a result, Lundy's theory is worth dissecting.

First of all, there appears to be an aversion to management types in general. They are seen as being too narrow-minded, and editors are worried they may be cast in the same mold. Alas, editors made one mistake too many in their careers, took the promotion, and became editors. At least they can now revel in the role of the cigar-chomping or chain-smoking newsroom dictator with, possibly, a heart of pure gold. They have seen it all and done it all and are now demanding, in an eccentric manner, that it be done their way, right now. Enter Walter Burns, the crusty editor of "Front Page" fame, exit Mr. Nice Guy. Reporters, they feel, may hate them now but will love them later and describe fondly to novice reporters what characters they were privileged to serve under. Anyone who has been in reporting very long has run into this type of editor.

It's not that there aren't legitimate reasons for editors to adopt this management philosophy. William Murray, senior research associate with the University of Chicago Human Resources Center and a consultant on newspaper management problems, feels much of the trouble editors have as managers stems from the nature of their work, past and present.

The "comfort level" for editors is the role of individual contributor which, as a reporter, they vacated and which they may revert to at any time. It is hard for them to leave their individual contributions behind and instead contribute through others as a manager. Journalists are unconventional managers, partly because the traditional role of a news person is to be skeptical of anything, even organizational policies.[2]

Murray's opinion is validated by the results of a supervisory styles inventory administered to thirty editors at a newsroom leadership seminar in Chicago. The inventory showed the fewest number of editors practicing the "Official," standard-operating-procedure style of management. Instead, more editors fell into the "Expert" category, managing on the basis of personal experience. These editors said they frequently use statements such as, "When I was on the street . . ." or, "Just hand it in; I'll fix it up." Looking at the group profile for the 30 editors, Murray said the percentage following the "Official" style was much lower that what he had seen of managers in the other professions. This, he said, added to his view of editors as being rather unconventional managers.

Harvard management specialist Chris Argyris found similar results when he conducted an intensive participant observation study of a major newsroom. The study led Argyris to conclude that newsrooms are run by managers who are reluctant to accept new ideas, reluctant to confront interpersonal conflicts overtly, and quick to centralize decision making and to pit reporters against each other in an arena of competition. Although this was the dominant style he discovered, he also found another style which was the opposite of this "controlling, directive style." This second style was characterized by passive managers who kept themselves withdrawn and distant from newsroom life.[3] His conclusions regarding these two styles were:

The aggressive leadership causes conformity, dependence, submissiveness, inhibits innovation and internal commitment. The passive leadership 'cops out' and encourages the more aggressive leadership to predominate. Thus, both styles feed back to reinforce the difficulties of the system. There are at least two difficulties involved with these policies. First, they help to reinforce the win-lose dynamics of a competitive environment. This in turn increases the subordinates' mistrust of each other and their dependence on their superior. Second, it becomes difficult for the superior to learn when the unmanageable point has been reached, because the persons involved will tend not to inform the leader.[4]

One thing many editors and publishers find themselves agreeing on in the 1980s is that editors must broaden their understanding of management styles. This is necessary not just to bring editors into twentieth-century management circles, but because of the following as well:

1. The best possible news product can only be obtained when the newsroom staff is effectively motivated and managed.
2. An editor's leadership style has a direct bearing on how well the newsroom is managed.
3. Every news operation should make use of effective supervisory styles gleaned from the results of systematic, scientific research carried out by management specialists.
4. An editor who knows the importance of understanding reporters, trusting them and trying to meet their needs, will become a more effective manager and will have more committed reporters at his or her disposal.

THE UNIQUE CHALLENGE OF MANAGING REPORTERS

If editors are not traditional managers, reporters are certainly not traditional workers. Since the successful motivation of workers springs from an understanding of those workers, editors would be wise to consider those whom they manage and their differences from other employees. The first thing most editors would see is that the attitudes editors seek in prospective reporters (aggression and skepticism most notably) are the same traits that make managing these people so difficult. Other such traits—so welcomed at hiring and so perplexing later—are idealism, creativity, individualism, and strong ego needs.

Several researchers have delved into the psyche of journalists and come up with some interesting findings. Recently David H. Weaver and Cleveland Wilhoit found that the two most important predictors of job satisfaction for journalists—especially younger ones—is their esteem for the job their organization is doing and the frequency of feedback received from supervisors. They also found that journalists still perceive substantial authority in their work, but there is a big decline in the number who feel they can determine a story's emphasis.[5]

Dr. John C. Merrill, of the School of Journalism at Louisiana State University, asserts there is a definite polarity among journalistic orientations and that the finished stories will reflect these orientations. Merrill says any reporter will adopt traits from one of two basic orientations, which he calls "Scientific" and "Artistic." Merrill feels the reporter who follows one or the other will operate from different sets of assumptions about the job, and will exhibit different reporting and writing styles as a result. The Scientific orientation—also called the "Aloof" orientation—is the orientation beginning journalism students find in most reporting textbooks such as one which states, "Objectivity is not only alive and kicking; it remains a 'glory' of American journalism."[6]

The Artistic orientation, however, represents the reporter who wants to bring all of his or her senses into the reporting. These senses go beyond the mind and include the reporter's emotional reaction to the event and, Merrill says, it looks at traditional reporting as being too sterile. These journalists believe reporters who are seeking truth should report it as they see, hear, and feel it. Merrill notes that both these orientations run in the blood of most reporters, but that one will usually dominate and define a particular interest.

Merrill also asserts that reporters will have one of four basic allegiances: to people, institutions, ideologies, or events and facts. As with the orientations, there is often an overlap, but, at any time, there is the tendency for one to dominate. It is worth noting that only one of these four allegiances is oriented toward the journalistic institution. The remainder are more individualistic allegiances.

To an editor, these orientations and allegiances can spell trouble. For instance, the Artistic reporter is the individualist who may not recognize an absolute set of rulers or the authority of editors, but the Scientific reporter can also cause management problems because of the sheer aggression and single-mindedness he or she possesses. After all, these traits can run counter to the editor's ideas. For example, the cautious editor may rebel at running information that he feels is undocumented, while the reporter who has worked all day preparing it may push hard for its publication. There is no reason to think that an uncompromising, aggressive, and outspoken reporter will act any differently toward the editor.

The point is that nowhere among the dominant traits of most reporters are such traits as group-centeredness, team-playing, or the like. Instead there is the individualist who shies away from becoming a joiner or conformist. Therefore, any attempt by a management-minded editor to force a reporter into organizational loyalty may be met with resistance. Many editors of smaller newspapers have found this out while trying to convince their reporters of the need to contribute ''fluff'' stories to an annual Progress Edition of the newspaper.

This does not mean that even idealistic, skeptical reporters cannot come to see their goals and the organization's goals as coinciding. Indeed there seems to be some evidence that the reporting ranks are becoming filled with more and more ''yuppies'' (young urban professionals). According to Susan Miller, director of editorial development for Scripps Howard Newspapers, there is a vast difference between the 25-year-old journalists now in the newsrooms and those aged 35 to 40. For one thing, more reporters today are interested in creative writing as opposed to investigative reporting; for another, they lack motivation to become consumed by the job; overtime is something many of them detest. There is more of a division between their private and professional life than has been exhibited by their older counterparts in the newsroom, and finally, many of these young reporters want to map out a career in journalism that has them behind an editing desk sooner rather than later.[7]

If yesterday's editor thought he has his hands full managing reporters, today's editor must really be a master of people skills. This is where effective management pays off and why a good understanding of leadership styles is so important.

REPORTERS AND STRESS

The subject of stress in the newsroom has drawn the attention of publishers and managing editors around the country as new findings suggest stress is a major contributor to burnout among journalists as well as a cause of serious health problems. Some psychologists feel newspaper people exhibit very high stress levels, but add that journalists are also stress seekers. Otherwise, they wouldn't crave the emotional high that comes from carrying out their creative acts under deadline pressure. Many journalists would, in all probability, experience withdrawal pangs and depression were they suddenly thrust into another type of job without daily deadlines.

Although some degree of stress can be healthy for journalists and act as a catalyst, too much of it can have negative effects and lead to depression. Many experts feel the frantic pace of reporting makes it especially difficult to rein in that daily tension. Journalists are, in effect, on call 24 hours a day, and never know what events might require their reporting talents from one hour to the next. In addition, not only must they worry about getting a story in under deadline, but they must also worry about the accuracy, fairness, balance—and truth—of the piece. They have a personal stake in their reporting, and they know that turning in an inaccurate piece may result in anything from a reprimand from the editor to being fired, being sued for libel, or going to jail on a contempt charge. To compound matters, reporters quickly find there are few universal rules to reporting—only guidelines that can vary from one story to the next. In other words, as Sally Fields says in her portrayal of a troubled reporter in the movie *Absence of Malice,* ''There are no rules; there's just me.''

If all this weren't enough, most journalists work under a kind of personal and professional code that prohibits any personal or emotional involvement in a story. It is not easy for a reporter to walk through the city slums doing a piece on the homeless while keeping his or her emotions in check. In fact, if that pattern is repeated on a regular basis, it is downright unhealthy, yet such is the working environment of the journalist.

Editors and reporters are often motivated by a strict allegiance to achievement. The problem is that they work in a profession that has few, if any, measurable standards of success. Certainly money is not such a standard, and how many press awards does it take to insure a reporter's job or convince him he has attained success in the newspaper business? Indeed, many journalists spurn reporting contests, feeling the judging is too ambiguous and that the whole pursuit of prizes deters reporters from their primary altruistic mission of informing the public.

One former reporter in St. Louis describes his road to burnout in the following manner:

You start out young and very idealistic. You think you're on some kind of mission. It's only when you get older that you realize it's only a business, like every other business, and that the object is to make money. When somebody comes to you and says, "We like you as a reporter, and can you do something for us"—it felt good. But after having had a lot of fights with editors, and all that, I said, what the heck. It's more of a young person's business, because you work so hard. Newspaper reporting involves a lot less stress [than television] . . . but newspaper people throw themselves into their stories a lot more than television people do.[8]

As a result of the stress problem, many newspapers are instituting programs designed to deal with encroaching burnout, yet much more should be done. More newspapers should hire staff psychologists to counsel reporters and editors on their stress and to show them how to deal with it positively. Management should encourage their journalists to use these psychologists. Editors should make sure that their reporters, copy editors, and photographers are not overworking themselves on a regular basis. More informal chats away from the newspaper may be needed between editors and their journalists to discuss things besides reporting and editing. Since physical exercise releases a great deal of pent-up tension, a great idea would be to encourage reporters and editors to form informal or formal intramural tennis, basketball, golf, and bowling teams to work out their tension and have fun in the process. The exercise need not involve competition at all. A simple aerobics class meeting a couple of times a week would be fine. The newspaper can also hold stress-management workshops—on company time—and urge the news staff to attend and participate.

If management chooses to ignore the newsroom stress problem and let the staff deal with it on their own, they may find many reporters and editors resorting to less satisfactory means, such as drugs, to lessen that tension. This is happening more often in newsrooms, and workshops for editors, such as the Associated Press Managing Editors Conference, deal regularly with this topic of drugs in the newsroom. What they find is that it is much more difficult to convince a reporter to give up drugs than to convince him or her to give up an afternoon and attend a newspaper-sponsored stress-management workshop or join an intramural exercise class or athletic team.

The newspaper business is charting new waters and encountering new icebergs. Newsroom stress is one of the obstacles resulting from the pressures of the 1980s. It must be dealt with effectively.

THE SPECIAL CHALLENGE OF COPY EDITORS

Excluding supervisory editors, there really are only two categories of wordsmiths within a newsroom: the reporter and the copy editor. Although working toward the same overall goal of an accurate and interesting story, many observers see the copy editor's job as having its own special set of frustrations. These frustrations become the responsibility of the editor to resolve. For instance, copy editors never get to cover new events, express themselves through the writing of a story, uncover wrongs in the community, or get any public recognition for their work. In addition, they seldom get their own desks (rather they get a spot on the universal desk), they have limited freedom to move about the newsroom during their shifts, and they generally have less autonomy in their work than do reporters as they are hovered over by copy-desk chiefs and news editors. Nevertheless, these newsroom employees have the same education, the same orientations and allegiances, and—in most cases—the same dreams as reporters.

It would be nice to be able to believe the perception of copy editors promoted by newspapers when they speak of them as having the respect of all in the newsroom. However, according to observers like Argyris, that respect stays hidden in the minds of those who hold it, if it is there at all. Argyris discovered in his newsroom research that the low status of copy editors in the newsroom was named by 37 percent of survey respondents as a major reason for low morale.[9] For years jokes have been widespread about reporters' fears of becoming washed up and winding up on the copy desk. Such was the doom of several hard-nosed courthouse reporters in the 1977 remake of the classic film, "The Front Page." Today, however, many copy desks are populated not with veterans, but with recent journalism graduates who may never have seen life as a reporter.

Chruden and Sherman, two personnel consultants, point out the importance of status to a job: "The status contributes significantly to the workers' feelings of self-esteem."[10] For the copy editor, however, there is an inconsistency about his or her status, and it comes because of the fact that his or her work is an important service in the newsroom, whether the copy editor is recognized for it or not. As Riblet puts it, "The copy editor wears neither star nor chevron, and his bosom never bulges with gold medals nor his pockets with coins, but he is the lifeguard of the newspaper office."[11]

Consequently, while the copy editor should be seen by others in the newsroom as a lifeguard, he is instead pitied by many as a frustrated reporter. To many, the copy editor is easy to find in the newsroom: he is the one always catching hell and never receiving praise. Considering these aspects of the copy editor's job, it is no wonder Baskette and Sissors point out, "The most important ingredient, after training and talent, is strong motivation. The copy editor must care. He must love his job. He must be motivated by a fierce, professional pride in the high quality of editing."[12]

With these considerations in mind, it is incumbent for the editor to seek to match the right person with the right job, especially if that job is copy editing. It is always easier to hire a person on the copy desk simply because of their educational background and ability to spell. As Ann Moritz, assistant to the managing editor of the *Boston Globe,* points out, "There is a real need for copy editors at newspapers today. But if we don't take people who love copy editing, we know they won't stay with us or do the best job possible."[13]

Even if a managing editor is fortunate enough to find a capable person in love with copy editing, he cannot ignore the conditions that one former St. Louis copy editor found existing in his job:

There is no privacy at all, especially if you want to make or take a personal phone call, which by the way, is discouraged. I don't even feel at liberty to walk away from the desk except on my dinner hour. Really. I feel I even have to hold up my hand if I want to go to the bathroom. The only real creative part of the job is in writing headlines, and that can be a lot of fun. But even in that you are at the mercy of the slotman who assigns stories to the copy editor. The whole tenor of the desk depends on who is in the slot. At many copy desks, there is a flurry of activity for maybe four hours, but then there is nothing to do the rest of the time. The problem is that we're professionals and we'd like to at least be able to keep busy and not feel like the doormat of the newsroom.[14]

Not all copy editors see their jobs so gloomily, but the atmosphere doesn't lend too much optimism. To see how poorly this job description fits work-related conditions deemed conducive to job satisfaction, one only has to look to management specialist William Glueck, who lists the following determinants to job satisfaction and the quality of production:

1. Degree of environmental pleasantness (freedom from unpleasant smells and noise).
2. Degree of job specialization (the more fragmented the job, the less satisfaction).
3. Degree of interpersonal conflicts (the fewer the better).
4. Degree of freedom to do the job (the more the better).
5. Degree of responsibility (the more the better).[15]

Most of these five standards conflicts with the copy editor's job. Some conflict with the reporter's job. Even interpersonal conflicts are bound to be at a high level on the copy desk because of the close proximity of copy editors to each other. Martin Gannon, an organizational behavioralist, points out that people dislike being forced to be too close to each other, and they especially dislike having their intimate space (up to 18 inches) invaded. Most interpersonal business, he says, should be conducted in the 4 to 12 foot range.[16]

The fact is that most of the working conditions on the copy desk could be brought into line with the above five standards, but it takes newsroom managers who are aware of the problems and who are willing to work to redesign the job. Again, this is a management function.

THE EDITOR AS A FRONT-LINE MANAGER

Day-to-day changes in newsroom life must be brought about by the front-line, departmental editors who have face-to-face contact with reporters and copy editors. In fact, the city editor is usually seen as the pivotal newsroom manager, since he or she usually runs the largest of the newsroom divisions. Unfortunately, front-line editors find managing a difficult task at this end of the organizational ladder. A survey done at the University of Missouri School of

Journalism found that editors feel restricted by their own supervisors when it comes to trying out new leadership styles on their subordinates. Many of the editors responding to the question, "What, if anything, prevents you from managing the way you would like to manage?" listed the policies and supervisory styles of their own superiors. Still others listed a simple lack of knowledge on how to manage effectively.[17] Nevertheless, the importance of the front line manager was aptly portrayed in a *Harvard Business Review* article stating, "Our front-line supervisors can probably have more influence on our productivity, worker absenteeism, product quality, morale of our work force, labor relations, and cost reduction than any other group of managers in the company."[18]

However, the front-line manager is caught between upper management, with its set of priorities and loyalties, and the workers themselves, who often have a different set of priorities and loyalties. An example from a St. Louis television station illustrates the point. A few years ago the station received several regional Emmy awards for a high-quality, monthly public affairs program called *Extra,* which it produced. Shortly after winning a Peabody Award for the program, the station's management decided to cancel it. It was proving too expensive to produce for the revenue it generated. It just was not cost-effective. The station manager told a local journalism review, "It's not good business sense to have 11 people produce a monthly show."[19] The program's director argued, "The program was quality-oriented. They [station managers] are just not interested in pursuing quality or spending money."[20] The front-line manager in this case was the station's news director, and he was caught in the middle. A former investigative reporter and producer, the news director was highly interested in quality news as a top priority, yet, as an executive with the station, he had to go along with upper-level decisions regarding the program and its cost.

As if this squeeze were not enough for a front-line manager, another burden is sometimes loaded on. Sometimes the front-line manager does not have the authority to implement the tasks for which he is given responsibility. Several years ago, while assigned as night city editor in Dallas, an editor recalled fielding phone calls nightly from the day city editor who was his superior. Several times the day city editor insisted the night city editor get certain stories on Page 1, when in fact only the news editor had the authority to designate their placement. However, the night city editor had the responsibility. The point is that the front-line manager needs authority commensurate with his responsibility if he is to satisfy the newspaper's goal of producing a high-quality news product.

Adding to the worries of the front-line manager is the fact that he must excel in at least two areas of supervisory competency instead of just one: technical competence and human relations. Argyris feels that the editor of a newspaper has a difficult job in facing a newsroom that is generally resistant to change and individual reporters who condemn the system but who would be threatened by changing it. After a while, he writes, "You wonder if this is all worth it.

. . . Is this what I should be doing? Maybe I should go back to my type-writer.''[21]

Fortunately, there is a way out of the trap many editors find themselves in, and that way out is in understanding and embracing the appropriate leadership styles. However, it is obvious from this discussion that the entire management team at the newspaper must understand and be committed to the right leadership style. It does little good—and it will cause inevitable frustration—if only the front-line editors attend leadership seminars. Their supervisors must also attend and become committed to developing the organization into a more effective one for all employees. That is one reason the phrase ''organizational development'' is so popular at many newspapers these days. In these papers, it is understood that different management styles must be system-wide and not just tried at one or two levels.

Before concluding this section, it seems appropriate to state what several front-line editors have to say about their jobs and see if this agrees with what the management experts have found. Most of these comments came from a recent newsroom leadership seminar in the Midwest that drew 30 editors to two days of discussion and role playing.

A Florida state editor said, ''My biggest challenge is to remain an editor who understands reporters without becoming too much of an administrator.''

A Michigan sports editor said his biggest problem as an editor was, ''They [management] come[s] in and make[s] you an editor and all of a sudden you're in charge of the guy you played second base with on the paper's softball team. Exerting authority becomes a problem.''

An Illinois editor saw a problem in the different goals among reporters and management. ''Too often we don't have common goals, and that's a problem. Maybe task forces of reporters and management would be a solution.''

A Chicago sports editor saw his biggest problem as ''motivating people and balancing fairly large egos.''

A Tulsa city editor summed it up by saying, ''The biggest problem I've found in newsroom management is the *lack* of management.''

THREE EDITORS OFFER ADVICE

David Lipman, managing editor of the *St. Louis Post-Dispatch,* saw some ''significant changes'' in 1982 in the way newspaper editors treat reporters, and he said these changes must continue if reporters are going to keep doing quality work.[22]

I believe the management of human resources in newsrooms is becoming more important. . . . And I believe more editors are looking upon their reporters as just that: human resources. We tell our editors here that our reporters are, in fact, the first line of editors. It is they who initially decide what to put in and what to leave out, and so our editors need their input.

In fact, Lipman set up various ways to get the input from his staff members. Included in the list are daily meetings with department heads to discuss the daily look of the paper, monthly meetings with department heads to go over recurring problems and new ideas, and quarterly "onward and upward" sessions at which a wider range of employees can add their insight to the operation of the news department.

Lipman sees problems with many decisions that are made today on metro dailies. He says newspapers are just not innovative enough in the types of stories they cover and in the way they cover them. "It sounds silly, but the most conservative organizations in the world are newspapers. There are too many editors who say, 'this is the way we've always done this and, by God, this is the way we're going to do it now.' " Lipman sees this lack of innovation tied directly to a lack of turnover on some dailies. He says editors or reporters who have held their jobs for 20 years are not likely to be open to suggestions from anyone, least of all younger reporters or editors. When newspapers reach this point, he says, tradition starts becoming a negative factor.

Regarding frustrations among reporters, the managing editor says there are several. "One of the main complaints from reporters is that their stories are edited too arbitrarily; that the editors don't take time to consult with them," he says. To deal with that problem, Lipman says he has counseled with editors to get back with reporters whenever possible before the stories go into print. This is especially true of major investigations and news features. "It has not been unusual for one of our reporters to get a call at his home at 4 or 5 A.M. from an editor who has a question about his story," Lipman says.

Adding to the difficulty of editor-reporter communications on 24-hour papers like the *Post-Dispatch* is the fact that editors and reporters come in on any one of three different shifts. Therefore, a reporter may file a story on one shift, have it edited on a second, and see it given final editing on the copy desk on the third, Lipman explains.

Thus, communications is one of two main areas he would like to see improved in newsroom management. The other is improving the newsroom's resources. "Too many reporters don't understand what the editor had in mind in assigning a story, and we must change that through better communication. In addition, we must provide the reporter with the necessary resources to do his job well," Lipman says. These resources run the gamut from a good reference library to working tape recorders to adequate time to do a story. Lipman feels the last item is very important. "We tell a reporter we want an in-depth investigative piece, and then give him one or two hours to get it in. That's frustrating, and it's also not possible."

Part of the time needed to do a story comes in first seeing if the story actually does exist. Consequently, Lipman likes his editors to provide reporters with ample time to research an enterprise idea to see if the story is really there. At the end of that time, the reporter and editor get together to discuss the viability of the piece. Most of this communication takes place between the reporter and

the assistant city editor. The *Post-Dispatch* has about nine assistant city editors.
"The really important communication in the newsroom takes place at this level,"
Lipman says. "I can go out there and give pep talks and listen, but it does
more good if there is good, everyday communication between the assistant
editors and the reporters they actually supervise."

As for reporters, most all have a beat to cover, and the division between
general assignment and beat reporter is not that evident in most cases. Frequently the *Post-Dispatch* will double up on coverage in any given beat area,
so the reporters need to have a certain degree of flexibility.

To meet the problem of reporter burnout, Lipman says the newspaper tries
to accommodate beat rotation whenever possible. Under the policy, editors try
to rotate reporters off their beats every few years, and it seems to work well
for both the reporter and the newspaper. "For one thing, it breaks up close
friendships that may be brewing between the reporter and his sources, which
may adversely influence the quality of reporting on the beat," Lipman says.
The newspaper also has what Lipman calls "cross-fertilization," whereby any
reporter can ask to sample another beat for a short time before committing
himself or herself to that beat permanently.

Concerning competition among reporters in the newsroom, Lipman feels,
"A certain degree of competition is good, but not so much between reporters
as *inside* an individual reporter." He feels an editor can get the most out of a
reporter by letting the reporter know how good he or she is and challenging
that reporter to show his or her best stuff.

The *Post-Dispatch* is also concerned about extramural competition. Lipman
says,

> We are very edition-conscious here. . . . We have not resigned ourselves to getting
> beat on a story by television. We try to get the story in our first edition, then update it
> as many times as needed in succeeding editions. We make over about 20 pages of every
> edition, and we try to force ourselves to beat the competition. When I go home and
> turn on the 5 P.M. news, I like to know we've already put those stories in our paper.

Overall, Lipman is concerned about the frustrations reporters have because
he believes reporter morale is tied to the quality of work the reporter produces.
"You have to grade it on an individual scale, this link between morale and
quality of work, but overall I think the happier a reporter is, the better work
he will do. That's partly because reporting and editing are as much emotional
tasks as intellectual tasks." Lipman says journalists involve themselves deeply
in their work, and the more satisfied they are with their jobs, the better they
will feel in performing them.

The managing editor feels it is the duty of the newspaper's front-line editors
to implement the management's policies, communicate with reporters, seek their
input, and provide them with the resources they need. However, he adds, few
reporters have the necessary management skills at the time they are promoted
to editing ranks. "What happens in most cases is that you have a good reporter

and you take and make him an editor. Now you've lost a good reporter and gained a bad manager,'' Lipman explains. To help solve that problem, Lipman tries to keep an eye open for reporters who have potential management abilities. These people become candidates for editing jobs, as the *Post-Dispatch* (like many other papers) likes to hire from within whenever possible. Once on the job, editors are expected to expose themselves to management instruction, whether it comes from within the newspaper in seminars by the employee relations department, or from outside in seminars by the American Newspaper Publishers Association, American Society of Newspaper Editors, or American Press Institute.

Further to the southwest, Executive Editor Jim Standard, a former Nieman Fellow, leads the news operation at *The Daily Oklahoman*. Some of his ideas on newsroom management are similar to Lipman's, and others are different.[23]

''Most frustrations among reporters are caused by the fact that you have creative people working for newspapers, and creativity many times is at odds with the small amount of available space most newspapers have to work with,'' Standard says. In short, the idealism of many reporters turns to frustration when it faces the reality of the news hole, yet Standard feels there is a solution to this problem. That answer is to communicate to the reporters the overall objectives of the newspaper and to show them the importance of their work to the overall newspaper operation. ''It sometimes helps if a reporter understands why the newspaper is put together as it is, and why the reporter is so essential to it,'' he says. In addition, the reporter should see the importance of the other departments to the finished product. The communication of this understanding is the responsibility of the editor who must pass it along to the reporters.

Standard casts a different emphasis on newsroom turnover than does Lipman. Whereas Lipman focused on the fact that too little turnover can cause too little innovation, Standard sees the darker side of too much turnover. Turnover is costly to the newsroom, he explains, both in dollars and in lost reporter-source relationships. While it may seem easier at the time to let a malcontent reporter go, Standard feels it may be better—in the long run—to try and convince that reporter to stay. To do that, the editor must do something about the causes of turnover in the newsroom. One such cause is reporter frustration over not having enough time to do important stories.

''Most reporters just don't feel they have the time they need on depth pieces,'' Standard explains. He adds that, unfortunately, this is a reality in the news business, but he sees some leveling-off in turnover because of the fact that more new reporters are concerned mainly about getting a job on a metro daily and holding on to it. This is even true among people signing onto the copy desk. ''We're finding now that many recent graduates don't mind working on the copy desk, and the frustration level there isn't as high as it once used to be,'' he says. ''In fact, many graduates see the copy desk as a way to advance into newsroom management, and that is becoming more important to this new breed of journalists.''

Like Lipman, Standard sees too much arbitrary editing contributing to reporter burnout. He feels arbitrary editing is not only a frustration for the reporter but also results in inaccuracy. Editors must do something about this problem, and the answer is, again, better communication in the newsroom.

You've just got to insist on better communication between the reporter and editor. Sometimes, we have found, an editor may edit arbitrarily simple because he does not want to confront a reporter about his story. The editor feels it will take too long, that a big argument may ensue, or whatever. But consulting with reporters about their copy is a necessity.

Standard is dubious about carrying the idea of newsroom democracy too far. Although he feels reporter participation is important, he feels the newsroom can't be run on a regular basis by committees. Standard notes,

The editor is still the boss. . . . Recently a journalism professor wrote in the *Wall Street Journal,* for instance, that editors should be elected. I cut the article out and sent it to my publisher asking if he would be my campaign manager. In short, I just don't take the idea too seriously.

Still, Standard does solicit input from his editors on major decisions affecting the newsroom. For instance, one decision the newspaper had to make was whether to combine the morning and evening staffs. (The *Daily Oklahoman* and *Oklahoma City Times* were merged into one paper recently.)

I've got enough knowledge of the newsroom that I could sit down and write out a plan on how to combine our staffs. But it might not be the best plan or totally complete. So I gathered my assistants together to have them put together their own plans as well, and then asked them to check with their editors on the various desks to get their input. But, after the plans were presented, it was still my decision on which one to implement.

A common complaint among editors is they don't have time to manage. Standard doesn't buy that line, however:

We insist that our editors take time to manage. We want them to learn basic management skills, whether they learn them in-house or take college courses. Our Personnel Department runs an excellent seminar on time management, and several of our editors have taken it. Although a newsroom is a different place to manage than your normal widget factory, so many management principles are universal and can be transferred to the kind of supervising the editor does.

Standard looks for several things in potential editors. Among them are excellent technical skills as a writer, reporter, and editor; maturity and general leadership characteristics; and one other important ingredient: respect. "I look for the person who has the respect of the other professionals in the newsroom," he says. "It's very hard for a reporter to go from being one of the boys to becoming a supervisor, and this respect among his colleagues helps a lot."

Standard doesn't expect new editors to have mastered the management skills when appointed as editor, but he does expect them to learn fairly quickly. He finds that one of the most difficult things for editors to do is to learn to criticize reporters and, in some cases, to praise their work.

The ability to criticize is a trait that eludes many new editors, partly because they have been one of the boys so long. Praising and disciplining are also important, because feedback is so vital to reporters. In addition, the business of firing reporters is something the editors have to learn. Some will never fire a reporter, and others will fire too many. They see it as the quickest way around a problem reporter, but sometimes it is very costly. Yet some editors never take the time to criticize a reporter, and they let the frustration build up so high that they actually become angry at the writer and fire him too quickly.

Bill Evans, managing editor of *The Dallas Morning News*, believes in the primacy of constant communication among editors, reporters, photographers, and artists involved in developing stories. When such communication is lacking, the story produced will not equal the story intended, he says.

In addition, management must stress the highest standards of accuracy, fairness, and balance in every story, and the newspaper must be willing to admit its mistakes when they occur.

"There must be a willingness to acknowledge errors by the staff and insist that these be corrected for the record and for the credibility of the publication," Evans says.[24] One way in which newsroom management can help insure such high-quality reporting and writing is by treating journalists as professionals and providing adequate and fair pay to attract and keep the best talent available.

Evans, who gained the Managing Editor's office after several years on the copy desk and news desk, also believes in constantly trying to avoid isolation of the working press from the newsroom management team. He feels that, when this occurs, there is an immediate breakdown in two-way communications. The quality of the news product then suffers, as does newsroom morale.

Finally, Evans sees the necessity of journalists developing a thorough understanding of their market. After all, he notes, these are the people the newspaper is reporting for; therefore, their wants and needs should be addressed in the news hole. "There must be a willingness by management to accommodate the ideas and interests of the community, while maintaining a proper perspective toward any special interest or prejudice," he counsels.

THE X, Y, AND Z OF NEWSROOM MANAGEMENT

In addition to the advice from Lipman, Standard, and Evans, and the practical tips to follow this section, editors should understand something of the three mainstream philosophies of leadership and motivation, and see how they relate to managing newsroom personnel. Regardless of the often-heard comment, "I have no management philosophy; I just do what has to be done," every manager (editors included) has a management philosophy. Even the above quote represents a philosophy, one that is task-oriented and contingency-based. Further, every editor manages on the basis of some assumptions about their reporters. The editor may think the reporter is lazy, so he will exert a heavy hand; the editor may trust the reporter implicitly, and so may exert a light management touch; or the editor may think the reporter is motivated only by money and will do what he can to meet the reporter's financial demands. These and many other assumptions form the basis of an editor's individual leadership style, and many editors get into management trouble by not really examining their assumptions about their reporters to see whether they are correct. Perhaps an editor has just inherited the assumptions that his own editor had about him. Perhaps the editor believes the only way to manage is by doing so autocratically, because that was his own editor's style years ago, and his own editor did very well on the career ladder. If this is the case, then Argyris's point about editors being slow to innovate in management styles is on target.

A more enlightened approach to people managing would be at least to look at the assumptions underlying a leadership style and see if they are pertinent to professional journalists. In looking for a way to study these assumptions and relate them to appropriate management styles, one can do no better than to examine Theories X, Y, and Z of management as they have evolved over much of this century.

Theory X

The first three decades of the twentieth century saw the rise in this country of the "Scientific Management Theory," developed by management specialist Frederick Taylor. Among the assumptions undergirding this leadership style are that the worker is lazy and is motivated only by money; that few workers want much responsibility or authority; and that most workers want direct supervision and are incapable of supervising themselves.[25] Thus, Theory X arose, giving rise to such practices as the piece-rate system, and fractionalizing jobs for maximum worker output. If it was true that workers were motivated only by money, why not give them the chance to make the most they could? Job simplification was the answer, regardless of its demeaning or boring aspects to the worker. Add a shop foreman, constantly monitoring and issuing orders, and you would have the perfect solution.[26] Casting doubt on the validity of Theory X, however, were studies like the ones conducted at the Western Electric Hawthorne Plant in 1939 by management researchers and analyzing the link between—of all things—worker satisfaction and productivity. The Hawthorne studies reached many conclusions, among them the following: that the failure to treat employees as human beings was largely responsible for such things as low morale and poor performance.[27] It was also during the 1930s that Abraham Maslow published his famous "hierarchy of needs" pyramid that showed workers' highest needs are not for money, but for self-actualization.

Theory Y

As a result, out of the 1930s came a revised line of assumptions, and a modified management theory, which came to be known generically as the "Humans Relations Model," or Theory Y. Among the assumptions underlying this management style are the following:

1. Many different factors influence worker behavior.
2. Different employees want different rewards.
3. Many workers are capable of directing themselves.
4. Most workers are competent and want to contribute.
5. Employees are every bit as much a company resource as the tools and machinery.

Management set a new goal of tapping these resources in a way that facilitated achieving both employee and organizational goals. Integrating personal goals with management goals became all the rage, and practices such as putting ad salesmen on commission and putting editors on MBOs (management by objective) were legitimatized with this theory. Some employee input into decisions was also seen as beneficial. Managers gradually came to feel that if the central principal of Theory X was authority, then the central principle of Theory Y would be integration of personal and company goals.

However, for all its rhetoric and good intentions, Theory Y still held onto a key feature of Theory X: the basic management goal was to secure employee compliance with management authority. Another problem was that almost no attention was given to changing the nature of the job itself; only the relationship between employee and manager.

If Taylor was the guru of Theory X, then MIT's Douglas McGregor was the champion of Theory Y. Through most of the twentieth century these two theories have vied for supremacy in the nation's workplaces. After all, Theory X and Theory Y seemed to address all imaginable assumptions about the worker and productivity. The problem was they did not stem the tide that took the United States into the modern period of stagnant productivity and substandard product quality. Could there be a missing link?

Theory Z

A growing number of management specialists, like UCLA's William Ouchi, and top corporate managers like AT&T's Charles L. Brown, agreed, and they felt that the link was represented by a leadership style now known widely as Theory Z.[28] Although components of this theory had been around since the turbulent 1960s, when editors began hearing the cries of "newsroom democracy," this new formalized leadership style encompasses much more. The assumptions underlying it are:

1. People want to work together for a common purpose.
2. Human resources are the most valuable resources.
3. Managerial decisions should arise out of a consensus of workers affected by those decisions. (Consensus, by the way is not synonymous with a unanimous vote. The important thing in consensus building is that every member feels his or her idea has been heard, even if the vote favors a decision other than theirs.)
4. There should be no sharp distinction between the actual work of producing the goods, and the planning and coordinating of that work.
5. The quality of work life is an important influence on the quality of the work produced.

The central principle of this theory is really an extension of a modern management truism: delegate to the lowest possible level for best results. Critics who see Theory Z as just another personnel program which seeks to coddle already over-indulged workers miss the point, Ouchi says. AT&T's Brown notes, "We are dealing with nothing less than management style here."[29] To be sure, Theory Z is a workplace philosophy that adapts best to the patient Japanese culture, and some of its features, such as lifetime employment and no promotions for the first ten years, would hardly adapt themselves to U.S. culture, but two key aspects seem to characterize Theory Z and make it worth noting:

1. It is a management style built on mutual trust between employee and manager.
2. Its decisions arise out of a consensus of workers impacted by those decisions.

These aspects do seem compatible with U.S. culture and, hopefully, with the newsroom as well. Management consultant Charles Bisanz has stated that the essence of Theory Z is that, "It is not a solution devised by management, so much as it is a decision by management to share responsibility with employees in designing solutions."[30]

The chief problem in implementing Theory Z has been that it does take so much time to do it properly and to have it truly accepted by both management and employees. General Motors, for example, took a decade to implement the Quality of Worklife program into two-thirds of its plants, and in the newspaper business, an Iowa daily laid out a five-year implementation plan a few years ago for introducing Theory Z into its newsroom. Unfortunately, at the end of the second year the managing editor quit, and much of the process had to be started over with a new managing editor at the helm.

One of the reasons it takes so much time is that a solid foundation must first be laid to establish a common philosophy, objectives, and beliefs among management and workers. These are necessary before trust can be established, and trust is vital to decisions by consensus, yet newspaper people are trained from the first day of journalism school to be skeptical of everything and everyone. In fact, most changes inside newsrooms are met with skepticism and resistance. Dan Warner, editor of the *Lawrence Eagle-Tribune* in Massachusetts, told a group of graduate journalism students in Boston recently, "If you want to start a lot of grumbling and rumors going among reporters, just change one little thing in the newsroom." Theory Z is no little thing.

Some editors are finding that Theory Z principles do work in the newsroom. Scott Bosley, managing editor of the *Detroit Free Press,* stated recently, "Some news people think they are different from people at IBM or Ford. I don't think they are. People in every industry have deadlines. We are people like everyone else."[31] Executives of Knight-Ridder newspapers began installing quality control circles in their newsrooms in 1981, and today have 90 such circles in operation.[32] These circles are made up of workers in each department—including the newsroom—who meet regularly on company time to address ongoing departmental problems and offer solutions to them. The *Philadelphia Inquirer* is also taking advantage of quality circles, and has one in its newsroom. In fact, during a recent strike at that newspaper, the newsroom's quality circle kept meeting on a weekly basis.[33]

THE MISSOURI STUDY ON NEWSROOM LEADERSHIP

A 1981 study done at the University of Missouri School of Journalism sought to ascertain which management styles editors were using in their newsrooms and which styles these editors would prefer to use if they could. It also asked reporters whether their perceptions of these management styles coincided with their editors' perceptions. For this study, Theories X, Y, and Z were translated into four separate types of manager. That translation was done by Fred Pearson, then of the University of Chicago Human Resources Center. Pearson felt that his own breakdown of the "Official," "Expert," "Counselor," and "Team-Builder" managers represents individual managers instead of management styles. Thus, they were easier to identify with. What he actually did was to split Theory X into two types of authoritarian manager (punitive and benevolent). The Counselor and Team-Builder roughly corresponded with Theory Y and Theory Z managers respectively. In diagnosing personal traits of each of his individual managers, Pearson listed the following attributes:[34]

OFFICIAL: This is the manager who relies on rules and directives, preferably in writing; uses an impersonal style of management; and knows the "right way" to get things done. This is also the punitive authoritarian manager.

EXPERT: This manager operates out of personal experience and has the skills needed to perform the work. As such, he tends to give directions based on "what I say," and acts directly to get results under pressure, tending to keep a hand in the business, even when not needed. This manager is also the benevolent authoritarian.

COUNSELOR: This is the manager who maintains personal relationships with reporters, tries to build trust, and sets mutual goals with each worker; he encourages, but also expresses disappointment when goals are not met.

TEAM-BUILDER: This is the manager who uses the work group for both motivation and discipline; stresses openness and consensus; and tries to achieve balance between group choices and organizational goals. He is ready to take a personal risk with his style.

The survey form used was developed by Pearson and revised for newsroom application by a Missouri researcher. It asked editors how they handle certain situations that arise in the newsroom, and how they would like to handle those situations if they could. Reporters were asked to comment on the same points. Editors and reporters did not know which leadership style their answers were casting them into, as these were tabulated later. Editors chosen to take the survey were city editors at 140 daily newspapers. Reporters were those who had been at their paper at least one year. In looking at the results of the survey, the following findings and interpretations stand out: [35]

1. Editors came up with almost 30 management techniques to improve morale in the newsroom, and several similarities were found in the editors' and reporters' suggestions. For instance, editors and reporters agreed on "praising reporters more, preferably in public"; "criticiz[ing] when needed, preferably in private"; and "inviting comments and listening to ideas." Also high on the agenda were "hold more staff meetings"; "establish better communications between editor and reporter"; "allow reporters more freedom to work on what they want"; and "share information on upper-management policies and decisions." Most comments thus related to involving reporters more in the overall operation of the news department.

2. Among the obstacles preventing them from managing the way they would like to, editors agreed most upon "attitudes and policies of my bosses," and "budget constraints." Reporters agreed these were obstacles for their editors, along with "a lack of time for supervision," and "the editor's fear of having his authority usurped."

3. The intensity of perceptions regarding current supervisory styles of city editors was different between reporters and editors. Significant differences were found between editors and reporters for perceptions of the Expert style, for instance. Both reporters and editors felt the Expert manager type predominated slightly among editors' current leadership styles, but reporters were less sure of that than were the editors. Reporters instead had a stronger feeling that their editors were using the Official style than did the editors themselves. Therefore, as Argyris suggests, it is possible that many editors are not managing the way they assume they are.

4. Some differences were noted between reporters and editors regarding preferred leadership styles. Differences were found between editors' and reporters' perceptions of- and preferences for- the Official and Expert styles and, to some extent, the Team-Builder style as well, with more editors appearing to prefer the three styles than did

reporters. No differences were found in preferences regarding the Counselor style, although editors' preferences for this style slightly outweighed their preferences for the Expert style.

5. A wide difference of opinions was noted on how certain managerial situations should be handled. For different situations, in fact, different leadership styles were preferred.

6. Neither the reporter nor the editor group cast strong votes for the Team-Builder manager. Both groups placed the Team-Builder third in overall preferences, ahead of only the Official manager.

7. In first place of preference was the Counselor style, just edging out the Expert.

In sum, editors and reporters appeared to see a primary need in the newsroom for an editor who is—first of all—technically proficient in reporting and editing. They see an editor's own experience in the field as invaluable and prefer an editor who bases his decisions on personal experience, yet they also want an editor who treats reporters as professionals, trusting them and consulting with them on decisions affecting their stories. Both editors and reporters seem wary of pure Theory Z managers, yet they see a need for an editor who pays attention to reporters' professional needs and consults them on decisions affecting them.

One could say then, a paradox exists to some degree between what many managers feel to be the optimal management style (Theory Z) and what is prevalent and preferred in the newsroom (Theory Y). However, the results of the Missouri Study show that reporters do really want more say in at least one thing: their stories and how they are done. Whether they make the decisions or the editors make them is not so much the point as is the fact that reporters are consulted before intelligent decisions are made. Again, reporters are cut from a different cloth than are other professionals who dream about a trip up the management ladder. Many reporters want to do just one thing: report accurately. Whatever stands in the way of that goal, be it a source who won't talk or an editor who won't listen, will cause that reporter frustration, lower his morale, and eventually result in a poorer quality story which that reporter produces.

WHICH STYLE IS BEST?

After reading this chapter and the suggestions from the various editors, the student of newsroom management might well ask, "Okay, but what is the best leadership style to use?" Unfortunately there is no one best style that seems to work in every newsroom situation. This is to be expected given the many variables that may influence the leadership style used. Some of these variables are:

1. The experience level of the news staff: rookie reporters may need more of an Expert editor running the show, while veteran reporters may need more of the Counselor editor.

2. The degree of time available for making a decision affecting the news staff: if the decision must be made immediately, then it must generally be made more arbitrarily by the editor; if there is time to consider the decision, a quality-circle approach could be in order.

3. The type of problems that need attention: if it is a long-term problem, such as newsroom morale or the way the newspaper has been defining news, it would seem wise to use a quality circle approach. If the problem is which story should go in tomorrow's paper, it is the editor's decision to make.

4. The type of story being done: if the story is an in-depth piece requiring more time than normal, many conversations can result between reporter and editor on how best to handle the piece. If the story is a recurring type emanating from a reporter's beat, editor and reporter can also get together to formulate a policy on how to deal with it when it arises again. If the story is an unexpected, breaking-news story, however, then decisions must be made quickly and centrally by editors who have a grasp of the overall situation and who have handled similar situations before. Even here, however, planning sessions for future disaster coverage can include the news staff for maximum input into decisions affecting such coverage.

5. The management expertise of the newsroom editors, or at least their willingness to expose themselves to more enlightened management styles: it does no good to innovate with a Theory Z style, for example, if the editors don't understand that style or how to implement it.

6. The tolerance of upper management and their willingness to experiment with different styles of management in the newsroom: also important is the involvement of upper management in such new styles. A Theory Y or Theory Z style of management needs the support of everyone in the management structure.

7. The level of turnover in a newsroom among the staff: if a newspaper, for low pay or whatever reason, has a history of high newsroom turnover, then a more participative style of management will probably not work well unless at least the newsroom managers can be convinced to stay long enough to give the new approach a chance to work.

These and other variables make it difficult to recommend any single leadership style for all newsrooms. It is possible, in fact, that none of the mainstream theories of leadership is totally adaptable to newsroom life, because of the nature of journalists and the nature of the job and daily deadlines. However, this is not a certainty by any means. What is important is that newsroom managers continue to address the issue of leadership styles and, taking into consideration the motivations and needs of their staff, carefully devise a style that is appropriate. Why not revise one of the mainstream theories, for instance, and tailor it to the general newsroom found in most newspapers? Perhaps this tailor-made theory could be called "Theory E" for application by editors. Certainly enough is already known about reporters, copy editors, and departmental editors—as well as the conditions of the newsroom workplace—to guide in preparing such a theory. Perhaps the assumptions and profile of this Theory E could be as follows:

Assumptions of Theory E

1. Regardless of the legal debates swirling around whether journalists are professionals, the important point is that journalists consider themselves to be professionals and expect to be so treated in the newsroom.

2. Evidence from available research indicates that reporters' frustrations center most strongly on anything or anyone who threatens the accuracy, fairness, or completeness of their stories.

3. Journalists are trained to be skeptics and individualists and are, by nature, creative artists. Therefore, any effective theory of newsroom leadership must take these traits into consideration.

4. Although journalists owe allegiances to several ends, good journalists share the same overall goals in the newsroom: to produce accurate, fair, and complete copy.

5. Any system of newsroom leadership must take into account the special problems experienced by copy editors as journalists who have chosen to contribute in a behind-the-scenes fashion, but who nevertheless need to know their contributions are appreciated by their peers in the newsroom.

6. Theory E, as are all leadership theories, is built upon the assumption that the basic needs of the employee are taken care of first, before the higher needs of self-actualization are addressed. These basic needs include a salary commensurate with their professional stature and good fringe benefits.

7. The newsroom is a workplace that produces voluminous pieces of communication for the world every day. Therefore, it is not unreasonable to assume that internal communication flows in an unrestrained fashion, so confusion is kept at a minimum among the staff.

Chief Characteristics of Theory E Editor

1. The Theory E editor understands the nature of reporters, copy editors, news photographers, subeditors, and their jobs.

2. The Theory E editor examines the causes of frustrations among the news staff and targets any initiatives for improvement at those causes.

3. The Theory E editor treats the newsroom staff as professionals.

4. The Theory E editor gets actively involved in the recruiting and hiring of new staff members to help insure the high quality of professionalism in the newsroom is maintained.

5. The Theory E editor has a high standard of accuracy, fairness, and completeness regarding all stories produced. He communicates those standards to the news staff in a specific fashion, seeks input to upgrade those standards when needed, and evaluates the news staff on the basis of those standards.

6. The Theory E editor leaves as much room as possible for reporters to develop stories in their own way.

7. The Theory E editor understands the training and experience the news staff has and trusts them to do the best job possible.

8. When reasons surface for the Theory E editor to doubt a journalist's capability, she discusses those reasons with the reporter, finds out what is causing the substandard performance, and works with the reporter to bring the work up to par. If subsequent work by the reporter does not improve, the editor realizes she doesn't fire reporters: they fire themselves.

9. The Theory E editor takes time to lead, and knows when it is time to take hands off and let the staff do the technical work.

10. Realizing the bind that front-line managers sometimes find themselves in between upper management on the one hand and the staff on the other, the Theory E editor works to educate superiors as well as the staff on the need for quality journalism.

11. When recurring or long-term newsroom problems occur, the Theory E editor sees the value in using quality circles of elected newsroom staff members to work for solutions to these problems.

12. Realizing the need to stay updated on findings regarding motivation and leadership styles, the Theory E editor commits herself to participating in regular seminars on newsroom management.

If recommendations like these were implemented, it wouldn't matter what the theory of leadership was called. The results would be the same: more enlightened leadership, a better workplace, higher morale, lower turnover, and improved quality in the stories produced.

NOTES

1. Walker Lundy, "How Should Editors Manage Managing?" *The Bulletin of the American Society of Newspaper Editors*, no. 640 (March 1981) p. 3.

2. William A. Murray, interview, May 1981.

3. Chris Argyris, *Behind the Front Page: Organizational Self-Renewal in a Metropolitan Newspaper* (San Francisco: Jossey-Bass, 1974), pp. 28–29.

4. Argyris, *Behind the Front Page*, pp. 28–29.

5. David H. Weaver and G. Cleveland Wilhoit, *The American Journalist: A Portrait of U.S. News People and Their Work* (Bloomington: Indiana University Press, 1986), p. 102.

6. John C. Merrill, *The Imperative of Freedom* (New York: Hastings House, 1974), pp. 144–145.

7. Susan Miller, "The Young and the Restless: Managing Yuppies in the Newsroom," *WJR* (October 1985), pp. 36–37.

8. Michael Wines, "Burnout in the Newsroom: Are Reporters Hooked on Stress?" *WJR* (May 1986), p. 38.

9. Argyris, *Behind the Front Page*, p. 35.

10. Herbert J. Chruden and Arthur W. Sherman, Jr., *Personnel Management*, 5th edition (Cincinnati: Southwestern Publishing Co., 1976), p. 32.

11. Carl Riblet, Jr., *The Solid Gold Copy Editor* (Washington, D.C.: Falcon Press, 1972), p. ix.

12. Floyd K. Baskette and Jack Z. Sissors, *The Art of Editing*, 2d edition (New York: Macmillan Publishing Co., 1977), p. 2.

13. Ann Moritz, interview, November 15, 1985.

14. Michael Killenberg, interview, September 8, 1981.

15. Glueck, *Personnel*.

16. Martin J. Gannon, *Organizational Behavior* (Boston: Little, Brown & Co., 1979), p. 236.

17. William J. Willis, *The Editor as a People Manager* (unpublished dissertation, University of Missouri, 1982).

18. W. Earl Sasser, Jr., and Frank S. Leonard, "Let First-Level Supervisors Do Their Job," *Harvard Business Review* (March–April 1980), p. 113.

19. Steven Means, "Extra: The Life and Death of Quality TV," *St. Louis Journalism Review* (September 1981), p. 8.

20. Means, "Extra," p. 8.

21. Argyris, *Behind the Front Page*, p. 32.

22. David Lipman, interview, July 12, 1982.

23. Jim Standard, interview, July 8, 1982.

24. Bill Evans, interview by mail, September 7, 1983.

25. Charles G. Burck, *Working Smarter* (New York: Viking Press, 1982), pp. 62–63.

26. Burck, *Working Smarter*, p. 63.

27. Burck, *Working Smarter*, p. 63.

28. William Ouchi, *Theory Z: How American Business Can Meet the Japanese Challenge* (Reading, Mass.: Addison-Wesley, 1981), p. 71.

29. Ouchi, *Theory Z*, p. 71.

30. Burck, *Working Smarter*, p. 68.

31. Kathleen Newton, "In Search of Excellence," *Editor & Publisher*, 23 November 1985: 9.

32. Newton, "In Search of Excellence," p. 9.

33. Newton, "In Search of Excellence," p. 9.

34. Fred Pearson, description of four leadership styles contained in training literature developed at the University of Chicago Human Resources Center, Chicago, Illinois.

35. Willis, *The Editor as People Manager*, pp. 112–148.

10

COMPETING IN THE MEDIA MARKETPLACE

Newspapers are finding themselves in a competitive paradox in the 1980s: while their traditional competition—other paid circulation newspapers—is decreasing, other new forms of competition have arisen to keep them on their toes. These newer forms of competition include television, shoppers, direct mail, and its stepchild, "marriage mail." In times past, an editor was pleased if there was just one competitor in the city, usually in the form of the rival crosstown daily. If he were lucky enough to score an exclusive over that rival, his day was a success. In the 1980s editors must not only worry about other newspapers in the area, but also about an increasing number of television stations—network and cable affiliates both—any one of which could steal the thunder the newspaper scoop used to generate. Inasmuch as shoppers and direct mail deal almost exclusively in advertising content, they also represent threats to the financial growth of the newspaper. As a result of these new competitors, many newspaper companies have found new sets of problems at their doorstep and are charting new courses for action in the 1980s and beyond. Some of these courses include taking a new look at the nature of the newspaper product and also at its physical form. Some paths of action also include paying more attention to the seventh day of the week—Sunday—as well as the other six. Some of the answers lie in the future, as with electronic publishing. Some of them lie in the present, as in devising ways to compete with shoppers and direct mail marketers.

COMPETING IN TWO-NEWSPAPER MARKETS

In 1923 there were 502 U.S. cities with competing daily newspapers. In 1986 there were fewer than 30. In addition, about 20 others are published under Joint Operating Agreements (JOAs), allowing qualified competing newspapers to pool circulation and production resources. Some newspaper analysts are skeptical about the ability of any city to support two daily newspapers in the future. "We're not sure any city can support two profitable newspapers indefinitely," says analyst Bruce Thorp of Lynch, Jones & Ryan in Washington, D.C.[1] Other analysts believe two-newspaper cities can survive only if (1) there are clearly distinct audiences for each paper and those audiences are of sufficient size and quality to attract advertisers, or (2) if one paper is clearly dominant and the other assumes a secondary position with fewer readers, fewer expenses, fewer resources, and lesser profits. As the E.F. Hutton Co. noted in an essay for newspaper investors, it seems advertisers are deciding a second daily in a market does not provide enough additional access to the right consumers. "We think it is clear that advertisers will be increasingly unwilling to pay twice for access they believe they can get more economically and efficiently from one newspaper," the essay states.[2]

To be sure, cities such as New York, Boston, Dallas, Chicago, Houston, Detroit, and others provide news consumers with two or more large dailies, but their ranks used to be joined by cities such as Memphis, Cleveland, Buffalo, and St. Louis, all of which have seen the loss of one competing daily each in this decade alone. It seems that, in the cities where the competition does still exist, each newspaper must, as E.F. Hutton infers, carve out different markets. Consequently, you have the obvious differences in format and emphasis between such competing papers as the *Boston Globe* and *Boston Herald, New York Times* and *New York Post, Chicago Tribune* and *Chicago Sun-Times,* and so on. This is good for the readers as well as the newspapers because it offers them alternative newspapers while still keeping alive the fieriest of competition between the competing newspaper staffs.

What does emerge in cities like Dallas and Detroit are circulation battles that harken back to the Pulitzer and Hearst days, with each paper trying to establish the idea that it has the larger share of the reading audience. Competition has become so fierce in Dallas that both newspapers have filed lawsuits against the other alleging puffery in the circulation figures and attending hype. *Time Magazine* noted that the circulation war between the *Dallas Morning News* and *Dallas Times Herald* resembles a "Texas-style shootout." The article continued,

> Locked in a struggle to become the best in the booming Southwest, both papers are rapidly piling up prizes as well as profits. At the same time they are proving, as the *Times Herald* put it in a nationwide help-wanted campaign, that "there's more to Dallas than the Cowboys and Who Shot J.R." . . . Clearly in a competition like the one between the *Morning News* and *Times Herald,* the real winner is the reader.[3]

The sad fact of dwindling competition is that, in some cities, the newspaper staffs lapse into a kind of drug-induced lethargy, despite the different type of competition television provides.

As mentioned earlier, several big-city dailies are managing to stay alive and compete under the auspices of the JOA. When a newspaper publisher decides to apply for the right to do business under a JOA, it is generally with the attitude of, "Well, if we can't beat 'em, we'll join 'em." To a certain extent, that is exactly what happens. Joint Operating Agreements are an outgrowth of the 1970 Newspaper Preservation Act, which was designed to preserve independent editorial voices in a community by allowing separately owned papers to merge advertising, circulation, production, and administrative departments for efficiency and economy. The JOA provision was aimed at keeping alive metro dailies that would otherwise go under. Not everyone was in favor of the act, however. The Justice Department was against it and argued that saving a failing newspaper by such artificial means really shut the city's doors to other possible newspaper publishers who otherwise might start up a new daily in a one-newspaper city. That argument, however, has not been proven by history. Only in Washington, D.C. has another newspaper (the *Washington Times*) dared to start up after the failure of one of the city's competing dailies (the *Washington Star*).

Among the cities where JOAs have been allowed are Birmingham, Tucson, San Francisco, Miami, Albuquerque, Cincinnati, Tulsa, Pittsburgh, Nashville, El Paso, Salt Lake City, and Honolulu. Showing that the JOA is not always enough support to save a daily, however, is the example of the *St. Louis Globe Democrat*, which was under a JOA with the *St. Louis Post-Dispatch*, yet folded in 1986.

TELEVISION AS A COMPETITOR

While newspapers continue to garner the largest single share of available advertising revenue (about 27 percent),[4] television is gaining fast in netting about 21 percent.[5] Television has its greatest impact on newspapers' attempts to increase their national advertising share, because national advertisers are primarily drawn to the electronic media. For instance, Delta Airlines—which in 1985 was the 20th largest national advertiser in newspapers—spent 47 percent of its total advertising budget in newspapers in 1982, but only 30 percent by 1987.[6] Delta officials have felt television offers better breakdowns of its demographics, more flexibility in its deadline structure, and volume discounts for national—as well as local—advertisers.[7] Even large regional and chain retailers, however, are moving more and more to local television as a means of getting their message out at a low cost-per-thousand figure.

In 1986, the growth rate of local spot television revenues (14 percent) over 1985 was virtually twice that of the growth rate of national spot television revenues.[8] During the same period, the Newspaper Advertising Bureau (NAB) estimates that retail and classified advertising in newspapers grew 6.6 percent (retail up 4.8 percent and classified up 9.2 percent).[9] Clearly television has emerged as a tough competitor not only for national but also for local advertising dollars. From a news standpoint, it is impossible to beat the immediacy television provides in breaking news events, 24 hours a day. To be sure, most television stations form their daily news budgets on the basis of the morning newspaper's offerings, but even for high-profile stories like major congressional hearings, assassination attempts, or key political press conferences, newspapers have had to find a way of providing a different type of coverage. Usually that has meant going into greater depth rather than rehashing the story that emerged on television. This type of coverage presents a problem, however, for newspapers that have opted for guidelines dictating shorter news stories in general. Some observers feel afternoon newspapers are more appropriate for the in-depth pieces because breaking news has a habit of occurring later in the day and so occupies more of the attention of morning newspapers.

Not all media observers see television as posing critical problems for the newspaper industry. Noted media critic Ben H. Bagdikian has stated,

Forty years ago, many people predicted that radio and television would kill printed news. In fact, they have had the opposite effect. Coverage of presidential press conferences and sports has *increased* sales of newspapers, to which readers turned the next day for a more comprehensive look. The most spectacular gains in newspapers have been made by those like the *Wall Street Journal* and *Los Angeles Times,* which present long stories that interpret and analyze recognized developments. Thus, the odds are strong that the daily newspaper will survive as a concurrent daily information source— even assuming widespread adoption of home consoles.[10]

Supporting Bagdikian's belief are surveys like the 1983 Merit report that sought to ascertain which medium among television, newspapers, radio, and magazines the public prefers as their means of getting local, national, and international news. The survey found that newspapers lead television as the favored source of local news. When the Merit report asked people where they get most of their local news, 50 percent indicated they prefer newspapers, 33 percent said television, and radio followed with 16 percent.[11] Fewer than 1 percent selected magazines. When the survey asked which medium the public preferred for national and international news, however, television emerged stronger, garnering 60 percent of the preferences, followed by newspapers with 28 percent, 8 percent for radio, and 3 percent for magazines.

Even though competing with such a live medium as television is difficult, many managing editors across the country refuse to give up trying to beat them with timely coverage. Jim Standard, executive editor at the *Daily Oklahoman,* for instance, says he is constantly exhorting his troops to do whatever it takes to scoop the local stations.[12] One of the advantages newspapers have going for them in reporting the news is that the news consumer can spend more time with the story, reading back over it for more detail, and filing pertinent pieces away for future use. As a result, newspaper readers have emerged more knowledgeable about state and local issues than have people who get their news more from television. A study at the University of Tennessee indicated that levels of knowledge of national or international affairs were not different for those who preferred newspapers and those who preferred television for their news. However, for state and local news, those who preferred newspapers for their news scored significantly better on a short test of public affairs knowledge.[13] The study was conducted in 1986 and was prompted by interest in the Roper polls which, since 1959, have shown television growing as the preferred source of news for most U.S. citizens.

THE OPPORTUNITY OF SUNDAYS

When the number of newspapers is tallied, they are most often divided into morning and afternoon newspapers. Then, almost as an addendum to some people's thinking, comes the list of Sunday newspapers. At last count, there were 770 Sunday newspapers with a total circulation of some 55 million.[14] Many times subscribers pay a separate charge for the Sunday papers and, at the newsstand, many are selling for $1 per copy or higher. Preprint advertisers love them. One issue of the *Boston Globe* alone featured 13 preprint circulars. It is important for publishers to realize, perhaps once again, how important the Sunday newspaper really is, both to the industry and to the public. Here is the newspaper that readers can really spend time with. It is not uncommon for some readers to come back to the Sunday paper several times throughout the day and even the following week. This is also the paper that has an abundance of space for reporters to treat subjects in depth, and, from a competitive standpoint, viewership of weekend television news is low. Therefore, newspapers have a real opportunity to score exclusives on Sunday morning.

Some industry observers are not happy with the current state of Sunday newspapers, however. Newspaper editor/consultant Jerry Bellune told a group of San Francisco editors that editors should ask themselves the following questions about their Sunday newspapers.[15]

1. How current is the news in our Sunday paper? Are we shutting out our main news sections too early and, if so, is it because of our own laziness instead of for circulation or production reasons?

2. What is our competition doing? How are they covering Saturday news? What aspects of those stories could we get exclusives on?

3. What types of coverage can we offer that will complement as well as compete with all-news radio and television networks like Cable News Network (CNN) on weekends?

4. How serious is our commitment to serving the foreign news and information needs of our Sunday readers? Is that degree of commitment reflected in our foreign coverage on Sundays?

5. Are our Sunday papers given over too much to advertising? Is our real reason for producing a Sunday paper in the first place to bring in more preprints? What about news content?

6. Are we doing a good enough job with enterprise reporting? Are we doing some well-documented and planned-out trend stories or are we simply being victimized by some deadly dull Saturday occurrences that we try to pass off as news?

Bellune, executive editor of the Camden, N.J., *Courier-Post* (which began its own Sunday edition in 1979) says if editors can answer affirmatively to the above questions, then their Sunday editions should be a hit and fill a needed gap among readers.

COMPETING WITH DIRECT MAIL

Direct mail advertising has become a force to be reckoned with for newspapers. Whereas a decade ago not a great deal was heard of this advertising medium, today it commands about 14 percent of total advertising revenue collected in the United States.[16] With the success of the largest of the direct mail firms, Advo, has come other direct mail marketing companies such as Hub Mail in Boston and many others. There is even a Direct Marketing Educational Foundation, Inc., that sponsors five-day seminars for talented college seniors and graduate students. Once not given much attention by college graduates, direct mail marketing is today becoming a viable alternative for college communications and business majors. The United States Postal Service in 1979 gave either an unconscious or conscious boost to direct mail marketing in this country by creating what has come to be known as "shared mail" or "marriage mail." Shared mail is a program whereby two or more advertisements or circulars can be sent out in the same package to split the postal charges involved in delivering it. By the mid-1980s shared mail firms were garnering good profits from the introduction of shared mail.

What should the newspaper's reaction be to direct mail advertising? Should publishers simply concede that this new, driving force is here to stay and instead concentrate on ways to protect the remainder of their newspaper advertising revenue, or is there a way for publishers to join in the battle for the advertising dollars going to direct mail companies? Many newspaper analysts are advising their clients to go on the offensive with direct mailers and begin incorporating shared-mail programs as part of their overall TMC plans. Among those newspapers which have followed this advice are the *Omaha World Herald, The Tacoma News Tribune,* and the *Bryan-College Station Eagle* (of Texas).[17] *The Houston Chronicle* also joined in the attack in 1981 by producing and distributing a vehicle called *Apartment Extra* to 249,000 apartments in four zones of Harris County. In Omaha,,the *World Herald* purchased a local direct mail firm and started selling the shared mail concept to area retailers before any other direct mail firm had a chance to enter the market. In Lincoln, Nebraska, the *World Herald*'s direct mail company was drawing linage away from the *Lincoln Journal & Star*. Meanwhile, in Tacoma, the *News Tribune* is using a mailed TMC shopper that can offer advertisers 90 percent penetration when used in conjunction with the daily. The paper, which has been working on its subscriber/nonsubscriber list for more than four years, covers three zones with zip code distribution.

"If you don't currently produce a viable alternative to marriage mail in your local market, I strongly recommend that it be implemented as soon as possible," retail ad manager Jim Pollard advises.[18] He adds that the success of any marriage mail program depends on the quality of the product's delivery. Because of this, newspapers must work hard to build strong relationships with local postal officials.

Conferences and seminars are being held regularly to introduce shared mail ideas to publishers. At one such conference in San Diego, members of the International Newspaper Advertising and Marketing Executives were advised to get into shared mail and augment it with ROP advertising. Members learned they could develop a nonsubscriber delivery program which can actually be a shared mail program to nonsubscribers mailed once a week in direct competition with any shared mailers in the market. Such a product could take the shape of a nonsubscriber shopper or entertainment guide used as a wrapper for other advertising inserts. It could be delivered either by mail or by carrier if the circulation were large enough.

One thing publishers might want to keep in mind is that not all stores—and shared mail programs are usually best-suited to the K-Mart and Sears types of stores—need real total market coverage. Instead what they need is total market coverage of their actual drawing area, which is probably much smaller than the entire newspaper market area. A solid review of each store in relation to its drawing area should produce the right TMC area and the optimal sales results.[19]

Many newspaper publishers involved in their own shared mail programs like to use a jacket or additional lightweight advertising pieces to supplement the insert package and make it more profitable. The *Sacramento Bee* has been wrapping advertisers' inserts inside an 11½ by 13½" advertising-only jacket. The jacket ROP rates are about the same in cost per thousand as the newspaper, and it has proven the most profitable portion of the product. The *Bee*'s shared mail program was working on an 8.7 percent profit margin in 1982 as a result of the program.[20]

Charles E. Hoonan, a California printing company executive, has pointed out that mass retailers have long shown their need to have saturation distribution of their circulars in the 80-percent or better range. He asserts that only marriage mail can work to produce that kind of saturation coverage.[21] It can work even better if combined with regular newspaper delivery systems. Hoonan and many others believe some large stores could be saved from failing by offering them combination advertising and high penetration. This could result from the newspaper's regular delivery to nonsubscribers plus a shared mail program to households on nonsubscriber lists. Hoonan feels the swing to marriage mail has had an immediate effect on area suburban dailies and weeklies as well as metros, and that newspapers had better go after these lost advertising dollars. Using a rule-of-thumb average of $30 per thousand for advertising inserts, marriage mail efforts in just the Seattle and Tacoma areas alone were pulling about $60,000 from those areas' newspapers, he says.[22]

However the individual newspaper or newspaper group chooses to shape its marriage mail program, the message is clear from these and other newspaper observers: the important thing is for the newspaper publisher to begin his own direct mail program as an adjunct to the newspaper's regular delivery system. If this doesn't occur, the direct mail marketing industry will continue to drain even more advertising revenue away from the newspaper industry.

COMPETING WITH SHOPPERS

Shoppers, or free-distribution weeklies that emphasize advertising almost exclusively, may be the brunt of numerous newsroom jokes, but in one sense the shoppers are getting the last laugh: they are highly profitable and their numbers are increasing. Why is this so? Regardless of the fact that they are free and provide little or no news content, they achieve high penetration into the households of the market area. In some cases the actual penetration is at high as 90 percent or more. No paid-circulation newspaper can touch that level of penetration unless they, too, field a supplemental shopper. That is exactly what many dailies and weeklies are doing. Strategies range from saturation of a targeted area or population group to total market coverage. The main thrust of these shoppers is to get the K Mart, J.C. Penney, Sears, and other large department store groups to see the attractiveness of newspapers as an advertising medium. If a newspaper can put the ads of these stores into most homes in the market, the point will be made.

Some shoppers more closely resemble traditional newspapers by carrying up to 30 percent or more editorial content consisting of mostly canned feature material from one of the various feature syndicates. In some cases there may actually be a locally originated feature prominently displayed on Page 1. Once inside, however, the reader finds mostly ads and canned feature material. It should be pointed out that many publishers offer free-distribution weeklies that field good news staffs. Generally these are new publications which the publisher feels can break into the market more easily—and with greater penetration—by going out to readers free of charge.

Some newspaper observers feel shoppers have arisen, not because of low daily penetration, but because entrepreneurial publishers have identified a new target market that no other newspaper was covering. Possibly a city has been experiencing rapid growth in one particular section where builders have developed hundreds of homes in a short span of time. Such is the case, for instance, in Indianapolis where the water-starved Hoosiers have been flocking to buy premium-priced homes on Geist Reservoir. An area like that is primed for the introduction of a shopper. Area residents become a special-interest group, so identified by their close-knit geographical features and—in this case—boating interests.

Whatever the exact configuration of the shopper, one thing is certain, profits have soared at many of them, and most of them are independently owned. While there is no exact total of the number of shoppers, media observers put their number at 10,000 or more. The National Association of Advertising Publishers, which is the trade association for free-distribution papers, experienced a 40-percent growth in membership from 1974, and now represents more than 1,100 such papers. Their total revenues in 1978 were $500 million, and circulation at the start of the 1980s was around 15 million.[23]

Shoppers are hampered, some feel, in that they cannot subscribe to the leading circulation auditing agency, the Audit Bureau of Circulation (ABC), which only audits paid publications. Consequently, many must produce their Post Office receipts to verify their circulations to wary advertisers, while others are audited by another auditing agency, Certified Audit of Circulations (CAC), which audits primarily independent, free-circulation papers. In 1979, CAC audited a total of 17 million free copies and found that 86 percent were delivered as publishers claimed.

Some shoppers and other free weeklies are distributed through the mails, while others are delivered by hand to doorsteps in the market. Third-class mailing is more expensive, but it is—at present—the only mail classification the shoppers qualify for, since they are not purchased by subscribers. More details about third-class mail, and the opportunities and problems it presents, can be found in Chapter 6.

Some publishers of paid-circulation newspapers have run afoul of antitrust laws in trying to compete with new shoppers in their market. The reason is the law stipulates that, in trying to compete, the established newspaper must be able to show a profit if it decides to drop its advertising or offer other incentives to advertisers to keep them from advertising in the shopper. If the paper's only justification for cutting its rates is to drive the shopper out of business, it violates the law. Lawyers are good people to consult here, because required combination rates (meaning advertisers must run ads in both the paid and free products) can also present legal problems for the newspaper.

Some publishers of shoppers feel dailies have taken unfair competitive steps despite what many daily newspaper executives consider to be stringent federal antitrust rules against dirty play. "Anti-trust laws require the paid newspaper that owns a free paper to compete fairly with the other free publication," ANPA staff attorney L. Peyton Hendricks says.[24] Several newspapers have found themselves in the throes of such antitrust battles. One was the *Daily Reflector* of Greenville, North Carolina. The competing shopper sued and charged that the daily set advertising rates which it considered less than competitive. The *Reflector*'s publisher denied the charges, but a U.S. Circuit Court of Appeals reversed a lower court decision that had favored the *Reflector* and remanded the case to trial. The case was settled out of court for about $25,000.[25]

One thing a paid newspaper can do to protect its franchise is not to wait until a competing shopper shows up on the market. Before that happens, the newspaper should itself unleash a supplemental shopper to discourage any future competitor. If funds are short, possibly the publisher can link up with other publishers in the county to produce a county-wide shopper. There is nothing wrong, of course, with a paid newspaper fielding its own shopper after another shopper has begun publication. The publisher of the paid newspaper, however, just has to keep in mind the federal antitrust guidelines.

THE ELECTRONIC NEWSPAPER

One of the topics of major discussion among newspaper publishers over the past decade has been electronic publishing. The idea of putting out a newspaper in some form other than its current physical form has captivated the imagination of many newspaper executives who see the problems involved in production and distribution of the traditional newspaper. The idea that telecommunication technology could be brought to bear on the problem, and that an electronic newspaper could be published was bound to catch their attention. In many cases it has done more than that. By 1985 there were more than 200 electronic publishing ventures involving newspaper companies in the United States.[26] The ANPA has reported that these ventures are broken down into the following categories:[27]

1. System Operators (13). This category defines newspaper companies that have developed their own in-house computer systems to distribute information to customers. These include all the videotex operations and on-line data bases such as Knight-Ridder's Vu/Text and the Oklahoma Publishing Company's DataTimes.

2. Information Providers (50). These prepare and sell information that is distributed by other electronic publishers. In late 1984, for example, Gannett Co. decided its Gannett News Media Services should start selling the *USA Update,* which was a compilation of information from *USA Today,* Gannett News Service, and wire and broadcast services.

3. Cable (84). Most of these companies provide text to local cable television operations. Some also provide video programming. One of the largest such ventures was by Cox Enterprise Inc. in Atlanta, Ga.

4. Public Access (12). These companies mostly provide text information to public electronic kiosks for passersby. One of the best operations is the *San Francisco Chronicle*'s system.

5. Affiliates (24). These include the newspapers that have signed joint venture agreements with videotex companies like Viewtron or Gateway or that have made their news copy available on Vu/Text or DataTimes.

6. Audiotex (19). Most of these companies provide information over a telephone service provided by someone else. Information could include stock or tourist information. Dow Jones and Lee Newspapers are examples.

Research done by the ANPA shows that most of the new newspaper ventures into electronic publishing are in the direction of videotex and decreasingly in the area of cable television. In addition, the majority of the new ventures are targeting specific markets.

Before going further, it might be wise to explain just what is meant by two of the terms most often heard in relation to electronic publishing: videotex and teletext. In its basic form, videotex is a computerized system which gives the user access to data in the form of text with graphics and color. The system is interactive, which means the user can interact with it and perform a number of functions from his or her own home. Videotex was originally developed by the British Post Office in the late 1960s and was seen as a way of making further use of telephone lines already existing. The British videotex system makes use of a modified television set with keyboard or keypad. Connected together and linked to one of several computers, the user can call up any of more than 220,000 "pages" in the British videotex system known as "Prestel" (for "press" and "television"). Early in this decade the Prestel system had more than 17,000 subscribers worldwide.[28] Development of videotex systems in the United States started in the 1970s as several large dailies computerized their information retrieval systems for their news staffs. These systems were first designed to service only dedicated terminals, but since have broadened to outside subscribers. Knight-Ridder started exploring the waters in 1976 through Viewdata Corp. of America, which sees the local information provider as the majority component in an offering of videotex services. Knight-Ridder conducted two years of research for its Viewtron from 1979 to 1981, and has been expanding the research ever since.

Teletext, on the other hand, has been called "Print TV." Teletext was introduced to the United States in June 1978 at KSL-TV in Salt Lake City, Utah. KSL's system utilized a sort of hidden transmission feature when formed that needed viewer decoders to call up 70 sample pages which were broadcast in a sequential order. The call-up was done by punching a three-digit page number on a selector that looked like a pocket calculator. Thus it was a subscriber system. The main difference between teletext and videotex is that teletext is noninteractive. Viewers must wait for pages to be presented to them in sequential order. When it began, KSL system pages were transmitted in sequence at an average of about seven pages per second.[29]

In 1982, two reports were published that gave somewhat opposing views of the feasibility of electronic publishing in the United States. First, a National Science Foundation (NSF) study unveiled the results of a research project entitled, "Teletext and Videotex in the United States." It concluded that electronic information systems will transform U.S. life-styles to the same degree that television did.[30] The study focused on videotex and predicted that 40 percent of U.S. homes would have terminals by the end of the century. The key driving force behind videotex's growth would be its ability to generate advertising and lower its cost to consumers, the study said.

"Individuals may be able to use videotex systems to create their own newspapers, design their own curricula, compile their own consumer guides," the study said. "On the other hand, these systems create new dangers of manipulation or social engineering, either for political or economic gain."[31] The study explained that while videotex will bring more information and news to the home, it will also "carry a stream of information out of the home about the preferences and behavior of its occupants."

Certainly the growth of home shopping on cable channels lends credence to part of the optimism found in the NSF study and to the importance that advertising would play in the new system of communication.

Just two months later, however, results of a two-year experiment in videotex journalism involving the Associated Press, ten newspapers, and CompuServe were published. They showed that the market was not there in 1982 for a profitable electronic newspaper, nor was it likely to be for some time.[32] RMH Research, Inc., hired to monitor the experiment, noted that, in general, videotex has a future, but it may depend much more on the continued advancement of technology. RMH President Richard Hochhauser said, "You have to have enough homes with computers. That does not exist today."[33] In other words, the market is still limited. The rapid growth in popularity of personal computers in the 1980s, however, may well change that and broaden the market. Personal computers are getting to the affordable stage for many families, and that means more potential customers for the various electronic information services. Since most of the conclusions of the RMH study were based on the limited number of homes with computers, it seems likely that—were such a study done in the late 1980s—the results might be different and show a wider market and thus more potential profit for electronic publishing ventures. Electronic publishing is thus an area of growth worth paying attention to and planning for.

ARE NEWSPAPERS LOSING THEIR GRIP?

John Morton, newspaper analyst with Lynch, Jones & Ryan (a member of the New York Stock Exchange) answered yes to this question, but he was quick to add there is something newspapers can do to retain their hold and even gain some ground.[34] He writes,

Year after year, the proportion of the population reading newspapers continues to drop, and year after year newspaper companies continue to make even more money. Has it occurred to anyone in the business to wonder whether there might be a connection between these two trends?[35]

Morton draws the analogy between the newspaper industry of the 1980s and the domestic automobile industry of the late 1970s that continued to blindly ride high profits into the sunset while turning out the huge cars and engines that just wouldn't succeed in a time of oil cutbacks. Everyone knows what happened when the gasoline shortages did occur. In one instance the government had to step in and bail out Chrysler. Morton and other analysts argue that it is time for the newspaper industry to take stock of itself and to see that poor quality and high profits will not continue forever. Eventually, it will be the poor quality that will cause the high profits to disappear.

Analysts see the key problem as being that fewer U.S. citizens are bothering to read newspapers. Today, as Morton points out, percentages of 55 to 65 percent have replaced former percentages of 80 to 85 percent of U.S. citizens regularly reading newspapers. Some newspaper observers like Philip Meyer even state that the big marketing problem for newspapers is not to convert nonreaders, but infrequent readers.[36]

Many analysts believe there is a definite link between declining quality in newspaper journalism and the rise of television, shoppers, and direct mail marketing as such strong competitive forces. Morton notes,

these competitive forces would not have arisen if newspapers had maintained a strong grip on their markets. The grip was weak because of too much devotion to profitability. The newspaper divisions of the major publicly owned companies on average keep in operating profits about 20 cents from every dollar taken in. That is two to three times higher than what other businesses keep.[37]

Morton says newspapers are skimping in investments that offer no clear payoff, even though they may be strategic in that they lay the groundwork for a better newspaper and for future profits. He cites areas such as higher pay, larger staffs, bigger news holes, and better market research.

Morton concludes some newspapers refused to skimp on strategic investments, and said those are the newspapers that have kept a strong grip on their readership. While their profits may be lower than some newspapers', their profits are growing and are derived from more—not fewer—readers.

The premise of this book has been that the newspaper which remains financially solvent has the best chance at being editorially independent as well. But remaining financially solvent does not mean a newspaper must make as much money as it possibly can make at the expense of the news product. As noted in Chapter 1, successful newspaper management in the late 1980s and beyond requires attention to both the market ethic and the service ethic. As it relates to this discussion, attention to the service ethic means that a newspaper publisher must devote adequate resources to insuring that his newspaper fulfill its editorial mission. This is the type of strategic investment Morton and others support and, in the long run, it is also the one readers and advertisers will support.

NOTES

1. Gene Goltz, "Where Newspapers Compete," *Presstime*, (November 1986), p. 38.

2. Patrick O'Donnell, *The Business of Newspapers: An Essay for Investors* (New York: E.F. Hutton, 1982), p. 2.

3. Janice Castro and Anne Constable, "Shootout in the Big D," *Time Magazine,* 7 September 1981: 58.

4. American Newspaper Publishers Association, *Facts About Newspapers, 1984,* brochure Dulles Airport, Washington, D.C.: American Newspaper Publishers April 1984, p. 8.

5. American Newspaper Publishers Association, *Facts About Newspapers, 1984,* p. 8.

6. Debra Gersh, "A Difficult Year for National Advertising," *Editor & Publisher,* 3 January 1987: 48.

7. Gersh, "A Difficult Year," p. 48.

8. John T. Mennenga, "Local Spot TV Ads Are Eating Up Newspaper Revenues," *Editor & Publisher,* 22 November 1986: 52.

9. Mennenga, "Local Spot TV Ads," p. 52.

10. Ben Bagdikian, "Newspapers Face Troubles, But They'll Still Be a Good Deal," *Next* (January–February 1981), p. 43.

11. "Newspapers Lead TV as a Source of Local News," *Editor & Publisher,* 6 August 1983: 7.

12. Interview with Jim Standard at the *Daily Oklahoman,* Oklahoma City, July 2, 1982.

13. Becky Menn-Hamblin, "Newspaper Readers Most Knowledgeable About State/ Local Issues," *Editor & Publisher,* 10 January 1987: 7.

14. American Newspaper Publishers Association, *Facts About Newspapers, 1984,* p. 2.

15. Jerry Bellune, "Are We Taking Sunday for Granted?" *Editor & Publisher,* 1 May 1982: 36.

16. American Newspaper Publishers Association, *Facts About Newspapers, 1984,* p. 8.

17. Bill Gloede, "Newspapers on Offensive in War With Shared Mail," *Editor & Publisher,* 24 October 1981: 15.

18. "Newspaper Urged to Embrace Shared Mail TMC Programs," *Editor & Publisher,* 31 July, 1982: 18.

19. "Newspapers Urged to Embrace Shared Mail TMC Programs," p. 18.

20. "Newspapers Urged to Embrace Shared Mail TMC Programs," p. 18.

21. Charles E. Hoonan, "If You Can't Beat 'Em, Join 'Em," *Editor & Publisher,* 20 February 1982: 52.

22. Hoonan, "If You Can't Beat 'Em," p. 52.

23. "Shoppers: Special Report," *Presstime* (October 1980), p. 5.

24. "Shoppers: Special Report," p. 5.

25. "Shoppers: Special Report," p. 6.

26. Tim Miller, "Newspaper Firms Involved in Electronic Publishing," *Editor & Publisher,* 9 March 1985: 28.

27. Miller, "Newspaper Firms Involved," p. 28.

28. R. C. Morse, "Videotex in America: The Birth of Electronic Newspapering," *Editor & Publisher* 26 June 1982: 41.

29. Milton Hollstein, "Teletext: Print TV," *Grassroots Editor* (Spring 1979), pp. 15–19.

30. "NSF Study Sees Videotex Transforming America," *Editor & Publisher*, 26 June 1982: 54.

31. "NSF Study," p. 54.

32. "Electronic Newspaper Found Unprofitable," *Editor & Publisher*, 28 August 1982: 7.

33. "Electronic Newspaper," p. 7.

34. John Morton, "Newspapers Are Losing Their Grip," *WJR* (September 1984), p. 52.

35. Morton, "Newspapers Are Losing," p. 52.

36. Philip Meyer, *The Newspaper Survival Book* (New York: Longman, 1986), p. 41.

37. Morton, "Newspapers Are Losing," p. 52.

APPENDIX

CASES FOR STUDY

The following hypothetical cases should help you in applying some of the principles discussed in this book and in other works cited in the Notes and Bibliography sections. In many cases there is no one right answer to a case, but there are specific problems inherent in the situations that should be addressed.

The *Pine Valley Daily Sentinel*

The *Pine Valley Daily Sentinel* is a newspaper of 30,000 circulation that services an East Texas area of four counties consisting of 75,000 households (135,000 adult population). It is located in the city of Pine Valley, population 50,000, about 50 miles east of another Texas city of 65,000 population. To its east, about the same distance, lies the metropolitan area of Shreveport, Louisiana. As yet, Pine Valley is not a part of a large enough SMSA (Standard Metropolitan Statistical Area) to command much attention from national advertisers, but it does do very well in attracting local retail advertising in its trading area. It could become part of a much larger SMSA if its four-county trading area could add another 50,000 population. That is not an unreal possibility, because the area has grown by 40,000 in the past ten years. Most of these new residents are young couples who have responded to a relatively recent emphasis by the Pine County Chamber of Commerce to promote the forested beauty of the area as a haven for young outdoor adventurers.

The publisher of the newspaper, which has grown about 10 percent in circulation over the past decade, is Helen Jackson, who took over the reins of the newspaper when her husband Tom passed away five years ago. Tom Jackson was a legend in Pine County, having moved to the area 30 years ago and used his entrepreneurial skills to bring new industry with him. With the industry came new residents, and both the county and city (as well as the *Sentinel*) grew accordingly. Tom was past president of the East Texas

Chamber of Commerce and East Texas Industrial Development Commission, and he became a legend in his own time as publisher of the *Sentinel,* although he had no journalistic background or strong reporting interests. He was an acknowledged leader among publishers in knowing how to relate to businesses and draw in advertisers.

His journalism was a journalism of optimism, and he always saw a bright future for the area and insisted his newspaper lead the cheerleading. One edition of the *Sentinel* had become a legend in Texas journalism: the annual 200-page Progress Edition. It consisted of several special sections celebrating the growth and prosperity of the eight-county East Texas region the newspaper services.

Pine Valley does continue to grow, and the *Sentinel* spotlights the industries that make it financially successful. Recently the newspaper dispatched a reporter to cover the shipment of some earthmoving equipment (made in Pine Valley) to the Contra forces in Nicaragua. The equipment was bought and paid for by the rebel forces in Nicaragua with the open support of the U.S. government. The reporter sent back a series of stories and pictures chronicling Pine Valley's contribution to the efforts to overthrow the government in Nicaragua.

As evidence of Pine Valley's growth, the East Texas Chamber of Commerce has made it the permanent home of its annual convention, drawing in visitors for one week a year from 100 area chambers of commerce.

The newspaper does a good job of maintaining relationships with the city and school officials. Several times a year, the education reporter and city hall reporter work directly with the appropriate public relations officials in preparing the stories of the school board and city council meetings. The newspaper feels the stories will be more accurate if officials like this sit with reporters while they prepare them, and act as consultants for points the reporter doesn't understand.

The *Daily Sentinel* has competition in each of the counties which it services. There are local dailies in each town of 10,000 or more population, and weeklies in most of the rest. The *Sentinel* is the largest paper in the region, although some of the competing dailies are group-owned (one is owned by a group of 50 daily newspapers). The *Sentinel* prides itself on being locally owned and operated. There is one network affiliate television station in Pine Valley and one cable station. There are also several radio stations in the region as well as a county-wide shopper, which is not owned by Mrs. Jackson. It has a penetration of 80 percent into the Pine County market, publishes every Wednesday, and is distributed by third-class mail, usually on Friday mornings. A direct mail service also operates in the area.

The total Effective Buying Income for the eight-county region, according to the *Sales and Marketing Management Survey of Buying Power,* is $1.5 billion. Total annual retail sales in the same area equals $900 million. Altogether, the competition media gross about $6 million in advertising annually, while the *Sentinel* grosses $8 million. Mrs. Jackson is proud of the fact that her paper grosses more than all competitors combined. The *Sentinel*'s advertising revenue has grown 12 percent over the past five years, and the state sales tax revenues have increased from $25 million to $35 million over the same period.

Mrs. Jackson's general manager at the paper is Cyril Sawyer, who has tried unsuccessfully to fill Tom Jackson's shoes as a magnet for new growth in the region. His heart is in the same place as Jackson's, but he doesn't have the dynamism. Still, he and Mrs. Jackson are longtime friends. He really runs the newspaper, even though he reports to her in the organization. Under him is Editor-in-Chief Mike Kenney, who has been with the paper 30 years. He feels his many years in the area qualify him to know what the readers want in news, and he bases most of the newspaper's new agenda on his experience. He knows the area extremely well, and has won several awards from the East Texas Chamber of Commerce, as well as the regional press association for feature stories and community service. The paper has been winning these awards for several years, and Kenney feels they validate his unchanging ideas of what Pine Valley readers want in news. He and Tom Jackson were great friends, and they shared the same ideas on upbeat journalism for the area. The newspaper has had little trouble in recruiting reporters, and it budgets $550,000 annually for a newsroom payroll that accommodates a staff of 38 editors, reporters, and photographers.

Although the upper newsroom management team has stayed relatively stable over the past several years, the reporter and departmental editor turnover has been 45 percent annually. One of the chief reasons given by reporters at exit interviews is that the newspaper does not allow them to do much investigative reporting in the city, county, or region, because of the "good-news myopia" of the management. Sawyer insists the newspaper can do solid investigative reporting once the area grows to the level needed to attract national advertising. He feels this revenue is necessary for the paper—and for the newsroom. He also believes people and industry are not going to move into an area in which there is crime and corruption.

Mrs. Jackson, deciding she should take a more active hand in managing and under-standing the newspaper, has decided to go against Sawyer's wishes and bring in a "newspaper doctor" to diagnose the central problems and related subproblems of the *Sentinel*, and to suggest alternative ways of addressing these problems. Her goal is to have a stronger newspaper (both in terms of finances and quality) emerge. She chooses Headline Newspaper Consultants, Inc., for which you work. The company selects you to look over the *Sentinel*'s situation and advise Mrs. Jackson, in writing, on what the paper's major and minor problems might be and how to address them. You should also address the strengths of the *Sentinel* and discuss both the positive and negative impli-cations of your recommendations. An accountant from your firm will be looking over the financial documents of the newspaper at a later date and making a separate report on the company's financial health. You need not concern yourself with this.

The *Springfield Star*

You are the advertising manager for the *Springfield Star* (a broadsheet with a circu-lation of 80,000 in an SMSA of 120,000 households), and the owner of the Chevrolet dealership comes in to see you. He wants to structure an annual advertising budget for his dealership, and he tells you his company did $4 million in gross sales last year. Checking information you receive annually from the Automobile Dealer's Association of America, you discover the average new dealer spends 1.5 percent of gross sales on advertising every year. Armed with this and other information in your possession, please respond to the dealer's questions which are as follows:

1. Why should I advertise in the *Springfield Star* instead of the county-wide shopper that has 80 percent penetration into the market?
2. What advantage do I have advertising in the *Star* as opposed to the local network affiliate television station which is watched by 60,000 households every night?

3. What steps do I take in setting up an annual advertising budget?

4. Assuming you talk me into spending 75 percent of my advertising budget with the *Star,* how many ads should I run during the year? What size would you recommend and why? Where should they be positioned in the paper, and what issues of the paper would bring me the best results?

5. Would there be any advantage to my using color in the ads?

6. What would an advertising calendar for one month out of the year look like?

7. Assuming I get cooperative advertising from Chevrolet, and assuming they will reimburse me for half of my advertising up to 1 percent of the autos sold last year, how much more advertising money would this co-op funding represent if I take advantage of it?

8. Based on the following excerpted data from the *Star*'s advertising rate card, please answer the following:

   A. Would I be better advised to use the Open Line rate or sign a contract? If I sign a contract, should it be an Annual Volume or Weekly Performance Contract? Why?

   B. Assuming I wanted to run regular quarter-page ads in the *Star,* how many could I buy based on the advertising budget you recommend and the rates quoted in the rate card data below?

   C. What SAU designation does this size ad represent?

Rate Card Data for the Star

Open Line Rate: $2.50

ANNUAL VOLUME CONTRACT RATE:

1,000–4,999 lines	$2.40
5,000–9,999 lines	2.36
10,000–19,999 lines	2.32
20,000–49,999 lines	2.28
50,000–99,999 lines	2.24
100,000 lines and over........	2.18

WEEKLY PERFORMANCE CONTRACT RATE:

(Assuming ads are run at least 48 weeks throughout the year)

1,000–4,999 lines	$2.25
5,000–9,999 lines	2.22
10,000–19,999 lines	2.18
20,000–49,999 lines	2.14
50,000–99,999 lines	$2.10
100,000 lines and over........	2.05

COLOR DIFFERENTIAL:

Four-Color	$800 per insertion order
Black plus two colors........	$400 per insertion order
Black plus one color	$250 per insertion order

Publishing in Holyoke

Referring to the *Editor & Publisher Market Guide,* answer the following questions about Holyoke, Massachusetts, as a place to publish a newspaper.

1. What is there about the general business conditions in this town that might interest you as a newspaper publisher?
2. What other sources might you consult to obtain trend data affecting business in Holyoke? Consult at least two of these sources and report on your findings.

Referring to the *Sales and Marketing Management Survey of Buying Power,* answer the following questions about Holyoke:

1. What is the median age of the population in the city? Is this important in any way for a newspaper operating in the area? Why or why not?
2. How does Holyoke compare with two other cities of its approximate size in the state, with regard to retail sales in the food and general merchandise categories?
3. How does the Median Household EBI in Holyoke compare with two other cities of this size in the state? Is that good or bad news for the Holyoke news media?
4. What is the approximate amount of money spent in the Holyoke retail market area?
5. What is the approximate amount of that money that, according to community averages, probably goes to retail advertising?
6. Assuming one newspaper in town is grossing, say, $2 million in annual retail advertising, and a local radio station is taking in $500,000, would there be any untapped advertising potential remaining in Holyoke? If so, approximately how much?

The Dying Dailies

During the years 1981 to 1986, several major daily newspapers including the *Philadelphia Bulletin, Washington Star, Cleveland Press, Memphis Press-Scimitar, St. Louis Globe-Democrat,* and *Oklahoma City Times* ceased publication or became merged with sister newspapers. Using information contained in such sources as *Editor & Publisher, WJR, The Quill, Presstime,* and *Columbia Journalism Review,* describe conditions that led to the demise of each of these newspapers, and project what things might have been done to save them. Do you notice any similarity of causes or did each newspaper seem to be victimized by the peculiarities of its own market? Explain.

Nagging Newsroom Problems

You are the managing editor of a mid-size daily newspaper that has witnessed a plethora of ongoing problems and changes in the newsroom. Among them are the following:

1. Overtime among reporters has gotten out of hand, although most of the overtime hours seem to be spent in the legitimate pursuit of news stories. In reality, you need a bigger staff to do the work in straight time, but you aren't likely to get a bigger staff because of budget cutbacks at the newspaper.

2. With the smaller news hole you have been assigned, many "softer" or non-breaking-news stories are being held in overset longer and longer. The reporters who put time in on these pieces are getting upset. They have been promising sources the stories would appear on such-and-such date, and they don't, and the reporters are embarrassed and generally tired of waiting for their pieces to see the light of day.

3. There seems to be a growing vagueness of how your newspaper is defining news. That is, the criteria for news value seem ambiguous and changing almost on a month-to-month basis. As a result, reporters are unsure as to which of their reporting efforts will pay off with front-page stories and which will wind up in overset.

4. A big problem has arisen with regard to scheduling for vacations and comp time for holidays. There seems to be no discernible system undergirding the assignment of such time off.

You have decided these are the kinds of problems that should be turned over to a group of reporters and editors to evaluate. Based on your understanding of quality circles, how would you go about setting one up, what results might you expect, and what would your role as managing editor be with regard to this newsroom quality circle?

Your Dream Philosophy

Once again, you are the managing editor of the *Pine Valley Daily Sentinel,* discussed earlier. Your quality circle, which you helped form a couple months back, has been meeting regularly and has decided your newspaper needs a written philosophy of news. The members would like to have a draft philosophy presented to them for their evaluation, and they have asked you to put this draft together. You now have the dream opportunity of your professional life: to write a philosophy of news that you believe should guide the editors and reporters at your newspaper. With what you know about the formation of such philosophies (Ouchi's *Theory Z* may come in handy here), prepare a formal, written philosophy that should guide your newsroom in its pursuit—and presentation—of news.

Troubleshooting Financial Problems

You are publisher of the *Banner,* a large daily newspaper in the Midwest. You have decided to take a hard look at your newspaper's income statement and balance sheet to assess just where your newspaper is financially. Using what you know about such troubleshooting techniques, analyze the following income statement and balance sheet and prepare to issue a report to the newspaper's board of directors concerning the financial status of the *Banner.* Included in your report should be an assessment of how appropriately the newspaper is being managed in its various departments and whether various expense levels are justified by the revenues received and the mission of your newspaper, which is to be the primary news channel for people in your part of the state and to continue making a profit that is at least as much as the newspaper industry average for large dailies. Based on these financial documents, what suggestions would you recommend to the newspaper's board of directors to help insure fulfillment of that mission?

Balance Sheet

ASSETS

Current Assets:

Cash................................	$4,700,000
Checking	500,000
Prepaids	700,000
Accounts Receivable	12,750,000
Newsprint Inventory.................	1,650,000
Ink Inventory	150,000
Job Stock	200,000
Misc. Inventory	210,000
Total Current Assets	20,860,000

Fixed Assets:

Building	14,000,000
Land	2,500,000
Machinery	4,500,000
Furniture	1,200,000
Cars, Trucks	1,000,000
Accumulated Depreciation	2,000,000
Total Fixed Assets..................	25,200,000

TOTAL ASSETS	$46,060,000

LIABILITIES

Current Liabilities:

Accounts Payable....................	$3,100,000
Notes Payable	5,100,000
Employee FICA Withheld	750,000
Accrued Payroll Taxes...............	850,000
Income Tax Payable	3,750,000
Accrued Salaries	1,750,000
Total Current Liabilities	15,300,000

Long-Term Liabilities:

Mortgage Payable....................	8,000,000
Notes Payable	3,500,000
Total Long-Term Liabilities	11,500,000

Owners' Equity:

Capital Stock.......................	9,260,000
Retained Earnings	10,000,000
Total Equities	19,260,000

TOTAL LIABILITIES..................	$46,060,000

Income Statement
Three-Year Summary of Operations

INCOME

ADVERTISING			
Retail	$22,264,000	22,464,000	23,813,000
National	4,464,000	2,996,000	2,120,000
Classified	9,792,000	10,483,200	9,677,500
Preprints	3,872,000	1,123,000	2,709,700
Legals	408,000	374,000	387,100
Total:	40,800,000	37,440,200	38,707,300
CIRCULATION			
City	7,310,000	7,000,000	6,850,000
County	1,690,000	2,300,000	2,430,000
State	690,000	780,000	800,000
Total:	9,690,000	10,080,000	10,080,000
OTHER INCOME			
Total:	510,000	480,000	210,000
TOTAL INCOME	$51,000,000	48,000,200	48,997,300

EXPENSES

DIRECT			
Editorial	$ 5,100,000	5,280,000	5,390,000
Advertising	3,060,000	2,400,000	2,450,000
Mechanical	4,590,000	3,360,000	3,430,000
Newsprint/Ink	13,260,000	13,440,000	13,230,000
Total:	26,010,000	24,480,000	24,500,000
INDIRECT			
Building	1,530,000	1,440,000	1,470,000
Circulation	5,610,000	4,800,000	4,410,000
Administrative	5,100,000	5,760,000	5,880,000
Total:	12,240,000	12,000,000	11,760,000
DEDUCTIONS			
Supplements	150,000	110,000	140,000
Bad Debts	120,000	200,000	200,000
Depreciation	600,000	730,000	710,000
Misc. Adjustments	150,000	400,000	420,000
Total:	1,020,000	1,440,000	1,470,000
TOTAL EXPENSES	$39,270,000	37,920,000	37,730,000
PROFIT BEFORE TAXES	11,730,000	10,080,200	11,267,300
PERCENT OF GROSS SALES	23	21	23
AVERAGE NET PAID CIRC.	311,500	317,260	319,600

Income Statement *(continued)*
Departmental Expense Breakdowns

Editorial Department

Salaries (Editorial)	$3,550,000	$3,800,000	$4,100,000
Salaries (Art & Photo)	375,000	380,000	400,000
Features	250,000	225,000	220,000
Wire Services	270,000	245,000	230,000
Telephone	120,000	110,000	105,000
Travel & Auto	260,000	280,000	125,000
Other	275,000	240,000	100,000
Total Editorial	5,100,000	5,280,000	5,280,000

Advertising Department

Retail			
Salaries	830,000	700,000	680,000
Other	200,000	175,000	140,000
National			
Salaries	250,000	190,000	155,000
Other	80,500	60,000	70,000
Classified			
Salaries	1,000,000	875,000	850,000
Other	200,000	100,500	80,000
Display/Make-Up			
Salaries	270,000	150,000	190,000
Other	30,500	80,500	30,000
Admin./Promotion			
Salaries	180,000	120,000	230,000
Other	14,000	9,000	20,000
Total Advertising	3,055,000	2,460,000	2,455,000

Mechanical Department

Composing			
Salaries	2,100,000	1,700,000	1,800,000
Other	490,000	300,000	400,000
Pressroom/Mailroom			
Salaries (Pressroom)	1,100,000	850,000	780,000
Salaries (Mailroom)	400,000	175,000	100,000
Other	275,000	185,000	195,000
Total Mechanical	4,365,000	3,210,000	3,275,000

Newsprint and Ink

Newsprint	12,560,000	12,610,000	12,350,000
Storage/Handling	250,000	300,000	340,000
Ink	450,000	530,000	510,000
Total Newsprint/Ink	13,260,000	13,440,000	13,200,000

Income Statement *(continued)*
Departmental Expense Breakdowns

Circulation

Salaries	$4,800,000	$4,100,000	$3,800,000
Other	810,000	700,000	610,000
Total Circulation	5,610,000	4,800,000	4,410,000

Maintenance/Security

Salaries	715,000	640,000	660,000
Utilities	515,000	525,000	500,000
Other	300,000	275,000	310,000
Total	1,530,000	1,440,000	1,470,000

Administrative

Business Office			
Salaries	900,000	960,000	1,100,000
Other	150,000	300,000	205,000
Executive Office			
Salaries	525,000	500,000	475,000
Other	75,000	40,000	35,000
General Unallocated			
Professional Services	700,000	750,000	660,000
Taxes	1,000,000	1,100,000	950,000
Insurance	450,000	450,000	550,000
Other	850,000	1,150,000	1,380,000
Total Administrative	4,650,000	5,250,000	5,355,000
TOTAL EXPENSES	9,300,000	10,500,000	10,710,000

The *Blue Eagle Bugle*

The *Blue Eagle Bugle,* a weekly newspaper in the county seat town of Cox County, is up for sale. The newspaper is one of the two largest in the rural county, with 2,400 subscribers. About 80 percent of these subscribers live in Blue Eagle (population 4,500 adults). The rest live in the rural area within a five-mile radius of the town. Population of this outlying readership area is about 2,000 adults. Blue Eagle is located just off a state highway, and is about five miles from the nearest interstate exit. About 80 percent of the newspaper's annual revenue comes from advertising and circulation sales. The remainder comes from job printing the paper does on a small job press and a large Xerox copying machine. In addition to its subscription sales, the *Bugle* logs about 300 single-copy sales per week.

The *Bugle* grossed $400,000 in revenues last year, $350,000 the previous year, and $360,000 the year before that. It netted out $40,000 last year, $30,000 the previous year, and $32,000 the year before that. The area, which has a median effective buying income of $22,000 per household and relatively stable retail sales averaging $50 million per year the past three years, features a large supermarket and two smaller groceries, two new car dealerships, two banks, and one savings and loan. There is one shopper in the county, four other paid-circulation weeklies in other towns, and one radio station. The town was a major Civil War site, and the local chamber of commerce is spearheading efforts to restore the downtown business area to its 1865 aura. A recreational lake is located eight miles from town.

The building is not included in the sale, although a personal computer system that allows for electronic editing and pagination is included, as is the job press and copying machine. The purchaser can lease the building from its present owners if he or she wishes. The current owner says he really would prefer not selling, because he and his family just moved to town two years ago and were just getting settled in the community. However, unexpected personal medical bills require more money than he can muster unless they do sell. The owner stresses the potential of the newspaper, as well as its performance record. He acknowledges that there has been some political corruption in the town's government, but that Blue Eagle is still a good place to live and raise a family. He has a price tag of $600,000 on the newspaper. Assuming you were an acquisition-minded newspaper publisher, would you consider buying the newspaper? If so, at what price and why? You should discuss any ways you see in which revenue might be increased and what factors are involved in your decision to buy or pass. Also, are there any other facts you would need to make a more informed choice on buying the newspaper? If so, what are they?

Encroaching Competition

Someone in your newspaper's market/research department has been asleep at the switch and failed to see the impending signs of a new shopper, which began publishing in your market last week. As a result, your competitive environment has changed. You publish the *Winton Daily News,* a 40,000-circulation newspaper that has 60-percent penetration into your market area. The new shopper, going through the third-class mails, is boasting 90 percent coverage in only its second week of operation. There is other competition in the area, but you have been successful in retaining your market advertising share against them. However, this shopper, named *Shopper's Delight,* threatens to give you trouble despite the fact that it carries no news content and goes free to households in the area.

The publisher of the shopper, Jack Harris, is an experienced hand at publishing other people's newspapers, but this is his first ownership venture. He has a small amount of capital behind him and feels he can lose money for a few months, if he has to, before breaking even. If his first issue is any indication, however, he may be breaking even sooner than he thinks. What do you do to protect your franchise?

SELECTED BIBLIOGRAPHY

BOOKS

Aaker, David A., and George S. Day. *Marketing Research*. New York: Wiley, 1980.

Aaker, David A., and John G. Myers. *Advertising Management*. 3d ed. Englewood Cliffs: Prentice-Hall, 1987.

Albrecht, Karl. *Successful Management by Objectives*. Englewood Cliffs: Prentice-Hall, 1978.

American Newspaper Publishers Association and the Newspaper Advertising Bureau. *Guide to Quality Newspaper Reproduction*. Washington, D.C.: Newspaper Advertising Bureau, 1986.

Argyris, Chris. *Behind The Front Page: Organizational Self-Renewal in a Metropolitan Newspaper*. San Francisco: Jossey-Bass, 1974.

Bagdikian, Ben H. *Media Monopoly*. Boston: Beacon Press, 1983.

Benjaminson, Peter. *Death in the Afternoon: America's Newspaper Giants Struggle for Survival*. Kansas City: Andrews, McNeel and Parker, 1984.

Broder, David S. *Behind the Front Page: A Candid Look at How the News Is Made*. New York: Simon and Schuster, 1987.

Byerly, Kenneth. *Community Journalism*. Philadelphia: Chilton, 1961.

Byron, Christopher M. *The Fanciest Dive: What Happened When the Media Empire of Time/Life Leaped without Looking into the Age of High-Tech*. New York: W.W. Norton & Co., 1986.

Carter, Nancy M., and John B. Cullen. *The Computerization of Newspaper Organizations: The Impact of Technology on Organizational Structuring*. Lanham Md.: University Press, 1983.

Christians, Clifford G., Kim B. Rotzoll, and Mark Fackler. *Media Ethics: Cases and Moral Reasoning*. New York: Longman, 1983.

Compaine, Benjamin. *Who Owns the Media? Concentration of Ownership in the Mass Communications Industry*. New York: Harmony Books, 1979.

―――――. *The Newspaper Industry in the 1980s: An Assessment of Economics and Technology.* New York: Knowledge Industry Publications, Inc., 1980.

Davis, Keith, and John W. Newstrom. *Human Behavior at Work: Organizational Behavior.* 7th ed. New York: McGraw Hill, 1985.

Emery, Edwin, and Michael Emery. *The Press and America: An Interpretive History of the Mass Media.* 5th ed. Englewood Cliffs: Prentice-Hall, 1984.

Emery, Michael. *America's Leading Daily Newspapers: A Media Research Institute Survey.* Indianapolis: R.J. Berg & Co., 1983.

Engwall, Lars. *Newspapers as Organizations.* Westmead, England: Teakfield, 1978.

Garcia, Mario R., and Don Fry, eds. *Color in American Newspapers.* St. Petersburg, Fla: Poynter Institute for Media Studies, 1986.

Ghiglione, Loren. *The Buying and Selling of America's Newspapers.* New York: R.J. Berg & Co., 1984.

Glueck, William F. *Business Policy and Strategic Management.* 3d ed. New York: McGraw-Hill, 1980.

Halberstam, David. *The Powers That Be.* New York: Alfred A. Knopf, 1979.

Hulteng, John L. *The News Media: What Makes Them Tick?* Englewood Cliffs: Prentice-Hall, 1980.

Hulteng, John L. *The Fourth Estate.* Englewood Cliffs: Prentice-Hall, 1984.

Isaacs, Norman. *Untended Gates: The Mismanaged Press.* New York: Columbia University Press, 1986.

Johnstone, John W. C., Edward J. Slawski, and William W. Bowman. *The News People.* Urbana: University of Illinois Press, 1976.

Kaufman, Louis C. *Essentials of Advertising.* 2d ed. San Diego: Harcourt Brace Jovanovich, 1987.

Kluger, Richard. *The Paper: The Life and Death of the New York Herald Tribune.* New York: Alfred A. Knopf, 1976.

Lavine, John M., and Daniel B. Wackman. *Managing Media Organizations.* New York: Longman, 1987.

Leapman, Michael. *Arrogant Aussie: The Rupert Murdoch Story.* Secaucas: Lyle Stuart, Inc., 1985.

Likert, Rensis. *The Human Organization.* New York: McGraw-Hill, 1967.

McCombs, Maxwell, Donald Lewis Shaw, and David Grey. *Handbook of Reporting Methods.* Boston: Houghton-Mifflin, 1976.

McGregor, Douglas. *The Human Side of Enterprise.* New York: McGraw-Hill, 1960.

Maslow, Abraham. *Motivation and Personality.* New York: Harper and Row, 1954.

Meeker, Richard H. *Newspaperman: S. I. Newhouse and Business of News.* New York: Ticknor & Fields, 1983.

Meyer, Philip. *The Newspaper Survival Book.* Bloomington: Indiana University Press, 1985.

Meyers, William. *The Image Makers: Power and Persuasion on Madison Avenue.* New York: Times Books, 1984.

Newsom, D. Earl, ed. *The Newspaper: Everything You Need to Know to Make It in the Newspaper Business.* Englewood Cliffs: Prentice-Hall, 1981.

Ouchi, William. *Theory Z: How American Business Can Meet the Japanese Challenge.* Reading, Mass.: Addison-Wesley Publishing Co., 1981.

Peter, Laurence J., and Raymond Hull. *The Peter Principle.* New York: William Morrow and Co., 1969.

Prichard, Peter. *The Making of McPaper: The Inside Story of USA Today*. Kansas City: Andrews, McMeel and Parker, 1987.

Quick, Thomas L. *The Quick Motivation Method*. New York: St. Martin's Press, 1980.

Smith, Anthony. *Goodbye Gutenberg*. New York: Oxford University Press, 1980.

Smolla, Rodney A. *Suing the Press: Libel, the Media and Power*. New York: Oxford University Press, 1986.

Sohn, Ardyth, Christine Ogan, and John Polich. *Newspaper Leadership*. Englewood Cliffs: Prentice-Hall, 1986.

Stidger, Ruth W. *The Competence Game: How to Find, Use and Keep Competent Employees*. New York: Thomond Press, 1980.

Talese, Gay. *The Kingdom and the Power*. New York: New American Library, 1969.

Udell, Jon G. *The Economics of the American Newspaper*. New York: Hastings House, 1978.

Vroom, Victor H. *Work and Motivation*. New York: John Wiley and Sons, 1964.

Weaver, David H. *Videotex Journalism: Teletext, Viewdata, and the News*. Hillsdale, N.J.: Lawrence Erlbaum Associates, 1983.

Weaver, David H., and G. Cleveland Wilhoit. *The American Journalist: A Portrait of U.S. News People and Their Work*. Bloomington: Indiana University Press, 1986.

ARTICLES

"A Chronology: The Demise of the Cleveland Press." *Editor & Publisher* (30 March, 1985): 11.

Adizes, Ichak. "Management Styles." *California Management Review* 19, no. 2 (1976): 55–70.

"A.M. Converts Laud Conversion from P.M." *Editor & Publisher* (10 October 1981): 56.

Anderson, Douglas. "How Managing Editors View and Deal With Newspaper Ethical Issues." *Journalism Quarterly* 64, nos. 2 and 3 (Summer–Autumn, 1986): 225.

Arvidson, Cheryl. "The Price That Broke the Register." *WJR* (April 1985): 20.

Ball, Robert. "Europe Outgrows Management American Style." *Fortune* (20 October 1980): 147–148.

Becker, Lee B., Idowu A. Sobowale, and Robin E. Cobbey. "Reporters and Their Professional and Organizational Commitments." *Journalism Quarterly* 56, no. 4 (Winter 1979): 753.

Blankenburg, William B. "Consolidation in Two-Newspaper Firms." *Journalism Quarterly* 62, no. 3 (Autumn 1985): 474.

"Buffalo Courier-Express Faces Sept. 19 Closing." *Editor & Publisher* (11 September, 1982): 13.

Burroughs, Ellis. "Readership Project: Looking Back and Ahead at Its Six-Year Run." *Presstime* (April 1983): 4–9.

Chamberlin, Anne. "You Love the Work—But How Soon Will You Starve?" *WJR* (March 1986): 12.

Cohen, Jack. "Advice for Shopper Newspapers." *Editor & Publisher* (24 March 1984): 48.

Cose, Ellis. "Keeping the Faith: Hiring and Promoting More Minority Journalists Is Not Only Right, It's Necessary." *The Quill* (October 1985): 8–13.

"Demise of Minneapolis Star Blamed on Life Itself." *Editor & Publisher* (17 April 1982): 12–13.

Dreier, Peter, and Steve Weinberg. "Interlocking Directorates." *Journalism Quarterly* (November–December 1979): 51–54.

Fitzgerald, Mark. "A Profitable News War in Denver." *Editor & Publisher* (15 September 1984): 12–15, 32.

————. "VDT Safety Still Up in the Air." *Editor & Publisher* (11 October 1986): 32.

Flowers, Vincent S., and Hughes, Charles L. "Choosing a Leadership Style." *Personnel* (January–February 1978): 27–38.

Frederick, Sharon. "Why John and Mary Won't Work." *Inc.* (April 1981): 70–84.

Freeman, George. "Antitrust Actions." *Presstime* (January 1985): 8.

Geltner, Sharon. "Two for the Job of One," *WJR* (September 1985): 38–39.

Genovese, Margaret. "Small Retailers: Newspapers Pay Special Heed to Local Clients." *Presstime* (December 1985): 12–13.

Goltz, Gene. "Where Newspapers Compete." *Presstime* (November 1986): 38–42.

————. "Today's Researchers Will Tackle Anything." *Presstime* (July 1987): 6–9.

Guest, David. "Motivation After Maslow." *Personnel Management* (March 1976): 89–92.

Henry, William A. "Learning to Love the Chains." *WJR* (September 1986): 15–17.

Herzberg, Frederick. "One More Time: How Do You Motivate Employees?" *Harvard Business Review* 46, no. 1 (1968): 53–62.

Hogan, Bill. "The Asset Test." *WJR* (July 1985): 38.

House, R., and J. Miner. "Path-Goal Theory of Leadership: A Theoretical and Empirical Analysis." *Contemporary Business* 3 (1974): 81–98.

Hynds, Ernest C. "Trends in the Daily Newspapers in the United States." *The Gazette* 42, no. 4 (1977): 135–149.

Lonergan, Wallace G. "Changing Approaches to Management." In *Readings in Management: Leadership,* 105–113. Chicago: Human Resources Center, University of Chicago, 1981.

Lucas, J. Anthony. "The Siege of Morrissey Boulevard." *New England Monthly* (August 1985): 26–38.

McNichol, Tom. "Drugs in the Newsroom: When Reporters Become Part of the Story." *WJR* (April 1986): 22–28.

Maguire, W. Terry. "Postal Affairs." *Presstime* (January 1985): 24.

Mallette, Malcolm F. "Dubuque Ties Into the Informal System." In *How Newspapers Communicate Internally,* 12–13. Reston, Va: American Press Institute, 1981.

"Managing the Newsroom." *The Bulletin of the American Society of Newspaper Editors* (March 1981).

Menzies, Hugh D. "The Ten Toughest Bosses." *Fortune* (21 April 1980): 62–72.

Mollenhoff, Clark R. "An Epidemic of Arrogance." *The Quill* (November 1986): 25–26.

Morton, John. "Dying Dynasties," *WJR* (March 1985): 60.

Morton, John. "The Price is Right Through The Roof." *WJR* (April 1985): 60.

————. "Counting on Readership." *WJR* (March 1986): 52.

————. "Games Newspapers Play." *WJR* (April 1986): 60.

————. "Too Much Too Soon." *WJR* (May 1986): 52.

————. "The Boom in Big-City Dailies." *WJR* (September 1986): 52.

————. "Trying for a Turnaround in Dallas." *WJR* (December 1986): 52.

———. "The Growing Giveaway Game." *WJR* (January–February 1987): 52.

———. "Winning Back the 'Burbs." *WJR* (June 1987): 52.

———. "Good and Bad Newspaper Deals." *WJR* (July–August 1987): 32.

"The New Industrial Relations." *Business Week* (11 May 1981): 84–88.

Newsom, Clark. "Quality Circles." *Presstime* (December 1986): 32–34.

Newsom, Clark, and Mark Ingham. "Checking References." *Presstime* (December 1985): 22–23.

Powell, Joanna. "Institutional Investor." *WJR* (July 1985): 44–46.

"Quality of Work Life: Catching On." *Business Week* (21 September 1981): 72.

Radolf, Andrew. "Psychographics and Advertising." *Editor & Publisher* (3 November 1984): 20.

———. "Standardization of Color." *Editor & Publisher* (26 January 1985): 8.

Rambo, C. David. "Newspaper Companies Go Back to Basics." *Presstime* (January 1987): 22–30.

Ramsey, Douglas and Donald Kirk, "Lessons From Japan, Inc." *Newsweek* (8 September 1980): 59–61.

Reed, Robert. "Audit Bureau Makes the Numbers Count, But Some Question the Worth of What It Prints Out." *Advertising Age* (9 January 1984): M-4-5.

Rothmyer, Karen. "Hot Properties: The Media-Buying Spree Explained." *Columbia Journalism Review* (November–December 1985): 38–43.

———. "Gannett in Detroit: Making Repairs on the News." *WJR* (July–August 1987): 16–18.

Rottenberg, Dan. "Missing the Message on Mergers." *WJR* (June 1987): 18–20.

Ruth, Marcia. "Co-Op Advertising." *Presstime* (May 1984): 12–13.

Schlosberg, Richard T., III. "A Management Training Program That Works." *The Bulletin of the American Society of Newspaper Editors* (March 1981): 12–13.

Sgarlata, Rob. "How Good Are Your Editors?" *Folio* (December 1980): 78–83.

Skylar, David. "Why Newspapers Die." *The Quill* (July–August 1984): 12–15.

Sohn, Ardyth B., and Leonard H. Chusmir. "The Motivational Perspectives of Newspaper Managers." *Journalism Quarterly* 62, no. 2 (Summer 1985): 296.

"Star's Closure to Make D.C. 1-Paper Town." *Presstime* (August 1981): 43.

Stout, Richard T., and Joseph Tinkelman. "Death in the Big City." *The Quill* (October 1981): 10–14.

Truitt, Rosalind C. "Interface '86." *Presstime* (July 1986): 34–48.

"Trust: The New Ingredient in Management." *Business Week* (6 July 1981): 104–105.

Vacha, J. E. "Dearth in the Afternoon." *WJR* (October 1981): 41–45.

Warner, Daniel J., Sr. "Readers (People) Respond Best to Messages From the Heart." *Presstime* (January 1987): 38.

Weiss, Bernard. "The Editor As Manager: How Do You Rate?" *Folio* (November 1981): 90–92.

Weiss, Philip. "Invasion of the Gannettoids." *The New Republic* (2 February 1987): 18–22.

Wilson, Jean Gaddy. "Women in the Newspaper Business." *Presstime* (October 1986): 30–37.

Wines, Michael. "Burnout in the Newsroom." *WJR* (May 1986): 34–38.

INDEX

About the Author

After six years as founding director of the Graduate Journalism Program at Northeastern University in Boston, JIM WILLIS is now Associate Professor of Journalism at Oklahoma State University. While at Northeastern, Dr. Willis helped create a graduate program that features a Master of Journalism in News Media Management, the only one of its type in the country at that time. Dr. Willis holds a B.A. degree from the University of Oklahoma, an M.A. from East Texas State University, and a Ph.D. from the University of Missouri. All three degrees are in Journalism. In addition to his teaching experience, Dr. Willis is a former editor with the *Dallas Morning News* and a former reporter with *The Daily Oklahoman*. He has also been managing editor of Texas' *Garland Daily News*, city editor of the *Columbia Missourian*, and news editor of Oklahoma's *Edmond Sun & Booster*. He has taught at the Southern Illinois University at Edwardsville and the University of Missouri, in addition to Northeastern and Oklahoma State. He has published articles on newsroom and newspaper management in *Editor & Publisher, Nieman Reports, Journalism Educator*, and *Grassroots Editor*. He has moderated sessions on newspaper management for the New England Press Association and on the teaching of newspaper management for the New England Newspaper Association.